Robert Marshall Offord

Life's Golden Lamp for Daily Devotional Use

A treasury of texts from the very words of Christ, with comments thereon by as many ministers of the gospel as there are days in the year

Robert Marshall Offord

Life's Golden Lamp for Daily Devotional Use
A treasury of texts from the very words of Christ, with comments thereon by as many ministers of the gospel as there are days in the year

ISBN/EAN: 9783337284947

Printed in Europe, USA, Canada, Australia, Japan

Cover: Foto ©Lupo / pixelio.de

More available books at **www.hansebooks.com**

For Daily Devotional Use.

*A TREASURY OF TEXTS FROM THE VERY
WORDS OF CHRIST*

WITH COMMENTS THEREON BY AS MANY MINISTERS OF THE
GOSPEL AS THERE ARE DAYS IN THE YEAR; AUTOGRAPH
OF EACH CONTRIBUTOR; SUGGESTIVE SCRIPTURE
HEADING AND APPROPRIATE LINES
FROM FAMILIAR HYMNS.

Edited by
REV. R. M. OFFORD.

NEW YORK:
NEW YORK OBSERVER.
37 AND 38 PARK ROW.
1889.

Copyright, 1888,
By R. M. Offord.

University Press:
John Wilson and Son, Cambridge.

PREFATORY NOTE.

THE peculiar features of this work would surely justify its production even though there were ten times as many daily text books in existence as there are. These features are apparent; and the constant use of the book will be likely to commend them more and more.

The words of our Lord and Saviour Jesus Christ furnish a text for each day of the year. Three hundred and sixty-five ministers of his gospel have paid tribute to their Master and rendered service to his people by their effort to emphasize and enforce his gracious sayings. May their reward for this service so cheerfully contributed be from the Master himself and be rich and abundant! Many denominations and various parts of the world are represented. Each contributor has signed his name to the material furnished by him, and the autographs have been faithfully reproduced by photography.

A stanza of poetry, generally from some familiar hymn, and as far as possible in harmony with the text and the comment, has been added, while each page opens with a suggestive heading. These headings, though invariably portions of Scripture, are not taken from the words directly spoken by the Saviour. The Epistles furnish many of them, while others have been selected from the Old Testament. The common English version has been drawn upon for all the texts and headings. A reference to the headings and their context will help to bring out the delightful harmony of Scripture.

An index at the close of the book will enable the reader to ascertain the particular church affiliations of each contributor.

It is hoped that Christians the world over may find the book to be a means of grace, and that the years as they pass may bring it an ever widening circle of readers. May the Lord whose words are the vital portion of the book grant that as these are read from day to day in its pages, they may not return to him void!

The task of selection, compilation, correspondence, and editing involved has been one of great joy. Though the work may not be the box of spikenard, exceeding precious, broken over the Master's feet, may he graciously regard it as a cup of cold water tendered his disciples "in his Name!"

Robt. M. Offord

DECEMBER, 1888.

THESE SAYINGS OF MINE.

———◆———

This is my beloved Son, in whom I am well pleased; hear ye him.
MATT. xvii. 5.

Whosoever will not hearken unto my words which he shall speak in my name, I will require it of him. — DEUT. xviii. 19.

The words that I speak unto you, they are spirit, and they are life. JOHN vi. 63.

Therefore whosoever heareth these sayings of mine, and doeth them, I will liken him unto a wise man, which built his house upon a rock: and the rain descended, and the floods came, and the winds blew, and beat upon that house; and it fell not: for it was founded upon a rock. MATT. vii. 24, 25

The Comforter, which is the Holy Ghost, whom the Father will send in my name, he shall teach you all things, and bring all things to your remembrance, whatsoever I have said unto you. — JOHN xiv. 26.

God, who at sundry times and in divers manners spake in time past unto the fathers by the prophets, hath in these last days spoken unto us by his Son. — HEB. i. 1, 2.

Therefore we ought to give the more earnest heed to the things which we have heard, lest at any time we should let them slip. — HEB. ii. 1.

And all bare him witness, and wondered at the gracious words which proceeded out of his mouth. — LUKE iv. 22.

For he taught them as one having authority, and not as the scribes. MATT. vii. 29.

Grace is poured into thy lips. — PSALM xlv. 2.

Never man spake like this man. — JOHN vii. 46.

Lord, to whom shall we go? thou hast the words of eternal life. — JOHN vi. 68.

How sweet are thy words unto my taste! yea, sweeter than honey to my mouth! — PSALM cxix. 103.

Lord, evermore give us this bread. — JOHN vi 34.

O send out thy light and thy truth: let them lead me. — PSALM xliii. 3.

Thy word is a lamp unto my feet, and a light unto my path. — PSALM cxix. 105.

✠

LIFE'S GOLDEN LAMP.

Let the word of Christ dwell in you richly in all wisdom.
COLOSSIANS iii. 16.

January 1.

The true light now shineth. — 1 John ii. 8.

As long as I am in the world, I am the light of the world. — John ix. 5.

THIS is one of those I AMS peculiar to John's gospel, by which Jehovah revealed himself through the manhood of Christ, even as he showed himself to Moses at the bush. "That which doth make manifest is light!" So Christ has revealed to us what, but for him, we had not known. By that one utterance to the woman at the well, "God is a Spirit," etc., he has told us more concerning the spirituality, the unity, and the fatherhood of God than the wisest of ancient philosophers had reached. By his sacrifice of himself upon the cross for the sins of the world, he has forever met the need which men were seeking to satisfy by the offering of bulls and goats upon the altar. By his resurrection from the dead and ascension into glory, he has brought life and immortality to light, and illumined for us the darkness of the future life. Nor is this all; everything that has brightened human life in the individual heart, in the family, in society, and in the nation has come from him. Truly this "light is sweet, and a pleasant thing it is for the eyes to behold" this sun. Let us therefore walk in its brightness, for he that followeth that "shall have the light of life."

Wm. M. Taylor.

I heard the voice of Jesus say,
  "I am this dark world's light.
Look unto me; thy morn shall rise,
  And all thy day be bright."
I looked to Jesus and I found
  In him my star, my sun ;
And in that light of life I'll walk
  Till travelling days are done.
                    H. Bonar.

January 2.

We preach Christ crucified. — 1 Cor. i. 23.

Verily, verily, I say unto you, except a corn of wheat fall into the ground and die, it abideth alone: but if it die, it bringeth forth much fruit. — John xii. 24.

HOW true this utterance in its application to him who gave it! He spake as never man spake, and lived as never man lived; yet his ministry was by no means fruitful. Crowds hung upon his lips, but their attachment was short-lived; and when he was put upon trial, few or none stood by him. Almost literally the corn of wheat abode by itself alone. But after the Saviour's death, at the first proclamation of the gospel on the day of Pentecost, three thousand souls were added to the Church, and on subsequent days "multitudes, both of men and women," — so that the crucified Saviour was more effective than the living Jesus. The blood of the cross is the great secret of awakening, conversion, and holy living.

How true is the saying in regard to all the followers of the Lord Jesus! Sacrifice is the indispensable condition of success. We must renounce in order to prevail. He that seeks his life loses it; he that loses his life finds it. One must sow in tears if he would reap in joy. Master and scholar have the same experience, — that suffering is required in order to fruitfulness and victory. It is the furnace that purifies and renders efficacious; the spices must be bruised to bring forth their fragrance. Happy they who recognize this law of the divine economy, and are content to suffer if only they may be made to bear much fruit!

Talbot W. Chambers

> Faithful cross! above all other,
> One and only noble tree!
> None in foliage, none in blossom,
> None in fruit, thy peers may be.
>
> J. NEALE *(Translation)*.

January 3.

Ye shall find rest for your souls. — Jer. vi. 16.

Come unto me, all ye that labour and are heavy laden, and I will give you rest. — Matt. xi. 28.

THIS is a tired world! Multitudes tired of body or tired of mind or tired of soul! Every one has a burden to carry, if not on one shoulder, then on the other. In the far East water is so scarce that if a man owns a well he is rich; and battles have been fought for the possession of a well of water. But every man owns a well, a deep well, — a well of tears. Chemists have tried to analyze a tear, and they say it is made of so much of this and so much of that, but they miss important ingredients. A tear is agony in solution. But by divine power it may be crystallized into spiritual wealth, and all burdens may be lifted. God is the rest of the soul that comes to him. He rests us by removing the weight of our sin, and by solacing our griefs with the thought that he knows what is best for his children. A wheat-sheaf cried out to the farmer, "Why do you smite me with that flail? What have I done that you should so cruelly pound me?" But when the straw had been raked off the wheat and put in the mow, and the wheat had been winnowed by the mill and had been piled in rich and beautiful gold on either side the barn floor, then the straw looked down from the mow and saw the reason why the farmer had flailed the wheat-sheaf.

T. De Witt Talmage.

    "Come unto me," — O precious words
      I hear the Saviour saying!
    He calls the weary ones to rest;
    He calls the toil-worn and oppressed;
      He calls the lost and straying.

    "Come unto me," — O gracious words
      Such tender love displaying!
    Dear Lord, I come — no merits mine —
    I come to trust thy love divine;
      I come thy call obeying.

R. M. Offord.

January 4.

Anointed . . . with the Holy Ghost and with power. — Acts x. 38.

The Spirit of the Lord is upon me, because he hath anointed me to preach the gospel to the poor; he hath sent me to heal the broken-hearted, to preach deliverance to the captives, and recovering of sight to the blind, to set at liberty them that are bruised, to preach the acceptable year of the Lord. — Luke iv. 18, 19.

"BY their fruits ye shall know them" is the test which our Lord asked to have applied to himself. When John was in prison and wondered whether Jesus was indeed Messiah, no direct answer was given. The messengers were kept near to Jesus for a time and then sent home with the command to tell what they had seen, from which John was to answer his own question. The Master applied this prophecy to himself and asked the people to believe he was Messiah, not because of what he said, but because of what he did. The best evidence of Christianity is what it does for humanity. Wherever there is good news for the poor, hope for the broken-hearted, deliverance for captives, a better physical life for the masses, there the Spirit of God is at work. The glory of Christ is that he saves men body and soul. Christianity repeats the claim of its Founder: it appeals for acceptance, not to any authority, but to a new life which has come to the world since the Advent. The Spirit is doing the same work through the Church that it did through Christ. Love and service for the children of God always follow the indwelling of the Spirit of God.

Amory H. Bradford.

Hail the heaven-born Prince of Peace!
Hail the Sun of Righteousness!
Light and life to all he brings,
Risen with healing in his wings.

C. Wesley.

January 5.

An inheritance . . . that fadeth not away. — 1 Peter i. 4.

Again, the kingdom of heaven is like unto treasure hid in a field; the which when a man hath found, he hideth, and for joy thereof goeth and selleth all that he hath, and buyeth that field. — Matt. xiii. 44.

IF our Lord calls the kingdom of heaven a treasure, what an unspeakable treasure it must be! In Romans 14, 17, the Holy Spirit through Paul tells us what the kingdom of heaven is. It is "righteousness, and peace, and joy, in the Holy Ghost." Just as there is a mutual indwelling between Christ and the believer, — he dwelling in Christ and Christ dwelling in him (John vi. 56), — so the Christian dwells in the kingdom of heaven, and yet the kingdom of heaven is in him. It is a treasure of protection around him and a treasure of experience within him.

When a poor sinner finds this heavenly treasure, he gives up everything to be fully possessed of it, for all else is of no account in comparison. It is alliance with God. It is to be partaker of the divine nature (2 Peter i. 4), to be partaker of God's holiness (Heb. xii. 10). For the "righteousness" is God's righteousness (Romans x. 3), the "peace" is God's peace (Phil. iv. 7), and the "joy" is the joy of the Lord Jesus Christ (John xv. 11), all given by the Holy Ghost.

Horace of Hosley

> He feeds in pastures large and fair,
> Of love and truth divine;
> O child of God, O glory's heir,
> How rich a lot is thine!
>
> LYTE.

January 6.

We which have believed do enter into rest. — Heb. iv. 3.

Why are ye troubled? and why do thoughts arise in your hearts? — Luke xxiv. 38.

TROUBLED by reason of their unbelief! How it resisted the testimony of those who had seen the risen Christ and yielded not, though he himself stood before them and spoke to them in tones of wonted greeting! "Terrified and affrighted" even in the presence of him whom they loved! Their minds were disturbed by "reasonings," — intellectual doubts as to the reality of his resurrection, and the fulfilment of his promise. Their unbelief, so obstinate and unyielding, may serve to establish our faith in their subsequent testimony, but brought to them only distressing unrest.

Intellectual doubt destroys the peace of the soul. We walk by faith, not by sight. Yet he who believes is more likely to see than he who believes not. Faith in God, in the certified truths of the gospel, in his promises, and in his overruling providence, brings rest. God reigns! Not a sparrow falleth on the ground without him. His kingdom is sure to come in spite of all obstacles. The darkest experiences are but the appointments of his infinite wisdom, and in the midst of them he will manifest himself. In every garden of Gethsemane an angel; in every lonely chamber the risen Saviour! Do not question, but trust. Be not troubled, only believe.

Henry M. King

While looking to Jesus, my heart cannot fear,
I tremble no more when I see Jesus near;
I know that his presence my safeguard will be,
For "Why are you troubled?" he saith unto me!

J. N. Darby.

January 7.

God shall wipe away all tears from their eyes.—Rev. vii. 17.

Blessed are they that mourn: for they shall be comforted.—
Matt. v. 4.

THE Master, when he said this, was fulfilling the prophecy,—"He hath sent me to bind up the broken-hearted" (Isaiah lxi. 1). He was speaking in the same line as when he said, "Come unto me, all ye that labour and are heavy laden, and I will give you rest!" (Matt. xi. 28).

The words reach beyond the mourners simply over sin. They indeed are blessed in their consciousness of pardon and safety, but there is more than that here. He, the infinite Saviour, came to bring the kingdom of heaven, God's reign in the soul. That is a kingdom of peace. The believer comes to him and is blessed in the coming. He comes with his heart borne down with earthly sorrow. Where else, to whom else in all the world can he go? Earth cannot help him. He comes to a sympathizing Saviour (Heb. iv. 15), and he is in a place of calm. He hardly knows why or how, but peace and rest are in his heart, and they are blessedness.

That is for to-day. But the "shall be" looks forward to a time when God shall wipe all tears away (Isaiah xxv. 8; Rev. vii. 17; xxi. 4). The anticipation of future blessedness touches and lightens the present sorrow.

William Aikman

> I've welcomed tears e'er since the day
>   I saw that by and by
> God's own dear hand will wipe away
>   The tears from ev'ry eye;
> And I have learned to welcome grief,
>   For grief doth bring me grace.
> I would not know the Lord's relief,
>   Had woe with me no place.
>   R. M. Offord.

January 8.

Whatsoever is born of God overcometh the world.
1 JOHN v. 4.

To him that overcometh will I give to eat of the tree of life, which is in the midst of the paradise of God. — REV. ii. 7.

HEREIN is Paradise regained! What was lost through the transgression of the first Adam is restored through the obedience and sacrifice of the second Adam, — the Lord from heaven. How inspiring to those who seek for glory and honor and immortality is this assurance of an eternity of blessedness in the presence of God himself! — for heavenward our best hopes tend.

We need, however, to be constantly reminded that it is through conflict we pass into this blessed inheritance. There is a victory to be won, — the victory over a sinful heart within, and a sinful world without. For this we need the whole armor of God (Eph. vi. 10-17), that with a steadfast, abiding faith, a faith that overcomes the world, we may attain eternal felicity through him who loved us and gave himself for us. The conflict may be long continued; but at last we shall be able to raise the glad shout of triumph, "O death, where is thy sting? O grave, where is thy victory? The sting of death is sin, and the strength of sin is the law. But thanks be to God, which giveth us the victory through our Lord Jesus Christ!"

Henry S. Burrage.

> Look up, ye saints of God!
>   Nor fear to tread below
> The path your Saviour trod,
>   Of daily toil and woe.
> Wait but a little while
>   In uncomplaining love;
> His own most gracious smile
>   Shall welcome you above.
>
> H. W. BAKER.

January 9.

What is thy petition? ... it shall be granted thee.
Esther vii. 2.

Ask, and it shall be given you; seek, and ye shall find; knock, and it shall be opened unto you. — Matt. vii. 7.

IN this most wonderful of sermons there are few words more wonderful; but disciples of Jesus verify them daily. " I love the Lord, because he hath heard my voice and my supplications. Because he hath inclined his ear unto me, therefore will I call upon him as long as I live." Asking, seeking, and knocking are the ways in which we reveal our desires; and desire is the key of heaven. "Blessed are they which do hunger and thirst after righteousness: for they shall be filled." We cannot refrain from asking for whatever we truly desire. We cannot keep from seeking what we know to be infinitely precious. We are sure to knock at the door which is between us and the object of our warmest affections. Father, I ask for thy loving-kindness, which is better than life. Son of God, I seek for thy grace, which in weakness makes me strong. Holy Spirit, I knock at the door which is always opened to the humble and the contrite heart. May all thy mercies and my infirmities constrain me to ask without ceasing until thou hast given, to seek without fail until I have found, to knock without fear until it has been opened unto me!

Wendell Prime

What various hindrances we meet
In coming to a mercy-seat!
Yet who that knows the worth of prayer,
But wishes to be often there?

Cowper.

January 10.

The Spirit of Life. — Romans viii. 2.

The wind bloweth where it listeth, and thou hearest the sound thereof, but canst not tell whence it cometh, and whither it goeth: so is every one that is born of the Spirit. — John iii. 8.

WIND, though invisible, is a tremendous power, moving commerce over the seas, bringing winter and summer, and mingling the germs of vegetation which cover the world with beauty. We see the effects, and know a few laws of the wind's action. Disregard of those laws involves discomfort, disaster, disease. and death.

The Chinese say wind is the key to nature. According to their Fung-Shway doctrine, the science of meteorology involves all knowledge.

Thus, but above all superstition, is the work of the Holy Spirit. His being and activities are full of mystery, yet their presence and power are felt in imperial sway by untold millions. Knowing God through the Spirit is entrance upon all knowledge. Born of the Spirit, mere existence has become life. Hitherto becalmed and drifting helplessly, we now full our sails and move forward. All the beauties of the revolving seasons come to the soul. Years that were a desert are now a paradise of Christ-like sacrifice and heavenward preparation. Unbelief is a vacuum which the Holy Spirit cannot enter. Violation of the laws of the Spirit involves sorrow, ruin, and despair; but trustful obedience, that stumbles not at the mysteries of the Infinite, insures peace, prosperity, and eternal joy.

W. F. Bainbridge.

> Eternal Spirit, we confess
> And sing the wonders of thy grace;
> Thy power conveys our blessings down
> From God the Father and the Son.
> Thy power and glory work within,
> And break the chains of reigning sin,
> All our imperious lusts subdue,
> And form our wretched hearts anew.
>
> Watts.

January 11.

Grieve not the Holy Spirit of God. — Eph. iv. 30.

Wherefore I say unto you, All manner of sin and blasphemy shall be forgiven unto men; but the blasphemy against the Holy Ghost shall not be forgiven unto men. — Matt. xii. 31.

WHILST all sins are mortal unless expiated and repented of, we are to beware of one that is so peculiarly virulent as to leave no room for repentance. The blood might cleanse it if applied; but the blood will never reach it, as it is beyond the jurisdiction of grace. Prayer for it is as unavailing as if offered for the impenitent dead, or for the conversion of Satan. It is like a disease from which no patient has ever recovered.

Whether the Pharisees had committed this sin, or were only forewarned of their peril, we are not informed. Perhaps no mere man can ever in this life be sure that his case is beyond hope. But as this sin is directed against the person and operations of the Holy Ghost, the terrible warning is still in season. We should fear to condemn a work because it fails to satisfy our prejudices or our sectarianism. Whilst professing to be only criticising human methods, we may be passing judgment on the Spirit, condemning his work as excitement and delusion, and ascribing it to Beelzebub. Our opposition may be in varying degrees, from mere grumbling to extreme blasphemy or persecution; but it is always mischievous in its effects and perilous to our souls.

George Maclaskie

Holy Ghost, with light divine,
Shine upon this heart of mine;
Chase the shades of night away;
Turn my darkness into day!

. . . .

Cast down every idol throne,
Reign supreme, and reign alone!   A. Reed.

January 12.

In whom I am well pleased. — Matt. iii. 17.

For the Father loveth the Son, and sheweth him all things that himself doeth: and he will shew him greater works than these, that ye may marvel. — John v. 20.

THE Father loveth the Son even as he loveth himself. One with him in essence and attribute, and at one with him in purpose and operation, the divine Father has loved his divine Son from the innermost eternity with infinite affection. From the Son of his bosom the Father has no secrets. He unveils to his Well-beloved the whole counsel of his will; and the Son comprehends all his intentions, coincides in all his purposes, and co-operates with him in all his actings. The works of the Father, existent in design from eternity, are executed, one after another, in time, through and by the incarnate Son in his official character of mediator. The successive disclosures of divine purpose are caused to progress from the great to the greater in ever-increasing majesty and glory, in order that those who witness them may marvel, — for though they may not constrain to faith, they compel wonder. This marvelling will attain its climax when the great works of Christ shall have reached their culmination in the final quickening of the dead and the last judgment. Then they who have recognized him as the Son of God shall be excited to a joyful ecstasy on being raised to eternal life, while those who have been wilfully blind to his sonship and Saviourhood shall be overwhelmed with everlasting dismay. "Behold, ye despisers, and wonder and perish!"

Robert T. Jeffery

Behold your Lord, your Master, crowned
  With glories all divine,
And tell the wondering nations round
  How bright those glories shine.
                              Anne Steele.

January 13.

How shall we escape, if we neglect so great salvation?
Heb. ii. 3.

Woe unto thee, Chorazin! woe unto thee, Bethsaida! for if the mighty works, which were done in you, had been done in Tyre and Sidon, they would have repented long ago in sackcloth and ashes. But I say unto you, It shall be more tolerable for Tyre and Sidon at the day of judgment, than for you. — MATT. xi. 21, 22.

THE sinner to whom no opportunities of repentance come is lost. Tyre and Sidon stand in the text as the terrible examples whose judgment measures the intolerable. But of how much sorer punishment is he worthy who has trodden under foot the Son of God! The sinner to whom opportunities come but pass unheeded, has his part in the more intolerable lot of Chorazin. Tyre and Sidon are cities in Satan's land; Chorazin and Bethsaida are Satan's strongholds, which he can trust to fortify themselves against every approach of the Saviour, and to repel his every advance. God grant that we have not Chorazin hearts!

How infinitely solemn a crisis the gospel brings to every city, household, life, to which it gains access! A sweet savor of Christ unto God, it is in all; but to one it is a savor from life unto life, to another a savor from death unto death. What a spectacle of mercy and judgment! Alas to us who have seen these mighty works, if they remain to us but a spectacle without us, and not a living power within!

Benj. B. Warfield

> Depth of mercy! can there be
> Mercy still reserved for me?
> Can my God his wrath forbear,
> Me, the chief of sinners, spare?
>
> C. WESLEY.

January 14.

Thou art my portion, O Lord. — Psalm cxix. 57.

But one thing is needful: and Mary hath chosen that good part, which shall not be taken away from her. — Luke x. 42.

Do not let me judge Mary lazy. She has done her work and "left" Martha to the cumbrous service she did not "choose" to do. Surely the Master had not favored neglected duty. Work we must, and that hard, for whatsoever our hand findeth to do, we must do it with our might. But let me never lose the one thing needful by choice, for that was Martha's fault. Martha *chose* excess of service. Mary *chose* "the one thing needful."

Every day brings its own cares and duties; every day, like Paul himself, we must serve God "with many distractions;" but amid them all, like him, we must be able to say, "This one thing I do . . . I press toward the mark."

Pause, O my soul, and consider! What life am I *choosing?* Fretful, irritable, do I make my much service an excuse for neglecting prayer and praise and God's word? That is Martha, — blamed. Calm, tranquil, do I do what I can in this life, yet careful to serve God always "with a quiet mind"? *That* is Mary, — praised. What shall I do to-day and always?

E Walpole Warren

Grant, we beseech thee, merciful Lord, to thy faithful people, pardon and peace, that we may be cleansed from all our sins and serve thee with a quiet mind, through Jesus Christ our Lord! Amen! COLLECT.

  Give me a calm, a thankful heart,
   From every murmur free;
  The blessings of thy grace impart,
   And make me live in thee! STEELE.

January 15.

Bought with a price: therefore glorify God. — 1 Cor. vi. 20.

Herein is my Father glorified, that ye bear much fruit; so shall ye be my disciples. — John xv. 8.

"MEET for use" seems to be the language of everything God has created. The Christian is no exception to this law. He, like the Master, is to be among men "as one that serves." Fruit-bearing is the sign of a thrifty life. By it the disciple knows he is abiding in Christ, and through it he brings help and cheer to others. "Much fruit," — it is the hope of this poor sinning world. There are so many needing help, opportunities for serving are so numerous, that only they who abound in good works fulfil the divine expectation. A true Christian should resemble a fruit-laden tree. We are taught here that God does what we are prompted to ask for in Christ's name, to the end that we may be useful, and because of our gracious attainments, beautiful. We become disciples by thus bringing forth fruit. Thinking Christ's thoughts, asking for things in his name, doing his will, and ministering through what we are, and by what we do, to others' good, we attest our discipleship. All forceful life springs out of union with Christ. We need not bring forth the self-same fruit, for the Father is glorified, not so much in the kinds of fruit, as in the all-essential fact that we are fruitful. Let each disciple serve in his or her own way, for it is the service that blesses. Fruit of every kind stands in evidence that we are rooted in Christ, and because of it is the Father glorified.

M. M. G. Dana

> Long as I live beneath,
>   To thee, oh, let me live;
> To thee my every breath
>   In thanks and praises give.
> Whate'er I have, whate'er I am,
> Shall magnify my Maker's name.
>
> C. Wesley.

January 16.

Neither is there salvation in any other. — Acts iv. 12.

I am the way, the truth, and the life: no man cometh unto the Father, but by me. — John xiv. 6.

THE heading of this chapter is, " Christ comforteth his disciples ; " and truly he gives the best comfort simply by telling about himself. The first verse begins, " Let not your heart be troubled." This verse seems to say to doubting Thomas, " Let not your mind be troubled." It is a release from perplexity. Heaven often seems distant and unknown, but if he who made the road thither is our guide we need not fear to lose the way. We do not want to see far ahead, — only far enough to discern him and trace his footsteps. Christ does not give us the full revelations of God and heaven at once; we could not bear them now. He gives us himself, and in that gift everything is secure. If you own the mines you will not lack treasure. If the fountain is yours you will have water day by day. Our peace lies not in believing much, but in believing well. If our faith in him is unwavering he will return it with knowledge. The way to escape from doubts is to think about Christ. What we need is not explanation, but confidence. Sometimes we know not what to believe, but always we know *whom* we have believed. Religion is not a theory, nor a doctrine; it is the coming of a person to a person, by a person. They who follow Christ, even through darkness, will surely reach the Father.

Henry van Dyke

I was not ever thus, nor prayed that thou
    Should'st lead me on ;
I loved to choose and see my path ; but now
    Lead thou me on.
. . . .
Keep thou my feet ; I do not ask to see
The distant scene, — one step enough for me.
Cardinal Newman.

January 17.

Do it heartily, as to the Lord. — Col. iii. 23.

Verily I say unto you, That this poor widow hath cast more in, than all they which have cast into the treasury: for all they did cast in of their abundance; but she of her want did cast in all that she had, even all her living. — Mark xii. 43, 44.

THIS incident of the third day of the Passion Week of our Lord suggests or vivifies many truths. It illustrates the thought that the apparent insignificance of our service makes the doing of it the more significant. It makes plain that Christ values our service, not by reason of its intrinsic merit, but by what it costs us. It shows that Christ sees and appreciates our service, though he may speak to us no word of commendation. It has for us a lesson of faithfulness in things secret. "The gods see it," said the Greek sculptor as he carved the part of the statue that was to be hidden from men's eyes. It teaches the duty of giving with each gift — ourselves. It proves that God is the supreme being to whom all service is to be given. The divine and not the human represents the ideal of humanity. This incident thus illustrates not a few of the truths of the atonement of him "who gave himself for us."

Charles F. Thwing

We give thee but thine own,
Whate'er the gift may be;
All that we have is thine alone,
A trust, O Lord, from thee!

W. W. How.

January 18.

Set your affection on things above. — Col. iii. 2.

He also that received seed among the thorns is he that heareth the word; and the care of this world, and the deceitfulness of riches, choke the word, and he becometh unfruitful. — Matt. xiii. 22.

HERE is a call to early soul-culture. The thistles from which our Lord fetches his illustration grow rapidly and in wild profusion on all ploughed fields of Palestine, springing up, however, after the wheat, which when white and dry and seen from a distance, they closely resemble. With these thistles, therefore, which all ploughed land bears, the wheat if it be late sown will have sore struggle for any vigorous and fruitful life.

We are thus taught to have divine truth timely sown and well advanced in the soul before the summer heat, so getting start of the weedy growths of our maturer years, — life's midsummer. The cares of this world and the deceitfulness of riches, which deplete the soil, outcrowd and overtop the tenderer and too late sown plant, destroying its worth and fruitfulness.

We should claim, seize, and improve for Christ first opportunities. The opening spring ought to find us beforehand with the weeds, early at work in our own heart's garden and the hearts of others, especially the young, getting start of the Devil by preoccupation of the soul for God.

Perhaps this opportunity may come to me to-day. The Lord help me to improve it, and forbid that either cares or riches choke his word!

Wm. T. Sabine.

Almighty God, thy word is cast
Like seed into the ground;
Now let the dew of heaven descend
And righteous fruits abound.
    Cawood.

January 19.

I know that my Redeemer liveth. — Job xix. 25.

Fear not; I am the first and the last: I am he that liveth, and was dead; and, behold, I am alive, for evermore, Amen; and have the keys of hell and of death. — Rev. i. 17, 18.

A SOLEMN exultation burns along these words. Each throws its light on some dark place in our thoughts, our lives.

I. "Fear not." Why should we fear? If Christ be the First and the Last, that secures that all between goes well. He is beginning and end, — "author and finisher." A strong, all-including hand bears us along, its grasp stronger than death, because it is the grasp of Life. "Fear not!"

II. "The 'Living One' was dead." How came one who was Life to die? Saint John, to whom these words were spoken, well knew, for he was with him in Gethsemane and at Calvary. So the reddened door opens into Atonement. Life was also Love, and therefore died for us. Now, he is "alive forevermore" to apply the atonement which he has made. On his work we may now rest in peace.

III. He holds in his imperial grasp the "keys." What are keys for? There is but one answer, — to lock in, and to lock out. O child of God, you cannot die until the time comes! You are locked out of your grave, and Christ has the key. No fierce disease or cruel accident can swing the door and thrust you in untimely. The key is in Christ's hand. He and he only can use it.

Mancius H. Hutton

> The First Begotten of the dead,
> For us he rose, our glorious Head,
>   Immortal life to bring;
> What though the saints like him shall die?
> They share their Leader's victory,
>   And triumph with their King!
>
>   KELLY

January 20.

He careth for you. — 1 Peter v. 7.

Therefore I say unto you, Take no thought for your life, what ye shall eat, or what ye shall drink; nor yet for your body, what ye shall put on. Is not the life more than meat, and the body than raiment? Behold the fowls of the air: for they sow not, neither do they reap, nor gather into barns; yet your heavenly Father feedeth them. Are ye not much better than they? — Matt. vi. 25, 26.

"TAKE no thought" (Revised version, "Be not anxious"), which means do not worry; and the reason is, you have a heavenly Father who can and will provide. Whatever betide, we must not lose confidence in God. When Abraham departed from the home where he expected to spend his old age, and turned his face toward the unknown scenes of Canaan, God said, "Fear not, I am thy shield," and this same "fear not," like a soothing refrain, purls to the end of Holy Writ.

The world tries to *cast away* care. Hence the endeavor to drown it in pleasures, to neutralize it by absorption in business, to amuse it with the aims of ambition. But care thus cast *away*, often returns like a boomerang. Scripture tells us, "Cast thy burden *on the Lord*, he shall sustain thee." The care is a care. Often it is a painful reality. We must have prudent thought about temporal affairs, and about our families. Scripture has no encouragement for lazy people, but it abounds in consolation for the toiling children of men. Now the true course is, not to cast *away* that care, but to consign it to God, who is as deeply interested in the objects of our care as we are; whose wisdom will direct what is best for them, and whose power can secure the accomplishment. Cares tend to crossness. Let us sweeten each cup of bitterness by some promise of our heavenly Father.

Geo. S. Mott

The birds without barn or store-house are fed;
From them let us learn to trust for our bread.
                                                              Newton.

January 21.

Fruit that may abound to your account. — Phil. iv. 17.

He that is faithful in that which is least is faithful also in much: and he that is unjust in the least is unjust also in much. If therefore ye have not been faithful in the unrighteous mammon, who will commit to your trust the true riches? — Luke xvi. 10, 11.

"TRUE riches!" Then there are riches untrue, — false, delusive riches, riches that mock the hopes of men, bringing disappointment, care, hardness, greed, instead of the liberation and repose they promised. There are such! Solomon describes them as winged. Jesus calls them deceitful. Paul pronounces them uncertain. But they have use. They are among those "least" things which may prepare the way for nobler trusts.

The chemical sunbeam, acting on the gross elements in the plant, produces color, fragrance, flavor, in flower and fruit; and the unrighteous mammon — wealth that has no moral worth and that tends so easily to evil — may be transmitted into the true riches of character, strength, achievement, heavenly treasures, under the constant touch of the actinic ray of fidelity.

All possessions are trusts, and all trusts are tests. The test both discovers the disposition and develops it. He who is faithful is advanced to larger service. He who is unfaithful is declared unjust; he wrongs all, the Master most, himself next; he is in danger of winning the curse of the fruitless fig-tree, the bitter doom of barrenness. The choice reward of faithful well-doing is increased opportunity to do good.

> Grant us hearts, dear Lord, to yield thee
> Gladly, freely, of thine own;
> With the sunshine of thy goodness,
> Melt our thankless hearts of stone.
>
> Mrs. Alderson.

January 22.

He that hath the Son hath life. — 1 John v. 12.

Verily, verily, I say unto you, Except ye eat the flesh of the Son of man, and drink his blood, ye have no life in you. Whoso eateth my flesh, and drinketh my blood, hath eternal life; and I will raise him up at the last day. — John vi. 53, 54.

THIS statement, so absolute, so authoritative, and so solemnly reiterated, was a fan with which the Saviour purged his floor. Many were so scandalized by it that from that hour they forsook him. So is it always. To declare in any age that for us sons of men there is no remission of sins, and no entrance into everlasting life apart from the death of the Son of man, is to rouse the repugnance of the natural heart. From the days of Cain, God's way of life by means of death has been an offence to many. Many also, like Abel, have by faith fed on the Lamb slain from the foundation of the world, and found his flesh meat indeed and his blood drink indeed. Thus they received and nourished eternal life, and lived in hope of the resurrection of the just.

How can I share this life, and attain to this resurrection? By no mastication of material elements, but by personal trust in an ascended Saviour. Jesus' words, being spirit and life, impart life wherever received. Hence his deepest complaint is, "There are some of you that believe not." He has the words of everlasting life. Here he speaks them. You may accept them! You may reject them! You cannot alter them!

A. B. Mackay.

> Extol the Lamb of God,
>   The all-atoning Lamb;
> Redemption in his blood
>   Throughout the world proclaim!
>
>   C. Wesley.

JANUARY 23.

Alway delivered unto death for Jesus' sake.—2 COR. iv. 11.

He that loveth his life shall lose it; and he that hateth his life in this world shall keep it unto life eternal. — JOHN xii. 25.

OUR Lord describes the career and close of two kinds of life, of which one is to love the present world with its pleasures, which is deplorable loss now, and will, unless faith and repentance prevent, lead to the fearful perdition of "the second death." The other is to hate life in this world by denying ourselves those delights which war against the soul, and to bear without shrinking reproach and suffering, to preserve the "inner man" unhurt and victorious.

The extent of the eternal life promised to self-denying believers is beyond our grasp of thought. There are some hints of its nature in the words of Christ and his apostles, of which the chief is the enjoyment of the glorified presence of the Redeemer, and the attainment of the promised recompenses of present sacrifices and faithful stewardship. Saint Paul's view of heaven was that of being with Jesus, while Saint John conceived eternal life to consist in being like him; and all who follow in their footsteps shall, after the wreck of all earthly things, escape with their life to the happy shore of perfect peace. They shall see him from whom shall flow those influences which shall change them "from glory to glory," and amidst the revelations of his love all life shall be Sabbath rest, all space temple, and all service adoring worship and praise.

J.J. Bright

We are the Lord's; then let us gladly tender
Our souls to him in deeds, not empty words;
Let heart and tongue and life combine to render
No doubtful witness that we are the Lord's.
C. T. ASTLEY *(Translation)*.

January 24.

What hast thou that thou didst not receive? — 1 Cor. iv. 7.

So likewise ye, when ye shall have done all these things which are commanded you, say, We are unprofitable servants: we have done that which was our duty to do. — Luke xvii. 10.

CHRISTIANS are at once sons and servants of God. This fact suggests the true measure of Christian merit. All ought to serve God; but the obligations of a redeemed soul are peculiarly tender. God's claims upon his time and talent are such that he can do nothing above what is required. None can put God under obligations. We are here warned against undue pride of achievement. Our best performance is imperfect. The servant's tasks are never finished.

The remembrance of this necessity of work laid upon us prevents undue self-complacency. Duty is a reality. "Stern daughter of the voice of God," says Wordsworth; while Schiller affirms, "When duty grows thy law, enjoyment fades away." The Christian who takes this view will render a servant's obedience. Gratitude and love change drudgery to voluntary service, while duty gives love character and lifts it above mere sentiment. Duty should be love's guide.

Strength increases with the performance of duty. Thus the willing servant grows in capacity and usefulness. The Lord graciously accepts the loving duteous service of him who humbly acknowledges his own unworthiness. He who obeys in such a spirit is already a child of God, a joint-heir with Christ.

Hubert W. Brown

When all is done, renounce your deeds,
  Renounce self-righteousness with scorn;
Thus will you glorify your God,
  And thus the Christian name adorn!

GIBBONS.

January 25.

First pure, then peaceable. — James iii. 17.

Blessed are the peacemakers: for they shall be called the children of God. — Matt. v. 9.

HE who speaks this blessed loving text is God incarnate, God the Son, Jesus Christ, the only all-sufficient Saviour. In the economy of God he is the greatest peacemaker known to earth. For this peace he was "slain from the foundation of the world." For this peace, in God's love for the world, his only begotten Son was given. For this peace as the only able one, he made the only propitiation for the sins of the world, and thus bought us, one and all, and thus became as the God-man our Lord under the exaltation of God, who gave him a name above every name as a reward of his infinitely humble, acceptable, and profitable work, that every tongue should confess Jesus Christ as Lord to the glory of God the Father. For this peace the Master sent his ministry forth and the Holy Ghost to bless them in the establishment of his Church for the salvation of men. For this peace he ascended into heaven to carry on his work in the presence of God, as the great Intercessor, with the marks of his love in his hands, with wounds in his feet, and with the open door in his side to his heart; and so he lives in the smile of heaven to the end of his mediatorial kingdom.

And now as is the tree so are the branches and fruit; they cannot help being blessed. It is in the very nature of things in the providence of God. And so we naturally read our text and learn our lesson, each in our own degree, as we faithfully apply its use.

Chas. H. Hoffman.

How sweet, how heavenly is the sight,
When those who love the Lord
In one another's peace delight,
And so fulfil his word!

Joseph Swain.

January 26.

Fruitful in every good work. — Col. i. 10.

Occupy till I come. — Luke xix. 13.

ACTION! — not that of the soldier fired with conquest, but of the merchantman, cool in brain, shrewd in judgment, augmenting invested capital. "Occupy" — do business herewith — "till I come." The Christian life is a service of usefulness. Gratuitously, every believer receives his "pound," then comes responsibility! An orthodox creed and a passive life may join hands. The mere culture of moods does as little for the soul as for the stock-market. Saved by faith, we must live by works! Duty slurred over robs the gospel of its power and the disciple of his reward!

To occupy, we must have knowledge. My successful business friend knows what he is about. He who negotiates for God must know God's word! Buoyant feelings are indispensable. The worried man falls out of the commercial arena. To win laurels in traffic, one must likewise curb his passions with bits of steel and reins of raw hide. "Whosoever will come after me, let him deny himself." We must die to the flesh to live to usefulness! Behold, moreover, the steadfastness of duty. "Occupy" — not till acclaim ceases or health loses its grip, but — "*till I come!*" "He that endureth to the end shall be saved!"

Alfred H. Moment.

> Go, labor on, spend and be spent,
>   Thy joy to do thy Father's will.
> It was the way the Master went;
>   Shall not the servant tread it still?
>
> H. Bonar.

January 27.

Ṩou hath he quickened. — Eph. ii. 1.

Verily, verily, I say unto you, The hour is coming, and now is, when the dead shall hear the voice of the Son of God: and they that hear shall live. — John v. 25.

WHO are the dead? Alas, we know but too well! Some of them have been carried from our homes. Their dust lies beneath the grass and the flowers in the cemetery. Their images haunt tenderly our memories. Their influence is woven, in many a golden thread, into our characters and lives. But these are not "the dead" of whom our Lord here speaks. He has reference to those who are "dead while they live," "dead in trespasses and sins," who have no perception of, or love for, or interest in, spiritual things, who do not "live unto God." Even heathen have had some perception of the possibility of spiritual death, present as well as future. "What," said Socrates to his disciples, — "what if some of those around us were already dead souls!" It is a terrible thought that even in the midst of the life and beauty of the world, over a vast multitude of souls "death reigns," and corruption is creeping. It may be that we ourselves are spiritually dead, or little better. But "the hour cometh," it is not far away, it "now is," for the dead to arise. Already it is the resurrection morn. Even now the Son of God is calling, and all around us men are coming to life. "Now is the day of salvation." "They who hear shall live." But how can the dead hear? Because he who speaks to Lazarus at the same time gives him the power to hear, and to obey, and to "come forth." O thou who art "the Resurrection and the Life," dispose us to hear thy voice and awake from spiritual death to life eternal!

John E. Todd.

Oh, let the dead now hear thy voice!
Bid, Lord, thy banished ones rejoice!
Their beauty this, their glorious dress,
Jesus, the Lord, our righteousness.

J. Wesley *(Translation).*

JANUARY 28.

God was manifest in the flesh. — 1 TIM. iii. 16.

Believest thou not that I am in the Father, and the Father in me? The words that I speak unto you I speak not of myself: but the Father that dwelleth in me, he doeth the works. — JOHN xiv. 10.

THE words and works of Christ were the words and works of God. We need not wait to prove the historic miracles which Christ wrought upon men's bodies. We have three greater miracles of his before us to-day, his matchless character, his matchless words, his matchless influence, — the miracle of a character too unique to be invented, too pure and mighty to be human; the miracle of teachings that the world's wisest men have almost universally admitted to be not only unequalled, but unapproached; the miracle of an influence upon individuals and nations greater than has been exerted by any other person that ever walked the earth. These present, indisputable evidences show that Christ is able as well as willing to save me and to save the world.

Christianity is a science, not a dream, because it is established in part, like law and history, upon abundant and reliable testimony; in part, like gravitation and the roundness of the earth upon a proved hypothesis that alone includes and harmonizes all the facts; in part, like medicine and chemistry, upon experiments and experience. No hypothesis but that of Christianity explains how an unlettered carpenter of Nazareth has become the best known, the most beloved, and the most obeyed of any being "that e'er wore earth about him." But there is yet stronger evidence in experience. "Come and see!"

Wilbur F. Crafts.

Show us thyself, for seeing thee
Do we, dear Lord, the Father see;
In all thy words and works we trace
The Father's heart, the Father's grace.
R. M. OFFORD.

January 29.

Your labour is not in vain in the Lord. — 1 Cor. xv. 58.

Well done, thou good and faithful servant: thou hast been faithful over a few things, I will make thee ruler over many things: enter thou into the joy of thy lord. — Matt. xxv. 21.

GOD has the highest possible claim to our services, and his claim is universal and constant. No peculiarity of natural endowment, great or small, nor diversity of opportunity or means of doing good, works any change in the matter of personal responsibility. All power and means of doing good are the gift of God, and to meet our obligations all must be consecrated to his services.

Christ teaches us that the grandest possibilities are wrapped up in every human life; that by the right improvement of the talents given, be they ten or one, we shall by and by become rulers over many things and enter into the joy of our Lord; that constant devotion to God is the true philosophy of a successful life: "For what shall it profit a man if he gain the whole world and lose his own soul?" Happy then the man who recognizes the will of God as the rule of his every-day life. It may, it will, require sacrifice, possible suffering, and failure in many worldly enterprises and prospects, but fidelity to God is assured success. To the faithful servant of God triumph is not far off. To-day improve the talents given; to-morrow the Master will say, "Well done," for the "Judge standeth at the door."

Martha Staple

<pre>
        Oh, may I, no longer dreaming,
          Idly waste my golden day,
        But, each precious hour redeeming,
          Upward, onward, press my way!
                                    H. Bonar.
</pre>

January 30.

Christ is the end of the law for righteousness.
ROMANS x. 4.

Think not that I am come to destroy the law, or the prophets: I am not come to destroy, but to fulfil. For verily I say unto you, Till heaven and earth pass, one jot or one tittle shall in no wise pass from the law, till all be fulfilled. — MATT. v. 17, 18.

HOW comforting are these words, which form a part of the Sermon on the Mount, in which our Lord sets forth the great principles of his kingdom! He founded redemption upon law as revealed to Moses and the prophets. Christianity thus stands upon the bed-rock of revelation as made before Christ; and the living Church, by its very existence, confirms every "jot and tittle" of the Old Testament. Law is love working out the eternal plan of God; its supreme, serene dominion over all things, material and spiritual, is the eternal repose of the universe. The gospel did indeed displace the types and shadows of the ceremonial only to reveal the grandeur of the moral law, as sunrise dispels the mists only to disclose more clearly the mountains, standing in all their rugged strength. There can in the nature of things be no redemption without law, no mercy without justice, no pardon without a stable throne; only a sound ship can save the wrecked. But Christ's expiatory death exalted the law. God incarnate added to it a glory impossible to be derived from the legal obedience or sufferings of mere creatures. The cross shows the granite foundations of the divine government in greater massiveness than they had before been seen. The heavenly hosts rejoice in obedience, as the planets in their swift courses. Grace and law are parts of the same complete sphere. All the redeemed sing the song of Moses and the Lamb.

Saml. W. Boardman.

But, fixed for everlasting years,
Unmoved amid the wreck of spheres,
Thy word shall shine in cloudless day,
When heaven and earth have passed away.
SIR ROBERT GRANT

JANUARY 31.

There is no want to them that fear him. — PSALM xxxiv. 9.

Labour not for the meat which perisheth, but for that meat which endureth unto everlasting life, which the Son of man shall give unto you: for him hath God the Father sealed. — JOHN vi. 27.

WE *must* do work to live *now;* we *may* so do it as to live forever. The body of Jesus was hungry for bread in the wilderness; but his soul was more hungry for that which came into his life through "every word of God." If we *will*, we *may* reap two harvests from every deed, — one in time, one in eternity. God has put the best things of earth right beside the path of duty, which leads to heaven; so Jesus says, " Seek first the kingdom of God . . . and all these things shall be added to you." Not because of your work, but your childhood. The prodigal started home to get bread for his labor; but he got the embrace, kiss, shoes, best robe, fatted calf, and father's heart, — not for his labor, but for his return to his father. As we lift life to God, we harmonize it with man. This wipes out "all inhumanity to man," reconciles all capital with labor, does away with all oppression, and makes "the kingdom come and the will be done on earth as it is in heaven." Thus the poorest task to human being given holds in it the possibility of an "heir of God, and joint heirship with Jesus Christ." The loneliest and most obscure lot in life can open into full fellowship with all the spirits of heaven.

Clifton Penick

Beneath the spreading heavens,
No creature but is fed;
And he who feeds the ravens
Will give his children bread.
COWPER.

February 1.

Truly this was the Son of God. — Matt. xxvii. 54.

If I do not the works of my Father, believe me not. But if I do, though ye believe not me, believe the works: that ye may know, and believe, that the Father is in me, and I in him. — John x. 37, 38.

THESE are remarkable words. Our Lord appeals to his mighty works as proofs of his divine mission, and as credentials that he came from God. Men resisted the evidence of his words; let them yield to the evidence of his works. If they were not convinced by what he said, let them be convinced by what he did. He had said he was the Son of God, — this they disbelieved; but how could they deny that he was one with the Father when he did the works of the Father, — works which none but God could possibly perform, and which proved his goodness, his mercy, and his love? Our blessed Lord again and again draws attention to his miracles. When John sent his disciples to ask him, "Art thou he that should come, or do we look for another?" he made answer, "Go and shew John again those things which ye do hear and see."

Let us mark, and rejoice that the Father and the Son are one, "The Father in me, and I in him." As Christ said again, "He that hath seen me hath seen the Father;" "I and the Father are one." One, — of a glory equal, of a majesty co-eternal; one in essence, one in purpose, one in working.

Blessed thought! For if Christ and the Father are one, then, believing in Christ, my salvation is secure, — for the Spirit proceedeth from the Father and the Son, and must therefore be one with both; so that the Triune God are all intent on my salvation, and nothing can separate me from their love.

Charles D. Bell

Christ our Lord and God we own,
Christ, the Father's only Son,
Lamb of God for sinners slain,
Saviour of offending man.   C. Wesley.

FEBRUARY 2.

By the power of the Spirit of God. — ROMANS xv. 19.

Verily, verily, I say unto you, He that believeth on me, the works that I do shall he do also; and greater works than these shall he do; because I go unto my Father. — JOHN xiv. 12.

THE words, "Verily, verily," render this verse emphatic. They show how deeply our Lord felt the truth he uttered. To him it was prophecy; to his disciples is given the blessed possibility to make it fact.

Living faith makes the disciple a branch of the true Vine, and on the branch we seek the fruit. The work is the same, for it comes from the same root. The disciple receives the grace of full obedience and consecration and of loving, willing service. That he should yield himself to such grace is no strain upon the gospel; it is the proper thing for the imitator of such a Saviour to do. Then comes the result. The branch bears fruit more abundant than the root.

"Because I go to my Father" gives the reason for these greater works. Our ascended Lord now works through the Spirit; and his disciples left on earth are made the instruments of greater spiritual results than any that attended the earthly life of Jesus: hence the greater works of Pentecost, of every true revival, of thousands of such disciples as Harlan Page. A few years ago, a poor humble Nestorian was followed to his grave by weeping crowds, who testified to a saving power in his life upon them, — a striking illustration of this verse fulfilled. ".Happy indeed is such a disciple; the same bringeth forth much fruit."

John A. Shedd

  Work, for the night is coming,
   Work through the morning hours;
  Work while the dew is sparkling,
   Work 'mid springing flowers.
  Work, when the day grows brighter,
   Work in the glowing sun;
  Work, for the night is coming,
   When man's work is done. ANNIE L. WALKER.

February 3.

Christ Jesus came into the world to save sinners.
1 Tim. i. 15.

For the Son of man is come to seek and to save that which was lost. — Luke xix. 10.

THE Son of God in his work for men identifies himself with them by becoming, and constantly calling himself the Son of man. He is among men and with men as a new power in the life of the world. For one purpose only could so great an event as the coming of the Son of man be demanded. For the ordinary regulation of life the resources of the earth and the activity of man are sufficient, as each new year of experience proves. But the fact that man was lost, that he had wandered from his Father's presence and from the knowledge of his Father's love, called for the coming of the Son of man to bring man back to his true position. The wisdom and love of the God of creation met the new demand.

Without the Son of man our daily duties and pleasures are the endless and aimless wanderings of men lost in a trackless existence. Under his guidance they are marches to a definite end. If that end is not always clear to us or to others, it is to him. He not only comes to seek, but to save. We respond to the seeking voice, and at once the work of salvation begins. It is sure of success, and every day that makes up a part of its story shares in that certainty, and has now in all its events the brightness of the sun which never shall set.

Arthur Brooks

> Jesus sought me when a stranger,
>   Wandering from the fold of God;
> He, to rescue me from danger,
>   Interposed his precious blood.
>
> Robert Robinson.

February 4.

Heirs of the kingdom.—James ii. 5.

Fear not, little flock; for it is your Father's good pleasure to give you the kingdom.—Luke xii. 32.

HOW like "the good shepherd!" What tenderness! What loving sympathy! "Seek ye the kingdom of God" as your life-work. Enemies and dangers will confront and oppose you. "Fear not them which kill the body." "Fear not" anything. "Let not your heart be troubled, neither let it be afraid."

"Fear not." "Your Father knoweth" your foes and your needs. It is his pleasure to give you the kingdom. His heart's joy is in it. His hand will accomplish it.

"Fear not, little flock." You may think I am sending you "as sheep in the midst of wolves," which rush with open mouth upon their prey. Seek and fear not; "for it is your Father's good pleasure to give you the kingdom."

"Fear not." Your Father gives. Ye are his children. Where should the sons and daughters of the King dwell but in the kingdom of their Father? How can the Father do otherwise than give you the kingdom?

"Fear not." Yea, rather, rejoice and be glad. Have confidence and expectation. Look for the coming of the King. Await the bestowment of the kingdom, with the throne and the crown, the sceptre and the glory everlasting.

Giles H. Mandeville

  Cease, ye pilgrims, cease to mourn;
   Press onward to the prize.
  Soon our Saviour will return,
   Triumphant in the skies.
  Yet a season, and you know
   Happy entrance will be given,
  All our sorrows left below,
   And earth exchanged for heaven.
        Robert Seagrave.

February 5.

God hath chosen the weak things. — 1 Cor. i. 27.

So the last shall be first, and the first last. — Matt. xx. 16.

WHOM God accepts the world rejects. To human eyes Dives was first and Lazarus last, but God saw differently. Nero had all the world offered, — health, an athlete's strength, intellectual culture, boundless wealth, absolute power, great honor. Paul was poor, old, sick, imprisoned, friendless. But the shout of triumph comes from the dungeon, not the palace; from the poor old sick man, not the athlete; from the apostle, not the emperor. "I have fought the good fight, I have finished the course, I have kept the faith." Who thinks of Nero to-day save with contempt? while Paul is loved and honored throughout the world, and will be to the end. Jonathan Edwards's congregation rejected him by a vote of two hundred to twenty. Even the King of heaven "was despised and rejected of men." Saved by grace, we are rewarded according to our faithfulness. The eleventh-hour laborers were as faithful as the rest, and so were paid the same. The weakest, obscurest child of God can be as faithful as Paul or Luther.

> "Within the smallest flower I often find
> A richer and more delicate perfume
> Than in the largest, most pretentious flower,
> That waves its petals in the summer wind."

The most beautiful window in the Lincoln Cathedral was made of rejected bits of glass. From material rejected of men, God will fashion some of the brightest and most glorious ornaments of the temple on high.

T. T. Eaton

> Let the world despise and leave me,
>   They have left my Saviour too;
> Human hearts and looks deceive me,
>   Thou art not, like man, untrue.
> And while thou shalt smile upon me,
>   God of wisdom, love, and might,
> Foes may hate, and friends may shun me,
>   Show thy face, and all is bright.   Lyte.

February 6.

Sealed with that Holy Spirit of promise. — EPH. i. 13.

And I will pray the Father, and he shall give you another Comforter, that he may abide with you for ever; even the Spirit of truth; whom the world cannot receive, because it seeth him not, neither knoweth him: but ye know him; for he dwelleth with you, and shall be in you. — JOHN xiv. 16, 17.

HOW replete with inspiration is every clause of this passage! What wealth of deep spiritual meaning does it convey! Take the very term "Comforter," a Latin derivative, — "con," "fortis," together with strength. Here is implied the Spirit companionship that is strength-giving, softened and sweetened by his tenderness and love. Christ here assumes that he was the first Comforter. His mission was to bind up the broken-hearted; to this end he held within his incarnate person all the treasures of wisdom, grace, and compassion. But the demands of his mediatorial work made it expedient that he should go away. Comfortless or orphaned he could not and would not leave his disciples, hence another Comforter is promised. Equal in his essence with the Father, yet was he officially subordinate in the redeeming order, and so he prayed the Father and his prayer prevailed. An abiding Comforter was sent as the final manifestation of God to the Church. Bereaved, desolate, forsaken, lone one, wearing around the heart the rustling, withered, dead leaves of departed joy, this is your great heritage, — a companion who shall abide with you along the untravelled eternities, even the Spirit of truth, who shall guide you up the steeps of time and on to the blissful forever.

Geo. Douglas.

I worship thee, O Holy Ghost,
I love to worship thee;
My risen Lord for aye were lost
But for thy company.

I worship thee, O Holy Ghost,
I love to worship thee;
With thee, each day is Pentecost,
Each night Nativity.

WILLIAM F. WARREN.

February 7.

The word of our God shall stand for ever. — Isaiah xl. 8.

Heaven and earth shall pass away: but my words shall not pass away. — Mark xiii. 31.

WHO could speak thus but a man who was God? The words cover everything that Jesus ever said. His doctrines can never pass away. Human philosophies may go out of date, the words of Jesus never; neither can the law which he declared. The Sermon on the Mount will never be toned down to the level of human morality; and the warnings of Jesus abide in force. Men may ignore them, if they like, or explain them away; but this will make no difference. They shall not pass away. But we need not stop with this. This mighty assurance covers also all the promises of Jesus. How many and how precious they are! — "Him that cometh unto me, I will in no wise cast out;" "I am with you alway:" and "I will come again, and receive you unto myself." Truly such promises as these are royal, godlike! so great that faith often finds it hard to believe them. But he abideth faithful. We feel that we can depend on the rising of the sun and the nightly shining of the stars and the order of the revolving year; yet he assures us these are not so certain as the fulfilment of his words. Let us then hold fast the doctrine of Jesus, obey his law, heed his warnings, and joyfully rest in his promises; and in the end we shall confess with Israel, "Not one good thing hath failed us of all that the Lord our God hath spoken."

J. H. Kellogg

> Wide as the world is thy command,
> Vast as eternity thy love;
> Firm as a rock thy truth must stand,
> When rolling years shall cease to move.
> — WATTS.

February 8.

Charity . . . thinketh no evil. — 1 Cor. xiii. 4, 5.

Judge not, and ye shall not be judged: condemn not, and ye shall not be condemned: forgive, and ye shall be forgiven. — Luke vi. 37.

NOT judged of God to whom all hearts are open and to whom all at last shall give account. These words are not to be understood to mean that the Church or the Christian shall pronounce no judgment against evil, — that duty is expressly enjoined in not a few places in the New Testament both by the Lord and the apostles. The Saviour's words in this text are not to be interpreted as permitting the easy-going indifference to evil which is so often simply moral cowardice. His thought is directed rather to censoriousness, — that captious, fault-finding spirit which is quick to see evil and overlook good. It is a spirit of rapid growth and wide opportunity. As we see it in others, we wonder at its proportions and its acuteness. It has an eye like a vulture's; and often when its possessor is thought to be enjoying the pure ether and the celestial radiance of the upper air in which at the time he is floating, it detects the single speck of carrion in the wide horizon and descends upon it as if it were the all-important object within its ken. The exhortation is, that we throttle this spirit within ourselves; that we cultivate an eye that shall be quick to discern good, a spirit always eager to wrap the work and the person of others in the mantle of generous charity. It is the command which gives birth to the virtue that Paul so beautifully describes as the pre-eminent grace of the Christian, the charity "that suffereth long and is kind, that taketh not account of evil, that rejoiceth not in iniquity."

Henry A. Stimson

Love is kind, and suffers long,
Love is meek, and thinks no wrong;
Love, than death itself more strong,
    Give us heavenly love!   C. Wordsworth.

February 9.

Lights in the world. — Phil. ii. 15.

Ye are the light of the world. A city that is set on a hill cannot be hid. Neither do men light a candle, and put it under a bushel, but on a candlestick; and it giveth light unto all that are in the house. Let your light so shine before men, that they may see your good works, and glorify your Father which is in heaven. — Matt. v. 14-16.

WE do not need to adopt any philosophical theory of light to perceive the beauty and pertinence of the figure by which our Lord represents his friends as the light of the world. The world is dark because sin dominates it. Sin darkens the mind so that God, truth, duty, the way of salvation by Christ, are obscured. Therefore it needs light, penetrating, revealing, awakening. Watch the earth when the light of morning breaks over it! So the moral world needs the spiritual light,— the light of Christian example, instruction, influence.

This light is not our light. It is given from above. Christ is the light of the world, and the light that is in us is from him, as the reflected light of stars is from the central sun. It is not given to be hidden, but to shine forth. The old Roman law maintained the right of citizens to unobstructed light. Light is for the world. If we have it we must let it shine. The light of the individual Christian should make an illuminated home. The light of the united Church should be like a lighted city at night, standing on a hill.

Burdett Hart.

> Oh, let our love and faith abound;
> Oh, let our lives to all around
>   With purest lustre shine, —
> That all around our works may see,
> And give the glory, Lord, to thee,
>   The heavenly light divine.
>
> C. Wesley.

February 10.

What persecutions I endured. — 2 Tim. iii. 11.

Think not that I am come to send peace on earth: I came not to send peace, but a sword. — Matt. x. 34.

THIS statement is in apparent conflict with other declarations of Scripture, and indeed with our cardinal conceptions of the design of the gospel. Jesus elsewhere says to his disciples, "My peace I leave with you; my peace I give unto you." The natal song of the Redeemer was, "Glory to God in the highest! On earth, peace!"

How shall we reconcile the seeming discrepancy? First, it is an inward peace and not external quiet that is promised.

Christ expressly tells his followers, "In the world ye shall have tribulation." But he adds, "Be of good comfort; I have overcome the world." The peace that he gives us, the world can neither give nor take away.

Next, the world will never be at peace until the world be subdued to Christ. A king can grant peace to his subjects only while they remain loyal; when they are in rebellion he must draw the sword. Our Saviour here represents himself as a sovereign come to recover a revolted province.

Satan has usurped dominion of this world; he must be dethroned. It is our noblest privilege to engage in this warfare under Christ's banner. To those thus enlisted he says, "Fear not, little flock; for it is your Father's good pleasure to give you the kingdom."

Thomas A. Hoyt.

> Fear not, O little flock, the foe
> Who madly seeks your overthrow;
>   Dread not his rage and power.
> What though your courage sometimes faints!
> His seeming triumph o'er God's saints
>   Lasts but a little hour.
>
>   Catharine Winkworth *(Translation)*.

February 11.

Whose end is to be burned. — Heb. vi. 8.

Ye are the salt of the earth: but if the salt have lost his savour, wherewith shall it be salted? It is thenceforth good for nothing, but to be cast out, and to be trodden under foot of men. — Matt. v. 13.

THE salt in Judea was native salt mingled with various earthy substances. When exposed to the atmosphere and rain, the saline particles in due time wasted away, and what was left was an insipid earthy mass, looking like salt, but entirely destitute of a conserving element, and absolutely good for nothing. It was not merely good for nothing, but actually destructive of all fertility wherever it might be thrown; therefore it was cast into the streets to be trodden under foot of men. The carcass of sheep or bullock might be buried deep in this worthless mass, and the process of corruption not be delayed a moment.

What an illustration is this of the absolute worthlessness of the form of godliness when the power is utterly lacking! If the salt have lost its savor, wherewith shall it be salted? How can its salting, conserving property be recovered? What can you do with it? So your savorless religion is not only worthless in its influence on others, but of no good to yourselves. It will save neither them nor yourself from corruption. How sad for one to have lost the power that belongs to the Christian calling, and instead of being the instrument of saving others, becoming a means of their perdition! Well does the Saviour say in another place, "Have salt in yourselves."

David D. Demarest.

Lord, to me more grace impart;
Make me faithful, Lord, I pray.
Purify and keep my heart;
Make me fruitful day by day.

R. M. Offord.

February 12.

He maketh the storm a calm. — Psalm cvii. 29.

Why are ye fearful, O ye of little faith? — Matt. viii. 26.

THE reproving question bears its own answer. The disciples were fearful because they had so little faith. How dull they were! How little they understood him! They did not really know who he was. Surely if they had taken in the evidences of his divine personality and authority, which had attended all he did and said in their presence, the sudden storm on the lake would not have affrighted them with Christ in the boat, although he were asleep. Were they not there by his command, and what were winds and waves to him? Could they perish with him on board? Alas that we are such cowards often in the face of danger, and forget who it is that commands the ship!

In recently crossing the Atlantic a group of passengers after a violent storm huddled together on their steamer-chairs condoling each other on their late fearful experiences, when a lady of the company addressed the captain, who had drawn near, and asked, "Captain, did n't you think we were going to the bottom?" Assuming an air of offended dignity, the master of the ship replied, "Madam, when I signed the ship's papers in the company's office, I agreed to carry this steamer across the Atlantic Ocean from Liverpool to New York. The bottom is not on my chart."

Now when Christ entered the ship with his disciples his purpose was to cross the lake. The bottom was not on his chart. But he answered their fears and bade the wind and storm cease; and there was a great calm.

F. Bottome.

Jesus Jehovah, be our stay
Over the dark and troublous way.
Embarked with him we need feel no fear
Though the storm, the trial of faith, be near.

February 13.

Let nothing be done through . . . vain glory. — Phil. ii. 3.

Take heed that ye do not your alms before men, to be seen of them: otherwise ye have no reward of your Father which is in heaven. — Matt. vi. 1.

GIVING and *serving* are the two thoughts of this passage. As to *giving*, Christ seems to take it for granted that his followers in every possible way will relieve human sorrow and want. He does not command them to feed the hungry, clothe the naked, and deliver the oppressed, but in his life shows how these exercises are the natural outcome of a loyal love. For the true Christian no commands are needed on these lines. There is, however, danger that men will give for the sake of attracting attention and securing applause. Here "take heed." He who gives from love to God shall have reward, and may not concern himself whether his gifts are unknown or known; but he who gives for the sake of human commendation, or human recognition of any kind, shall have no reward, save such as comes from the hollow praise of men. All truly Christian giving is spontaneous and self-forgetful. As to *serving*, this is to spring from the same unselfish motive. We are not to do righteousness that we may be personally commended, but that we may commend Christ. In all our deeds our one aim should be to lead men into the acceptance and obedience of the gospel. The more vital our Christianity the more completely do we lose ourselves in the one purpose to attract men to Christ and cause them to share in his great salvation.

J. E. Twitchell

Mean are all offerings we can make;
Yet thou hast taught us, Lord,
If given for the Saviour's sake,
They lose not their reward.

WILLIAM CROSSWELL.

FEBRUARY 14.

How long halt ye between two opinions?—I KINGS xviii. 21.

He that is not with me is against me; and he that gathereth not with me scattereth abroad.—MATT. xii. 30.

CHRIST had come to an issue with the leaders of the Jewish people. He claimed to be their Messiah. To disregard that claim was to reject him. This they did, and called his power satanic. The common people looked to these leaders for guidance, and followed their indifference.

We all influence each other. Influence is like force. It always acts *in some direction;* and the direction is not affected by its strength. A west wind is a west wind, whether it is a cyclone or a zephyr. A great man and a child may both work for Jesus, and the child just as truly as the man.

Some railroad men are on a hand-car. Whoever does not work at the lever adds to the load. A poor family are struggling for a living. Such of the children as earn ever so little are doing a share, but those who earn nothing eat up the earnings of the rest. The policeman that so far befriends a thief as not to arrest him is the thief's ally. The army officer who tolerates mutiny is guilty of helping it on.

No man can sit on the edge of a sword-blade; his attempt would be his destruction. There is no half-way place there; so God calls for open, active friendship. As you cannot stop breathing and not die, so you cannot neglect Christ and not perish.

Geo. P. Hays

Lord, I am thine,—entirely thine,
Purchased and saved by blood divine;
With full consent I thine would be,
And own thy sovereign right in me.
SAMUEL DAVIES.

February 15.

Be clothed with humility. — 1 Peter v. 5.

Whosoever will be great among you, let him be your minister; and whosoever will be chief among you, let him be your servant: even as the Son of man came not to be ministered unto, but to minister, and to give his life a ransom for many. — Matt. xx. 26–28.

OUR Lord did not reprove the desire to be great. He taught by what means greatness can be secured. These men were not to make this the thought and purpose of their life, nor were they to regard it as the unconditioned gift of God. They could have it by becoming ministers to others. This is not an arbitrary rule, but a necessary principle. Greatness is not of bargain or reward, but the natural result of a great life. Usefulness wins the honor which it does not seek. Nothing less than this gains our lasting homage. We bow before high authority; we admire great attainments; but it is service to which we give real honor, and render sincere allegiance. To this we build monuments. We gain our own approval when we have made ourselves of use. This is in accordance with the divine nature, of which we are partakers. God has revealed himself as love. As a father he ministers to his children, and even to birds and flowers. When the Christ came into the world it was to give his life for men. It is through this gift that he has made himself our Redeemer and our Lord. He taught that this is the law of heaven. Those who "for the sake of the Name" have ministered to others with the cup of water and the personal helpfulness are his disciples, whom he receives into the kingdom prepared for them.

Alexander McKenzie

> O wondrous Lord, my soul would be
> Still more and more conformed to thee,
> And learn of thee, the lowly One,
> And like thee, all my journey run.
>
> Bishop A. C. Coxe.

February 16.

Able ... to save ... to the uttermost. — Heb. vii. 25.

My sheep hear my voice, and I know them, and they follow me: and I give unto them eternal life; and they shall never perish, neither shall any man pluck them out of my hand. My Father, which gave them me, is greater than all; and no man is able to pluck them out of my Father's hand. — John x. 27–29.

THE characteristics of the Saviour's sheep are presented in these words, and their secure and happy condition is also set before us. In the attitude of a shepherd, the Lord Jesus shows us how near he comes to the needs of our sinful humanity. This is presented in the former part of this chapter, where we are taught that he calls and names his sheep, that he leads and feeds them, and also that he gives his own life for them. On the other hand, the sheep are brought before us in these most interesting and touching verses, that we may understand what they are in character, and what they shall be in the future of Christ's kingdom and glory. It should be realized that these are the permanent and universal traits of true discipleship. Whenever and wherever one of the Saviour's true sheep is found, he will be one who receives him as Master and Lord, and who hears his word and follows him; and the result will be that Christ will know him in the way of recognition and of gracious assurance, and will give to him eternal life.

Rob.t Russell Booth

> Oh, what glory, far exceeding
>   All that eye has yet perceived!
> Holiest hearts for ages pleading
>   Never that full joy conceived.
> God has promised, Christ prepares it,
>   There on high our welcome waits;
> Every humble spirit shares it,
>   Christ has passed the eternal gates.
>
> WILLIAM J. IRONS.

February 17.

Our fellowship is with the Father, and with his Son.
1 JOHN i. 3.

If a man love me, he will keep my words: and my Father will love him, and we will come unto him, and make our abode with him.— JOHN xiv. 23.

THIS fourteenth chapter of John is full of comfort for the troubled Christian: 1. Heaven is certain (v. 2). 2. The way is plain (v. 6). 3. Power for service is granted (v. 12). 4. Our prayers will be answered (v. 13). 5. The Comforter will come (v. 16). 6. Christ will return (v. 18). 7. Fellowship with the Father is promised (v. 23). What more could we ask? Not only is the future home assured, but here in this life we are promised fellowship with God. But remember, this is conditioned on our loving the Lord and keeping his words. The Person and the Book — the incarnate Word and the written Word — should be the centre of our thoughts. If then, "the words of Christ dwell in us richly in all wisdom," we can appropriate this beautiful promise and say with joy, "Truly our fellowship is with the Father, and with his Son Jesus Christ."

Wm. Walton Clark.

    Love divine, all love excelling,
      Joy of heaven to earth come down,
    Fix in us thy humble dwelling;
      All thy faithful mercies crown.
    Jesus, thou art all compassion,
      Pure unbounded love thou art.
    Visit us with thy salvation;
      Enter every trembling heart.
                        C. WESLEY.

February 18.

God for Christ's sake hath forgiven you. — Eph. iv. 32.

Son, be of good cheer; thy sins be forgiven thee. — Matt. ix. 2.
Thy sins are forgiven. — Luke vii. 48.

HOW happy the child who knows he has been forgiven! Especially is this true if he is conscientious,— one who has been taught the truth by the Spirit of God.
A Christian is a child redeemed. He has the simplicity, the trust, the joy of a child, not only at his conversion, but often after he hears the voice of Jesus saying to him, "Thy sins are forgiven thee." The moralist, the socinian, the worldling, the formal professor, knows nothing of this; but the true disciple does.
Let me give an illustration. A theological student just completing his course was a good prey for the adversary. Satan told him he was not a Christian; how then could he consistently preach the gospel? For days he was in darkness. At length his burden became intolerable. This matter must be settled. He shut the door of his study and tried to pray; the heavens seemed to him like brass. In his distress he opened the Bible. The first verse he saw was, "Son, be of good cheer; thy sins be forgiven thee."
Light came, and with it joy. Was it a chance? Was it a delusion? No; forty years have passed, and that student now testifies in this sermonette the Lord is true. They that trust in him shall not be confounded. When Jesus says the word "forgiven," he seals the truth with his Spirit. Has he spoken this word to you?

Peter Stryker

My burden at his feet I laid,
   And knew the joy of heaven,
As in my willing ear he said
   The blessed word, "Forgiven."

P. STRYKER.

FEBRUARY 19.

Christ who is our life. — COL. iii. 4.

I am the living bread which came down from heaven: if any man eat of this bread, he shall live for ever: and the bread that I will give is my flesh, which I will give for the life of the world. — JOHN vi. 51.

AS our bodies need bread for the sustenance of the physical life, so also do our souls need their proper food. In response to this profounder need, our blessed Lord graciously offers himself. He came down from heaven that he might make this offer. As in the olden time the manna fell from the skies to feed the people of God, so has Christ descended from his throne to be the spiritual food of humanity. The manna was only a feeble type of the nobler sustenance given us in our Lord. It was itself corruptible, and administered merely to the necessities of the corruptible nature. Christ is the living bread.

Let us remember, however, that the Christ who is the living bread for humanity is not the pre-existent Son of God, nor even the man of Nazareth, but the crucified and risen Saviour. The bread which Christ offers to men is his flesh given in atoning sacrifice upon the cross, and carried through the grave. As grain must be ground in the mill and pass through the oven before it can become bread, so Christ to become the true bread of humanity must be subjected to the tribulations of an earthly life of loneliness and persecution, and pass through the fiery furnace of suffering and death. They only are nourished by the bread of life who by faith receive and assimilate the crucified Christ.

A J Rowland

Bread of heaven, on thee we feed,
For thy flesh is meat indeed.
Ever let our souls be fed
With this true and living bread.

JOSIAH CONDER.

February 20.

I was set up from everlasting. — Prov. viii. 23.

Your father Abraham rejoiced to see my day: and he saw it, and was glad. . . . Verily, verily, I say unto you, Before Abraham was, I am. — John viii. 56, 58.

THE continuous life of Christ in creation and in the history of this world from first to last underruns various questions as to redemption and salvation, solving many such problems satisfactorily. The work of Christ through the Divine Spirit is potent alike in external and indwelling Christian life. The lack of the Christ-life among professing Christians, as it seems, causes Tolstoï and other able leaders to question whether true Christianity as yet exists to any considerable extent on this planet. Far from being a religion worn out and ready to pass away, the perfect day of Christ, the true Christendom, is yet to come: for the real Christian's true life has this unmistakable quality, — it is inevitably and invariably manifest in the self-sacrificing, self-effacing devotion to God and humanity of Christ-like living. The ground of Christian missions then is not so much the fear of hell as the love of God. The Church's missionary charter is our Lord's commission, "Go ye into all the world and preach the gospel to every creature: go, teach all nations!" Christians, incited to daily Christian living at home, are thus directed to undertake devoted efforts reaching far abroad, for those enlightened by the gospel day owe a vast unpaid debt to Abraham and the past. To Greece and Rome and Egypt, to learning, whether of the orient or occident, as well as to Mahometan scholars and the Jewish Scriptures, Christians owe a *debt of honor*, to be paid in proportion as we teach all that they may come to see and know the truth as it is in Jesus, and that so finally may be fulfilled our Lord's high-priestly prayer that "all may be one."

February 21.

Forbearing one another, and forgiving one another.
Col. iii. 13.

Moreover if thy brother shall trespass against thee, go and tell him his fault between thee and him alone: if he shall hear thee, thou hast gained thy brother. — Matt. xviii. 15.

"THY brother," — this brings to mind the relationship which all Christians sustain. "One family we dwell in him," "of whom the whole family in heaven and earth is named." What a privilege to be recognized as a "brother" in it! "If thy brother trespass against thee!" Alas, how liable we all are by word or act to commit this offence! "To err is human." "In many things we offend all." "If a man offend not in word, the same is a perfect man." This fact is the basis for mutual charitableness. If when another has thus trespassed against us, we can forgive it without a word being said about it, we ought to do so; but if we cannot, then our elder Brother saith, "Go and tell him his fault between thee and him alone." Do not *tell* any one else about it. We must remember, however, that to secure a successful hearing, we must "go" in a Christian spirit and at a proper time. "If he shall hear thee, thou hast gained thy brother." What a blessed result to both parties, and to the cause of our Redeemer! "*Brethren*, if any of you do err from the truth, let him know that he which converteth a sinner from the error of his ways, shall save a soul from death and hide a multitude of sins." "*Brethren*, if any man be overtaken in a fault, ye which are spiritual restore such an one in the spirit of meekness, considering thyself, lest thou also be tempted."

Geo. C. Baldwin.

Oh, give us hearts to love like thee!
Like thee, O Lord, to grieve
Far more for others' sins than all
The wrongs that we receive.

Sir E. Denny.

February 22.

Whatsoever is not of faith is sin. — Romans xiv. 23.

O thou of little faith, wherefore didst thou doubt? — Matt. xiv. 31.

PETER'S perilous enterprise had in it a good deal of presumption, and very little faith. Happy he who has been taught to discern the difference between these two. Faith accepts duty even when there is danger. Presumption accepts danger even when there is no duty. True faith is never foolhardy. It may dare anything at the call of the Master, but it may dare nothing recklessly. He who trusts God need not fear. He who tempts God need not hope.

But there was an element of vanity as well as of presumption in Peter's behavior. It would be a great feat if he could walk on the tempestuous waves. Mingled with the enthusiasm of his affection was an ambition to exhibit his bravery. This neutralized what little faith was in him. Faith will have nothing to do with display. When self-conceit enters in, the virtue of faith oozes out. Self-trust and Christ-trust are mutually exclusive. Vanity forestalls victory. True faith, like true charity, vaunteth not itself, is not puffed up, doth not behave itself unseemly. Fear and trembling are the steadfast friends of triumphant faith. If when the difficulties of life thicken, we have nothing to support us but our own ardent feelings and enthusiastic resolves, we must surely be overcome; but if we can look away from our troubles to Christ, and say, though heart and flesh faint and fail, "Thou art the strength of my heart and my portion forever," we will walk unflinchingly on the floods. "This is the victory that overcometh the world, even our faith."

Jhr= B. M. Leod

Increase our faith, and clear our vision, Lord,
Help us to take thee at thy simple word;
No more with cold distrust to bring thee grief,
Lord, we believe, help thou our unbelief!   W. F. Sherwin.

February 23.

Hungry and thirsty, their soul fainted in them.
Psalm cvii. 5.

And when he had spent all, there arose a mighty famine in that land; and he began to be in want. — Luke xv. 14.

HOW graphically our Lord portrays human experience! Every turn in this most simple and yet most marvellous of all his wondrous parables delineates some phase of practical truth. When the prodigal had spent all that he called his own, *then* arose the famine.

Possessed of wealth, surrounded by affluence, the thought of want had never presented itself. Soon, however, he discovered the exceeding deceitfulness of sin. It not only palls on the taste, but destroys, alienates, and produces irremediable want where before had existed profligate abundance.

What words can depict the hunger of the soul! The figure of the poor outcast, envious even of the swine that he herded, is unequalled in its power to set forth the unutterable misery of the soul when bankrupt in truth and love and all that really sustains life.

Note well that the famine was in *that* land. O soul, ahungered, needy, and despairing, in thy native land want never comes! Only because thou hast turned thy back on thy Father's house and hast wandered beyond his domain, in the forbidden territory of lust and sin, has thy patrimony failed thee and want consumed thee. In that home which thou didst so lightly abandon, there is unfailing plenty and room for all.

John Howland.

Thou who homeless, sole, forlorn,
Long hast borne the proud world's scorn,
Long hast roamed the barren waste,
Weary pilgrim, hither haste.
Anna L. Barbauld.

FEBRUARY 24.

𝔏ord, teach us to pray! — LUKE xi. 1.

After this manner therefore pray ye: Our Father which art in heaven, Hallowed be thy name. — MATT. vi. 9.

WHO as Jesus can teach us to pray? Only the Son of God knoweth the Father, and only the Son of man — the man Christ Jesus — knoweth the depths of the human heart. Christ is light. He is love also, and as he alone knows our need, so he only knows the fulness of blessing and glory to which divine love has chosen us in him.

The invocation is the countenance of the prayer, in which its very soul and heart shine forth! Jesus *reveals*, gives us the Father. He is the *only* begotten; but he became man and died for us, and by his resurrection he became the first begotten, the first born among many brethren. The Holy Ghost, who brought you to Jesus, cries in you, Abba Father! Look thou to Jesus, and then in him say, Father. It is the word of faith; and faith cannot be without love, and therefore you say, Our Father. The filial spirit is the brotherly spirit; and hope beholds heaven, for there is our treasury, our future inheritance.

Our first petition, fundamental and comprehensive, is, Hallowed be thy name. To know God is eternal life. Every name of God by which he revealed himself to Israel is precious. Every name is substance; but his perfect name is Jesus. May his name be a strong refuge of safety to us, an all-sufficient consolation and joy, a bright light and perfect standard, a victorious weapon against temptations and worldliness, summary and seal of all the blessings of the new covenant!

Adolph Saphir.

"Abba, Father," Lord, we call thee,
 Hallow'd name from day to day.
'T is thy children's right to know thee;
 None but children "Abba" say.
ROBERT HAWKER.

February 25.

Of thine own have we given thee. — 1 Chron. xxix. 14.

Verily I say unto you, Wheresoever this gospel shall be preached in the whole world, there shall also this, that this woman hath done, be told for a memorial of her. — Matt. xxvi. 13.

THESE words were spoken to comfort one in distress. Simon had invited Jesus to supper. Seeing Lazarus, — once dead — and Simon cleansed of leprosy, type of sin, Mary longed to express her love to the conqueror of natural and spiritual death.

She took an alabaster box of precious ointment and poured it on his head. John characteristically shows her depth of love by adding, "She anointed his feet and wiped them with her hair." Judas, hypocritically, and "some of the disciples," honestly, reproached Mary for not selling the ointment and giving it to the poor. There was apparent good reason for the reproach, for the Master had often commended in word and in deed the care of the poor. Mary was troubled lest she had made a mistake, but she was comforted by the prophetic promise that in the whole world, wherever the gospel shall be preached, her act would be told for a memorial of her. "More than three hundred pence" would have relieved much distress, and the ointment poured upon Christ's head was of little material use. But an act is estimated not by its results, but by its prompting motive. Mary's motive was to honor her Lord. Recognizing the motive, he commended the act. And so he will recognize and commend every act, great or small, springing from a like impulse.

Daniel Bliss.

We lose what on ourselves we spend;
We have as treasure without end
Whatever, Lord, to thee we lend,
  Who givest all.

C. Wordsworth.

February 26.

A wholesome tongue is a tree of life. — Prov. xv. 4.

But I say unto you, That every idle word that men shall speak, they shall give account thereof in the day of judgment. For by thy words thou shalt be justified, and by thy words thou shalt be condemned. — Matt. xii. 36, 37.

HOW tenderly and tragically impressive are these words of Jesus! They surely do not come under the idle category. We are amazed at the minuteness of the divine inspection. Does God care for the divisions and subdivisions of things in this world?

The Old Testament declares that "the *steps* of a good man are ordered by the Lord," and the New Testament adds that the "hairs of your head are all numbered." It is not strange, then, that *words* should be taken into the scale of judgment, — for words are the betrayal of nationality even here. With the eyes shut we can classify talkers. So too are words the betrayal of companionship. Watchful parents quickly trace the friendships of their children by the words they use; and words also indicate the thoughts and inward character. Hot, hasty words reveal the spirit's life; so idle words, betraying a careless, indolent spirit, become the evidence of a just condemnation at the great assize. Idle words caught from the lips and repeated, penned, and printed give to strangers their estimate of their author. Words are more than air vibrations. They build up and demolish, strengthen and discourage, drive to despair and lead to Christ.

Oh, what need of pardon, of blotting out the records in atoning blood, when we remember that all the idle words have been registered! Not by what another has said of us, but by our own words shall we be justified or condemned.

Samuel H. Virgin

Take my lips, and let them be
Filled with messages from thee.   F. R. Havergal.

February 27.

Come ye to the waters. — Isaiah lv. 1.

Whosoever drinketh of this water shall thirst again: but whosoever drinketh of the water that I shall give him shall never thirst; but the water that I shall give him shall be in him a well of water springing up into everlasting life. — John iv. 13, 14.

ENLIGHTENED by the great Teacher the woman of Samaria saw that no fountain of earthly joy could satisfy her immortal spirit. Would that all who thirst for riches, honors, pleasures, could have their eyes thus opened! The principle of divine grace, implanted in our hearts, becomes "a well of water springing up into everlasting life." Our merciful Saviour invites, yea, urges us all to come to him and assuage our thirst. Have we done this? If so, we are sure of heavenly support amid earthly trials, and of eternal bliss. An African missionary of my acquaintance exclaimed when dying, "How grand a thing it is to have the certain consciousness of everlasting life!" He had quenched his thirst at this wonderful fountain. It bubbled up in his glad experience, as he bade adieu to sublunary scenes. Friends, drink yourselves, freely, and persuade others to do likewise. The four lepers at the gate of Samaria said one to another, "We do not well; this is a day of good tidings, and we hold our peace."

Josiah Tyler

Come to the living waters, come;
 Sinners, obey your Maker's call!
Return, ye weary wanderers, home,
 And find his grace is free for all.

J. Wesley.

February 28.

Kept by the power of God. — 1 Peter i. 5.

Are not two sparrows sold for a farthing? and one of them shall not fall on the ground without your Father. But the very hairs of your head are all numbered. Fear ye not therefore, ye are of more value than many sparrows. — Matt. x. 29-31.

THIS is an argument from the less to the greater. Does God care for oxen? For *our* sakes, no doubt, this is written. "Much more," is the frequent formula by which God proves to us from what we already know and clearly see what he desires to teach us regarding his providential care. *We* are of great worth because we can know God, can love God, can serve God; because we shall live forever. Therefore God cares for us. "The redemption of their soul is precious."

God's providence is *universal*. "His kingdom ruleth over all." He can govern all only by controlling each. He manages the stream, because he presides at the fountain. God's providence is *minute and specific*. Great doors swing on small hinges. God's very greatness enables him to care for the little; only the Infinite can pay attention to infinitesimals. It is "trifles that make perfection." Telescopes reveal the magnitude of God's creation; microscopes, the minuteness of his care. God's providence is *beneficent*. "All things work together for *good*." "As for you, ye thought evil against me, but God meant it unto good." Even the wrath of man is made to subserve God's beneficent purpose. "All things are yours." "Fire and hail; snow and vapor; stormy wind, fulfilling his word." "I know the thoughts that I think toward you; thoughts of peace and not of evil to give you an expected end." "Trust in the Lord."

Henry M. Sanders.

The soul that on Jesus hath leaned for repose,
I will not, I will not desert to his foes;
That soul, though all hell should endeavor to shake,
I'll never, no never, no never forsake. George Keith.

February 29.

Incline your ear, and come unto me. — Isaiah lv. 3.

And the Spirit and the bride say, Come. And let him that heareth say, Come. And let him that is athirst come. And whosoever will, let him take the water of life freely. — Rev. xxii. 17.

THE Bible is God's message to mankind, and its contents may be summed up in a word, — come. We have "Come," in Genesis and in Revelation; "Come," in the prophets and the gospels. Under righteous sentence of death on account of sin, God bids us come into the Ark for shelter. Though he is holy and just, and we are guilty, yet may we come to him, — for he can make away with the crimson of our guilt and the scarlet of our transgression. Athirst for peace and rest and joy and bliss, he bids us come to the never-failing, the ever-satisfying waters. We have nothing to give him in return, but he bids us come without money and without price. To every soul burden-worn and weary, Christ says, "Come unto me and rest." Burden of sin, burden of sorrow, burden of care, burden of temptation, each may be brought to him. None can be turned away, for he says, "Him that cometh to me I will in no wise cast out." Nor shall any coming one fail to find satisfaction, for Christ says again, "He that cometh to me shall never hunger." The last chapter of the Bible, almost the last verse, repeats the call. It is the call of the risen Christ now. He came from heaven to give once more heaven's invitation to earth, God's message to man. Let us therefore come.

Robt. M. Offord

Come, ye dying, live forever;
  'Tis a soul-reviving flood.
God is faithful; he will never
  Break his covenant sealed in blood,
Signed when our Redeemer died;
Sealed when he was glorified.   J. Montgomery.

MARCH 1.

Beloved, let us love one another. — 1 JOHN iv. 7.

A new commandment I give unto you, That ye love one another; as I have loved you, that ye also love one another. By this shall all men know that ye are my disciples, if ye have love one to another. — JOHN xiii. 34, 35.

NO one can really love the Saviour without loving those for whom he died; and we are bound to love one another *as* Christ loved us. His love is not dependent upon our worthiness, — alas for us all, if it were! He loved us before we loved him, and having loved his own, he loves them to the end in spite of all their frailties. We are called to love the fallen all the more, because they so much need our love, and should continue to love our brethren, although we may see that they are full of infirmities.

True love is always faithful, as well as charitable and tolerant; but it ceases to rebuke as soon as the signs of penitence appear. When Jesus met the disciple who had just before denied him, he had no word of reproach to utter, because he had seen the poor man's bitter tears. Those whose lives had been crimsoned with sin Jesus forgave, because they "loved much." True love is always forgiving as well as faithful.

"Greater love hath no man than this, that a man lay down his life for his friends;" and this is what Christ did. He even laid down his life for his enemies, and prayed for his murderers as he hung upon the cross. Our love for those around us is to be measured by what we are willing to do for them. True love is always ready to make sacrifices. It rejoices in the opportunity of helping others. Faith may languish and hope grow dim, but love outlasts them both, "for the greatest of these is charity."

Thomas M. Clark.

> Love is the golden chain that binds
>   The happy souls above;
> And he's an heir of heaven who finds
>   His bosom glow with love.   JOSEPH SWAIN.

March 2.

This is the true God, and eternal life. — 1 John v. 20.

And this is life eternal, that they might know thee the only true God, and Jesus Christ, whom thou hast sent. — John xvii. 3.

CHRISTIAN philosophy epitomized! Two thoughts appear, shining like upper and lower harbor lights to guide the mariner home. Life! — creation's great fact, riveting attention in every leaf and flower, demanding thought with every breath and heart-beat, questioned by every longing hope of humanity, — what is it, not alone physically and mortally, but spiritually and eternally? Science hangs her head and answers evasively, or in a circle. Human philosophy confesses ignorance. We grope unsatisfied; not a ray of light till it bursts resplendent from the life and lips of Christ! This is not mere eternal existence of which Jesus speaks. Lost souls, fallen angels exist in living death forever. Real living, worthy living, is no question of years, but of growing character and quality of being. "To be spiritually minded is life." Immortal souls live only as they commune with God.

But how may I attain it? Seeking to know God is the only way. But human searching cannot find out the infinite. To our unaided sense he is "the unknown God." Hence we need Immanuel, God revealed. Now, to know Jesus Christ, whom he hath sent in all his fulness as redeemer, teacher, and king, is to know the only true God, and thus is life eternal within our reach, for "he that hath the Son, hath life."

Henry M. Ladd

  Life's but a means unto an end; that end,
  Beginning, mean, and end of all things, — God.
              BAILEY.

March 3.

God is not unrighteous, to forget your . . . labour of love.
HEB. vi. 10.

And whosoever shall give to drink unto one of these little ones a cup of cold water only in the name of a disciple, verily I say unto you, he shall in no wise lose his reward. — MATT. x. 42.

"IN the name of a disciple." How carefully our Lord distinguishes between deeds and motives! A little deed of kindness from a great motive reveals nobility of character. To do it for Christ's sake reveals the loftiest nobility. A little act is often a surer test of character than a great one, because it is spontaneous. So-called great occasions often complicate our motives. Ambition or love of praise try to insinuate themselves.

"A cup of cold water." How much it does! It refreshes the whole physical man; and because the giver of it shows thought which is wide awake, and tenderness and sympathy, his "over soul" wakens the higher nature of the thirsty man, and so a cup in Christ's name is a double cup. "Everything for Christ." That makes the whole life kingly. The buckles upon the girth of the king's saddle are royal. This spirit gives by unconscious influence a thousand cups of comfort and inspiration. We are handing them out because giving is the spirit of our life. We shall not know while here about all the refreshing cups we have given; but the record is made in heaven: "Inasmuch as ye have done it unto one of the least of these my brethren, ye have done it unto me."

Edward P. Ingersoll.

Blessings abound where'er he reigns;
The prisoner leaps to lose his chains;
The weary find eternal rest,
And all the sons of want are blest.
C. WESLEY.

March 4.

Healing . . . all manner of disease.—Matt. iv. 23.

Rise, take up thy bed, and walk.—John v. 8.

DIVINE authority and divine love are beautifully mingled in this short, simple command. Jesus, the friend of the friendless, addressed it to a wretched sufferer beside the pool of Bethesda, who had long waited in vain for some one to help him into the healing waters. The reader of this paragraph may be a sin-diseased lingerer who is wasting life in waiting for — you can hardly tell what or whom. Why waste another moment? Jesus stands beside you. He bids you repent, trust him, and follow him. As soon as you are willing to obey, he gives you strength to obey. That poor cripple had only two weak and withered limbs to "rise" with, but the instant that his will obeys Christ, a divine power shoots through nerves and muscles, and he stands erect. He wanted to arise, made the honest effort, and divine strength did the rest. His part in the blessed transaction was *faith;* Christ's part was saving *grace.* The two combined make the biography of every converted sinner on earth or in heaven. The first act you perform, the first sin you refuse, and the first effort you make simply to please your Saviour, puts you on your feet. Thenceforward the Christian life is a walking with Christ and a working for Christ until you reach the Father's house in glory.

Rev. T. L. Cuyler.

Thy work alone, O Christ,
 Can ease this weight of sin;
Thy blood alone, O Lamb of God,
 Can give me peace within.

H. Bonar.

MARCH 5.

Who will go for us? — ISAIAH vi. 8.

Say not ye, There are yet four months, and then cometh harvest? behold, I say unto you, Lift up your eyes, and look on the fields; for they are white already to harvest. — JOHN iv. 35.

IN the natural world there are four months, more or less, after the seed is sown before the harvest can be expected. In like manner, months and years sometimes elapse between the preaching of the gospel and the gathering of converts. But, as at Sychar, it is not always so. "Behold! lift up your eyes, and look on the fields"— these fields of human souls — in many lands. The sowers of the Word have gone forth. Much seed has been sown. Some gospel sheaves have been gathered. But the sphere is widening; many fields are already white for the harvest. Multitudes in many heathen lands are even now ready to renounce idolatry, and like the Samaritans, to receive Jesus as the Saviour of the world. But, while some fields are ripe and others are ripening, much ground is still unsown. God calls for both sowers and reapers. "Who will go for us?" Yes, "*Who?*" One may sow and another reap; but when sowers and reapers see the fruits of their joint labor safely garnered in heaven, they will "rejoice together." They will together share the joy of their Lord.

John Newton

Where are the reapers? Oh, who will come
And share in the glory of the harvest home? .
Oh, who will help us to garner in
The sheaves of good from the fields of sin?
EBEN E. REXFORD.

March 6.

Jesus Christ maketh thee whole. — Acts ix. 34.

Daughter, be of good comfort: thy faith hath made thee whole; go in peace. — Luke viii. 48.

THIS potent touch which Jesus honored was prompted by a realization of present and pressing need. The woman fully understood the malign nature of her ailment, and was persuaded that it was incurable unless Christ should interpose for her relief.

This realization of need and helplessness was the result of repeated trial and failure. Only after that she had spent all her living upon physicians and grew nothing better, but worse, was she persuaded that her case was hopeless unless the great Physician would aid her. Under constraint of these convictions she came to Christ, she touched, and was healed.

Jesus never rejects us because we insist upon making trial of every conceivable device that gives promise of relief before we intrust ourselves to his care; but when we come to him with the conviction of helplessness that sin engenders, and touch him by that simple faith which relies solely on him, he will speak to every sin-sick soul those words of cheer: "Go in peace: thy faith hath made thee whole."

D. R. Frazer.

> Heal me, O my Saviour, heal;
> Heal me, as I suppliant kneel;
> Heal me, and my pardon seal.
>
> . . . . .
>
> Thou the true Physician art;
> Thou, O Christ, canst health impart,
> Binding up the broken heart.
>
> Godfrey Thring.

March 7.

They shall be mine, saith the Lord of hosts. — MAL. iii. 17.

Thou hast a few names even in Sardis which have not defiled their garments; and they shall walk with me in white: for they are worthy. — REV. 3, 4.

THE Sardian Church, nominally alive, was dead. But a few lived righteously, as a few bowed not the knee to Baal in the days of Elijah; as in all times and in all churches, doubtless, a remnant is, in which truth survives to become the seed of future generations of faith. God never leaves himself without a witness.

2. The few, in contact with a body of nominal Christians "who have the name, but deny the power," have been kept by God's grace in their faith. They have been alive to God and his works, — have been letting their light shine so that men seeing their good works have glorified their Father in heaven. Though hindered and stumbling, they have been faithful; though imperfect, they are taught to look toward perfection.

3. Shall followers of Christ stop following him because the church to which they belong dies to spiritual life? The pressure of a tendency will be present to push them down into spiritual sleep. But the grace of Christ is sufficient for them. *There is no environment of evil so bad as the environment of God's grace is good.* He who is faithful in the midst of unfaithfulness is walking worthily and advancing toward that purity which is moral whiteness and light.

Myron Adams.

Courage, faithful souls and tried,
Ye who in his truth abide,
Keeping near the Saviour's side!

Ye shall walk with him in white;
Ye shall reign with him in light;
Ye shall share his glory bright.   R. M. OFFORD.

March 8.

He ever liveth to make intercession. — Heb. vii. 25.

And I knew that thou hearest me always: but because of the people which stand by I said it, that they may believe that thou hast sent me. — John xi. 42.

CHRIST possesses all the incommunicable attributes of proper, personal divinity. He is called the Son of God with reference to an order of subsistence we cannot comprehend, — an official subordination cheerfully accepted for our sakes, and the assumption of a human nature provided by the Father. No essential inferiority is intended; Christ and the Father are one. This fact explains the prevalence of his intercession.

In order that the Jews might know that he was one with God and wrought all his works in him, Christ preceded the raising of Lazarus with an audible address to the Father, adding, "And I knew that thou hearest me always."

It is a pleasant and inspiring thought to us who believe that the High-Priest of our profession, now in heaven, continues to appear before God for us. This assures us of necessary temporal good, and of spiritual blessings in adequate measure at appropriate seasons and in unfailing supply. In our experiences of temptation, conflict, sorrow, and fear, when burdened with responsibilities and worn with care, and in the closing moments of earthly life, Christ will ask that we may receive the grace we need and at last be received to glory. Blessed be God for the hope of heaven through him who ever liveth to make intercession for us!

Robert F. Sample,

> The atoning work is done,
> The Victim's blood is shed,
> And Jesus now is gone
> His people's cause to plead.
> He stands in heaven their great High Priest,
> And bears their names upon his breast.
>
> KELLY.

March 9.

His commandments are not grievous. — 1 John v. 3.

Take my yoke upon you, and learn of me; for I am meek and lowly in heart: and ye shall find rest unto your souls. For my yoke is easy, and my burden is light. — Matt. xi, 29, 30.

IT is the within that makes the without. If the soul be jarring, no circumstances can be chiming. If the inner life be smitten with winds and tossed, the brightest and stillest outward prospect will look stormy. If the soul but know how to sing inwardly, there shall be birds enough outside to sing, even amid the most wintry weather. The great trouble is heart trouble.

It is the philosophy of Christianity that it searches for the soul; if that be made right, prisons will become palaces. Rest for *souls* is the supreme gift.

The great Teacher tells us that the way of the reception of this supreme gift is the way of the *yoke*. This is the inexorable way. The lawless soul must be the clashing soul. I was riding smoothly and easily sixty miles an hour; the reason was, the train submitted to the yoke of the rails. What crash and destruction had the train determined on a way of its own! If I would have rest I must come under the yoke of the divine will. There can be no other path. Sings the Psalmist, "I will walk at liberty because I keep thy commandments."

And if we need teaching and direction along this road of the yoke, we are to look to Christ: we are to emulate his lowliness and meekness. Instant submission to the Father's will was the meaning of his life. "My meat is to do the will of him that sent me, and to finish his work." He was under the yoke and so at rest. What was for the elder Brother is also for the brethren.

Wayland Hoyt

Rest is not quitting the busy career;
Rest is the fitting the soul to its sphere.   Goethe.

March 10.

Ho, every one that thirsteth. — Isaiah lv. 1.

All that the Father giveth me shall come to me; and him that cometh to me I will in no wise cast out. For I came down from heaven, not to do mine own will, but the will of him that sent me. — John vi. 37, 38.

WHEN Jesus said, "Him that cometh to me I will in no wise cast out," it was a statement of such breadth that it was difficult for the human mind to receive it. That the most abject, forlorn, far-straying sinner would be received if he came back to Jesus, required that it should be supported by what would overwhelm all the infidelity and depravity of the heart of a sinner who had the slightest desire to return to God. The proofs which he affords are in the statement, first of all, that "God so loved the world that he gave his only begotten Son, that whosoever believeth in him should not perish, but have everlasting life." Now he adds that the Son also loved the world, and that therefore he had come down from heaven so as to put himself in such a position that man might come to him. To remove every scruple and silence every doubt, he asserts that his coming was under the double motive of love for mankind and devotion to the Father; that what the Father willed he willed, and he came down from heaven to carry out that will; and the Father's will was that he should lose nothing of what had been given him, and the Father had given to him every single human being that would come to him. And so the blessed Jesus gives to mankind the most overwhelming assurance that none should be lost except those who would not come unto him.

Charles F. Deems

> If I ask him to receive me
>   Will he say me nay?
> Not till earth, and not till heaven
>   Pass away.   J. Neale *(Translation).*

March 11.

Purge out therefore the old leaven. — 1 Cor. v. 7.

Take heed and beware of the leaven of the Pharisees and of the Sadducees. — Matt. xvi. 6.

ACCORDING to Luke's record, the "leaven of the Pharisees" is *hypocrisy*. A hypocrite is one who acts a part. The signification of the word has only that of evil in it. That being so, it is quite easy to be a hypocrite, — a Pharisee; the difficulty is not to be one. There is constant need of the warning, Beware of hypocrisy. Social influences are ever at work to convince men and women that their business is to make their life a masquerade. Worst of all is this when, as with the Pharisees, one's religion is but acting a part, an outside show, a seeming, a masquerade.

God is light. Light reveals. Shine into our hearts. O Light, that all darkness may be dispelled. Make us children of light, since it is a God of light we serve.

If children, then heirs. God is our Father. He is the living God. He is the God of the living. We are united to his Son. He ever liveth. Every true soul lives with him, lives like him, lives as long as he lives. We will beware of the "leaven of the Sadducees" by always keeping in grateful, happy memory that we belong to the race of which Christ is head; that we are one with his family in heaven and earth.

Nathl. W. Conkling.

I am trusting thee for cleansing
   In the crimson flood,
Trusting thee to make me holy
   By thy blood.

I am trusting thee, Lord Jesus,
   Never let me fall;
I am trusting thee forever,
   And for all.

F. R. Havergal.

MARCH 12.

He satisfieth the longing soul. — PSALM cvii. 9.

They that are whole have no need of the physician, but they that are sick: I came not to call the righteous, but sinners to repentance. — MARK ii. 17.

THE truth taught in these words is apparent in the experience of Christian workers in every land. Where there is no conviction of sin there can be no fitness to hear the Saviour's call to repentance. Many a man will admit that he is not in robust health who does not feel ill enough to call a physician, and there is an every-day sense of the need of food and drink, which is easily satisfied. But the feeling that one is sick unto death, and the sense of hunger and thirst such as one has in the heat of a desert with no knowledge of a supply at hand, are very different things. So many a man will admit in a general way that he is a sinner, when the admission only means that he is not so good a man as he ought to be; but to realize that one is really guilty before God and needs the Son of God to save him from eternal punishment is a very different thing. It is only when the Holy Spirit brings the soul to a sense of its sinfulness in the sight of God that it is ready to hear Christ's call to repentance and obey it.

The gospel call is addressed to the hungry, thirsty, burdened, and weary. These words all denote feeling a deep sense of want.

James L. Amerman.

His name is Jesus, and he died
For guilty sinners crucified;
Content to die, that he might win
Their ransom from the death of sin.
No sinner worse than I can be,
Therefore I know he died for me.   G. W. BETHUNE.

March 13.

And took upon him the form of a servant. — Phil. ii. 7.

I am among you as he that serveth. — Luke xxii. 27.

HERE is the true criterion of greatness, — willingness to serve. Judged by the canons of the gospel, the most illustrious life is that which has in it the largest ingredient of sacrifice. "O God, author of peace," runs the old prayer, "whom to know is to live; whom to serve is to reign."

Even in the traditions and mythologies of the old heathen races, the heroes are men who proved themselves such by their readiness to dare and to suffer in the service of others. The legend of unselfish, much-enduring love has always been the fascinating one, has always laid hold of the imagination and swayed the heart as none other does or can do. Whether the central figure be that of the warrior going out unattended into the wilderness to fight the dragon which has laid the country waste, or that of the brave youth leaping full-armed into the gulf, because the soothsayers have declared that only the sacrifice of the best will suffice to save the city, the secret of the story's power lies in the spectacle of a life laid down in order that other lives may be lifted up and blessed. To be as Christ was in this world, we also must serve.

W. R. Huntington.

O Lord, with sorrow and with shame
  We meekly would confess
How little we, who bear thy name,
  Thy mind, thy ways, express.

Give us thy meek, thy lowly mind;
  We would obedient be,
And all our rest and pleasure find
  In fellowship with thee.

J. G. Deck.

March 14.

Be careful for nothing. — Phil. iv. 6.

Which of you by taking thought can add one cubit unto his stature? Take therefore no thought for the morrow: for the morrow shall take thought for the things of itself. Sufficient unto the day is the evil thereof. — Matt. vi. 27, 34.

CHRIST'S teaching is this: "Ask questions; question anxiety out of existence." There is no power equal to a question. A question walks right into the soul and compels it to think. See God amid the majesty of the whirlwind, firing a volley of questions at the self-sufficient Job! That volley did what the combined learning of the Orient failed to do. It brought down *self-sufficiency*. Christ in the Sermon on the Mount has given us a volley of questions wherewith to bring down *anxiety*. Ask yourselves, What reason is there for anxiety? God has given you the higher gifts, "life and body." Is it reasonable to suppose that he will deny you the lower gifts, "food and raiment?" Ask yourselves, What profit is there in anxiety? Can it sweep away the limitations in which men find themselves? Ask yourselves, Does anxiety accord with the teachings of nature? What do the flowers, robed in their golden garments, say? What do the birds, picking their daily food out of the ground, say? Does anxiety accord with your divine sonship, or with God's fatherhood, or with the future which God has depicted for his people? That future is all golden. It is full of promises and songs and glories. It carries in it an endless heaven.

David Gregg

We expect a bright to-morrow; all will be well.
Faith can sing through days of sorrow, All, all is well.
  On our Father's love relying,
  Jesus every need supplying,
  Or in living, or in dying,
    All must be well.   Mrs. M. B. Peters.

MARCH 15.

The Lord looketh on the heart. — 1 SAM. xvi. 7.

Ye are they which justify yourselves before men; but God knoweth your hearts: for that which is highly esteemed among men is abomination in the sight of God. — LUKE xvi. 15.

"JUSTIFY yourselves;" that is, pass yourselves off as righteous. Pretended righteousness often deceives men, and the pretender is able to win on their esteem. But such a man is an "abomination in the sight of God."

How easy to justify ourselves before men! for "man looketh on the outward appearance, but the Lord looketh on the heart." And how difficult to justify ourselves before God! I was once resting on my oars on Lake George. Glancing over the gunwale of my boat, I found that I could look through the crystal water for at least fifty feet, to the bottom of the lake, and I could see stones, trunks of fallen trees, and the fish darting through the water hither and thither. So God looks into our hearts. His eyes search out every secret thing, whether it be good or bad. Then let us pray, " Create in me a clean heart, O God, and renew a right spirit within me."

A pretence of righteousness is not righteousness. It was the publican who went down to his house "justified" after prayer, and not the man who piously thanked God that he was a model of observance of religious and ethical proprieties.

Spirit of purity and grace,
Our weakness pitying see;
Oh, make our hearts thy dwelling-place,
And worthier thee!

HARRIET AUBER.

MARCH 16.

Let your speech be always with grace. — COL. iv. 6.

But let your communication be, Yea, yea; Nay, nay: for whatsoever is more than these cometh of evil. — MATT. v. 37.

WHAT gift so valuable and such a source of pleasure as that of speech, conversation, — the expression of thought between man and man! And yet what gift so liable to abuse! The Teacher who "spake as never man spake" here, in his Sermon on the Mount, shows us how to beware of this evil. He warns us to let our words be few.

Careless speech tends to *frivolity*. He who utters many words will speak many ill-advised, foolish things.

We should be on our guard also against rash, *hasty* speech. This is the most frequent source of unkindness, of uttering angry, heart-aching words. "A soft answer turneth away wrath: but grievous words stir up anger" (Prov. xv. 1).

Heeding this precept will, too, keep us from *impiety*. It was because he reflected before he spoke that Job "charged not God foolishly" with unjust providential dealings, and "in all this did not sin with his lips" (Job ii. 10).

Few words, again, are the more likely to be *resolute*, decisive words. A positive "Nay" to the tempter, how often it has rescued a youth from vice, or saved a soul to heaven, where compromising speech would have lost both!

Let us remember then, each day, this counsel of Jesus and begin it with the Psalmist's prayer: "Set a watch, O Lord, before my mouth; keep the door of my lips" (Psalm cxli. 3).

Junius B. Remensnyder.

Direct, control, suggest, this day,
All I design, or do, or say,
That all my powers, with all their might,
In thy sole glory may unite.
    BISHOP KEN.

March 17.

Not willing that any should perish. — 2 Peter iii. 9.

For God sent not his Son into the world to condemn the world; but that the world through him might be saved. — John iii. 17.

HOW unlike the usual ways of subduing rebels was that taken by God! Daring insurrections against law and order commonly meet with tremendous retribution among men. " Clemency," we are told, " would be misplaced kindness ; severity is kindness in the end. Show no mercy to old or young till you have stamped out the last ember of rebellion."

"As the heavens are higher than the earth, so are my ways higher than your ways and my thoughts than your thoughts." "God sent not his Son into the world to condemn the world, but that the world through him might be saved."

Did ever messenger from an offended king cause his advent among rebels to be proclaimed with songs of "glory to God in the highest, on earth peace, good-will to men"?

What a gift God gave to the world when he gave his Son! What store of heaven's light and love and joy, of all that heals our disorders, brightens our life, sweetens the breath of society, mitigates the gloom of suffering and death and throws brightness on the eternal future, came into our world with him! O blind foolish world, that will not receive the gift, and like the poor worldlings of Gadara, entreats God's Son to depart out of its coasts!

W. G. Blaikie

Delay not, delay not ; O sinner, draw near !
The waters of life are now flowing for thee ;
No price is demanded, the Saviour is here,
Redemption is purchased, salvation is free.

Thomas Hastings.

March 18.

Open to me. — Solomon's Song v. 2.

Behold, I stand at the door, and knock: if any man hear my voice, and open the door, I will come in to him, and will sup with him, and he with me. — Rev. iii. 20.

BEHOLD the dignity of man! The heart is a palace barred and bolted, kept by man, and Christ his Maker allows him to hold the key, and will not force a way in. Behold the interest in man! Gracious powers from above gather about him in pity and love, and out of the midst of these Christ knocks and asks admission. No other being is the centre of such interest. Behold the privilege of man! If he hear the entreaty and open the door, the Son of God will come in and dwell with him. Behold the blessedness of man! The soul into which Christ thus enters has Christ sup with him and he with Christ. Note the order: Christ first comes down and sups with him and then takes him up to sup with himself, — Christly communion with Christ as leader, up the ever-higher Christly ranges. Here is the highest bliss, and Christ stands at the door of our hearts and knocks, offering it.

Israel E. Dwinell

> O Jesus, thou art knocking;
>   And lo! that hand is scarred,
> And thorns thy brow encircle,
>   And tears thy face have marred.
> O love that passeth knowledge,
>   So patiently to wait!
> O sin that hath no equal,
>   So fast to bar the gate!
>
> W. W. How.

MARCH 19.

God loveth a cheerful giver. — 2 COR. ix. 7.

Freely ye have received, freely give. — MATT. x. 8.

SIR ISAAC NEWTON said that matter is capable of such condensation that the whole earth might be compressed into the size of a cannon-ball. Here are two words that contain the whole gospel, both of salvation and service: *receiving, giving.*

Imparting is both the end for which we receive and the condition upon which we receive more. The inflow of a fountain is in order to its outflow, and must cease when the outflow stops. He is but a "dead sea" who receives without imparting. As Canon Wilberforce says, the substance of all duty is, "Admit, submit, commit, transmit."

We have received freely. The priceless boons of nature — sunshine, rain and dew, atmosphere — are without price, while beyond price. Heaven itself may be had for the asking. God lives to give; and all true living is free and constant giving. The godlike soul is not a cold and barren peak or arid desert, but a broad and beautiful valley with waving harvests and singing streams.

Giving is the secret of joy. "It is more blessed to give than to receive," for it is the bliss of God!

Arthur T. Pierson.

That man may last, but never lives
Who much receives, but nothing gives;
Whom none can love, whom none can thank, —
Creation's blot, creation's blank!

GIBBONS.

March 20.

In him dwelleth all the fulness of the Godhead.
Col. ii. 9.

I and my Father are one. — John x. 30.

WE have here one of the briefest and yet sublimest words spoken by the Son of God concerning his blessed person. A colossal word, akin to another, "Which of you convinceth me of sin?" and alike in majesty to his declaration, "I am the light of the world."

The Jews understood, for they answered, "Thou makest thyself God;" but they were hardened in unbelief, and took up stones again to stone him.

The rock of offence to the Jews is our unspeakably precious treasure. *We know* what Jesus designed to teach. One with the Father, so spake he, one in life and one in love, and gave as proofs his stupendous works as Saviour of mankind, — one in grandeur, power, and glory with the Father, of whom John also testified, "And we beheld his glory."

Concerning his redeemed the voice of Jesus says, "I give unto them eternal life. They shall never perish." Wherein lies the pledge that God will do as he has engaged? Where is our hope securely anchored? Who guarantees to the believer perfect assurance of salvation through life and through the swelling waves of Jordan?

"My Father, which gave them me, is greater than all." He gave them to be redeemed and "kept," and "I and my Father are one!"

Rudolf Koenig

> Teach us to know the Father, Son,
> And thee, of both to be but One,
> That through the ages all along
> *This*, this may be our endless song:
> " Praise to thy eternal merit,
> Father, Son, and Holy Spirit."
>
> Bishop J. Cosin *(Translation).*

March 21.

Watch unto prayer. — 1 Peter iv. 7.

Be watchful, and strengthen the things which remain, that are ready to die: for I have not found thy works perfect before God. Remember therefore how thou hast received and heard, and hold fast, and repent. If therefore thou shalt not watch, I will come on thee as a thief, and thou shalt not know what hour I will come upon thee. — Rev. iii. 2, 3.

IN his counsel to his disciples, as he was about to die, Jesus repeatedly used one memorable word, Watch! After sixty years he renews this solemn counsel, Watch! So then, all with us depends upon watchfulness.

Watchfulness remembers. It recalls the two cardinal facts, — our sin, God's grace in Jesus Christ. The Holy Spirit's office is to stimulate the memory of these central facts. Thus he daily renews the soul.

Watchfulness holds fast its grasp of the faith once delivered to the saints, its conscious clasp of the hand of the Saviour. We ever tend to lose our hold. It needs ever to be renewed.

Watchfulness repents. Life begins anew, as it began at the first, with penitence. Observe the sequence of experiences, — remembrance, a new resolution, repentance.

Watchfulness makes ready for the coming of the Lord. We must be ready at the hour. He comes suddenly to all men; to the watcher as a bridegroom, but to the careless as a thief. What I say unto you, I say unto all: Watch!

George R. Leavitt.

Christian, seek not yet repose;
  Cast thy dreams of earth away.
Thou art in the midst of foes;
  Watch and pray.

Charlotte Elliott.

March 22.

His compassions fail not. — Lam. iii. 22.

Fear not: believe only, and she shall be made whole. — Luke viii. 50.

THIS word "Fear not," of our divine Lord, is one many times repeated in his life and ministry. It is full of compassion, comfort, and cheer. When the sad message came to the ruler of the synagogue, "Thy daughter is dead, trouble not the Master," the words sprang from Christ's lips at once, so that the faith of Jairus had no time to waver: "Fear not: believe only." Jesus immediately summons him to a trust in the almightiness of him to whom he had appealed.

Our Lord in this incident joins himself in tender sympathy to the sorrows of *home life*. He crosses the threshold of the domestic sanctuary, and with divine power and divine love brings "beauty for ashes, the oil of joy for mourning, the garment of praise for the spirit of heaviness."

Here we learn the tender compassion of Christ, the all-sufficiency of Jesus, and the reality of faith, as a personal trust in a personal Saviour, who is able and willing to heal, to help, and to save. Jesus is just as real, as personal, as near, as loving to-day as in the days of his flesh. He hears your cry, and feels the clinging of your faith about his heart.

John E. Cookman.

> But warm, sweet, tender, even yet
>   A present help is he;
> And love has yet its Olivet,
>   And love its Galilee.
>
> The healing of the seamless dress
>   Is by our beds of pain.
> We touch him in life's throng and press,
>   And we are whole again.
>
> John G. Whittier.

March 23.

No condemnation to them which are in Christ Jesus.
ROMANS viii. 1.

Verily, verily, I say unto you, He that heareth my word, and believeth on him that sent me, hath everlasting life, and shall not come into condemnation; but is passed from death unto life. — JOHN v. 24.

"HATH eternal life," is the reading of the Revision. The phrase thus comes into accord with John xvii. 3, "This is life eternal," etc. Eternal is a better word than everlasting, and has a richer meaning. Everlasting makes us think only of time endlessly prolonged, which is dull and dreary. Eternal has to do with a region of condition in which the hour-glass and the curfew are irrelevant. Years do not add themselves together to make eternity. The eternal is not a matter of addition or multiplication, but is as simple and uncompounded as is he who inhabiteth eternity. The real genius of the eternal may all be comprised in a single instant, as the real totality of God's presence may be contained in a cubic inch. Hence Christ does not say, shall have, but hath; will be life eternal, but, this is life eternal. Christ thus conjugates eternal life in the present tense for the reason that it has no tense; just as no one would ever think of dating honesty, or labelling righteousness 1888. Eternity is a divine attribute; by derivation we become eternal in Christ. In Christ we become seasoned with the eternal, and are eternal, — an instant matter, not a thing to hope for. "This *is* life eternal." He that believeth *hath* eternal life.

C. H. Parkhurst.

'T is eternal life to know him.
  Oh, how he loves!
Think, oh, think how much we owe him!
  Oh, how he loves!
With his precious blood he bought us,
In the wilderness he sought us,
To his fold he safely brought us.
  Oh, how he loves! MARIANNE NUNN.

March 24.

Written in the Lamb's book of life.—Rev. xxi. 27.

Notwithstanding in this rejoice not, that the spirits are subject unto you; but rather rejoice, because your names are written in heaven.—Luke x. 20.

THE desire of power is not wrong in itself. Power may be desired from the purest motives and exercised for the noblest ends. The seventy found the demons subject unto them through the name of their Master, and it was natural that they should rejoice therein. It was, no doubt, a *benignant* joy with them. But the exercise of this power might be associated with vanity and self-seeking; nay, it may consist with the utter absence of saving grace (see Matt. vii. 22, 23). Therefore, says the Lord, " Rejoice not that the spirits are subject unto you." There is a ground of joy so superior to the exercise of any miraculous powers, that our Lord would have his followers forget them all in view of a purer and far better prerogative: it is that their names are written in heaven. Their citizenship is there. Here, indeed, is cause for joy,—joy that swallows up every other joy; a joy, too, that sweetens the bitterest cup on earth. The humblest believer in Jesus may say, *My* name is written in heaven!

Yet, amid this rejoicing in hope, the devout and thoughtful believer will also say, But is *my* name verily written in heaven? What evidence have I of it? Have I the witness of the Spirit that I am born of God? Do the principles of the gospel of Christ control my heart and my life? If so, well may I rejoice: heaven is assured to me.

Stephen Yerkes.

In thy fair book of life and grace,
 Oh, may I find my name
Recorded in some humble place,
 Beneath my Lord, the Lamb!

WATTS.

March 25.

Your life is hid with Christ in God. — Col. iii. 3.

For as the Father hath life in himself; so hath he given to the Son to have life in himself. — John v. 26.

THE gospel assumes and illustrates the doctrine of the Trinity. The ineffable relations of the Father, Son, and Holy Ghost are all recognized and embodied in the structure of the economy of grace. As in the constitution of the Godhead the Father is first, the Son second, and the Holy Ghost third, — the Son being from the Father, and the Holy Ghost from the Father and the Son, — so in the arrangements into which they have entered for the salvation of men, the Father stands at the fountain-head carrying out the eternal purpose of mercy through the Son and Spirit. The text carries us back into the fathomless depths of this glorious mystery, and represents the Son as the God-man, as receiving from the Father for redemptive ends a life which is as truly divine and self-contained as that possessed by the Father himself. This life, in all its divine vigor, is exercised by him in the impartation of spiritual life to souls dead in trespasses and sins, and shall at last be revealed with majesty and power in the resurrection of the dead. Truly " our life is hid with Christ in God." Its guarantee and pledge are bound up indissolubly by covenant with the vital relations of the Godhead itself.

Robert Watts.

> Jesus is God! Oh, could I now
> But compass land and sea,
> To teach and tell this single truth,
> How happy should I be!
>
> Oh, had I but an angel's voice
> I would proclaim so loud:
> Jesus, the good, the beautiful,
> Is everlasting God.
>
> FABER.

March 26.

Who art thou that judgest another? — James iv. 12.

And why beholdest thou the mote that is in thy brother's eye, but perceivest not the beam that is in thine own eye? — Luke vi. 41.

TO see a mote in my neighbor's eye when a beam is in mine own eye is physically impossible. To see and measure my neighbor's sins when I am committing sins myself, is morally impossible. The Pharisee deciding that he was not "as other men are" was a blind man passing himself off for a professor of ophthalmology. No wonder that Christ says to such, "Thou hypocrite, first cast out the beam out of thine own eye; and then shalt thou see clearly to cast out the mote out of thy brother's eye."

Judging how far my neighbor's soul is wanting in conformity to God's law will become my business when there is no longer in me any want of conformity; hence it will never become my business. "Let us not therefore judge one another any more." The judgment seat is reserved for the holy Christ, whose eyes without beam or mote see all things perfectly.

This much however I may decide now, — that never can my neighbor's sin, viewed as to its power to obscure my vision of things worth seeing, be to me more than a mote. But my sin, because it is my sin, becomes a beam preventing my seeing God and the pure and heavenly.

"Search me, O God, and know my heart: try me, and know my thoughts: and see if there be any wicked way in me, and lead me in the way everlasting."

Henry M. MacCracken.

> Forget not thou hast often sinned,
> And sinful yet must be;
> Deal gently with the erring one,
> As God has dealt with thee.
>
> **Fletcher.**

March 27.

Come boldly unto the throne of grace.—Heb. iv. 16.

And whatsoever ye shall ask in my name, that will I do, that the Father may be glorified in the Son. If ye shall ask anything in my name, I will do it.—John xiv. 13, 14.

THE connection of this absolute promise shows its immense value. Many stumble at the words of the previous verse: "Verily, verily, I say unto you, He that believeth on me, the works that I do shall he do also; and greater works than these shall he do; because I go unto my Father." They fail to see the connection of the last clause, "Because I go unto my Father." Christ is not dead, but *alive* again from the dead, with all power in heaven and earth. Therefore he says, "Whatsoever ye shall ask in my name I will do." This is present *supernatural power* through the believer that is promised. The secret is in verses 10, 11: "Believest thou not that I am in the Father, and the Father in me? the words that I speak unto you I speak not of myself: but the Father that dwelleth in me, he doeth the works. Believe me that I am in the Father, and the Father in me: or else believe me for the very works' sake." This is the mystical union of the Father and the Son. He prays for the same in us (John xvii. 21).

This unity means that the will of God is our will, and our obedience means such a ready listening to his voice from abiding in him that he answers us by doing that which we desire of him (1 John iii. 22). *Our* works are to reveal Christ to the world, as his works reveal God to us.

H. M. Parsons

Come, my soul, thy suit prepare;
Jesus loves to answer prayer.
He himself has bid thee pray,
Therefore will not say thee nay. NEWTON.

March 28.

Let this mind be in you. — Phil. ii. 5.

Wist ye not that I must be about my Father's business? — Luke ii. 49.

OUT of all the gracious words which hallowed the childhood of Jesus, these alone have been preserved. The link of golden speech seems to bind the incarnate Christ-life to that mystery of eternity, when the "Only Begotten of the Father" assumed the right to become a ransom for fallen man. "Lo! I come. I delight to do thy will, O my God."

Whether as a key to all the obedience and sacrifice of the mediatorial work, or the motto of every consecrated life, the sublime sentence is lovingly cherished.

Happy are we when we apprehend as Jesus did the fatherhood of God.

In that supreme hour when filial love, born of the "spirit of adoption," cries "Abba, Father," we will realize, as did the holy Child in the temple, that the all-absorbing business of life is our "Father's business." We should have no business which may not with its best results be offered upon the divine altar; while all that work which is peculiar to his kingdom we should make our own.

As of such a service, one says, *I must*, compulsion ceases, and the word glows with the enthusiasm of a voluntary sacrifice.

"'T is love, not duty," shall we sing? Nay, rather, "Love *is* duty." When love commissions a child of God, the sweetest companionship and highest earthly joys fail to call him from the delighted service.

Cornelius Brett

Such was thy truth and such thy zeal,
Such deference to thy Father's will,
Such love and meekness so divine,
I would transcribe and make them mine.
— Watts.

MARCH 29.

For your sakes he became poor. — 2 COR. viii. 9.

Foxes have holes, and birds of the air have nests; but the Son of man hath not where to lay his head. — LUKE ix. 58.

IT is the glory of faith that it "esteems the reproach of Christ greater riches than the treasures in Egypt; for it looks away to the recompense of the reward." Thus Jesus, the Son of God and the Son of man in his one person, when on earth as our good Shepherd and great Captain, to seek and save the lost by his life of self-sacrifice and sufferings, was able to "endure the cross, despising the shame," by looking to "the glory that should follow." No person can be trained for the service of Christ and follow his example without the discipline of tribulation and faith fixed on Christ in his glory. In union with him through his Holy Spirit, we will make cheerfully any sacrifice, and rejoice in toil and tribulation to "follow him fully," as did Caleb and Joshua.

Then at length shall we feel as Caleb and Joshua felt, when, as Israel were on the bank of Jordan, these two old soldiers with armor on were at their post in the ranks, waiting for the sound of the trumpet, the signal for the advance in their last march across, dry-shod, into "the good land beyond Jordan." This King of glory, the Conqueror "crowned with many crowns," — once the poor man of Galilee, — is still in tender sympathy with his redeemed ones, and as the good Shepherd will ever "lead them to living fountains of waters and wipe away all tears from their eyes."

Geo. Burrowes.

> Who suffer with our Master here,
> We shall before his face appear,
>   And by his side sit down;
> To patient faith the prize is sure,
> And all that to the end endure
>   The cross, shall wear the crown.
>
> C. WESLEY.

March 30.

Having loved this present world. — 2 Tim. iv. 10.

Yet lackest thou one thing: sell all that thou hast, and distribute unto the poor, and thou shalt have treasure in heaven: and come, follow me. — Luke xviii. 22.

LACK of *one* thing *may* be fatal, — lack of one stone in the arch; of attention to one leak in the ship; lack of saving faith in the soul. Lack of one thing led the young ruler to make "the great refusal," and turn his back on the Redeemer.

No sacrifice, needful to the following of Christ, to be withheld; all sacrifice in vain without the following. Sell *and* follow.

To every life marred by a single sin or by a single imperfection, and to every service of heart, lip, or hand, comes the word, "One thing thou lackest."

Self-denying distribution to the needy in the name of Christ is a deposit laid up in heaven to be received again with usury.

Had this young man obeyed, possibly he had been called to some high and incalculably useful office in Christ's kingdom, — perhaps to be an apostle in the place of Judas; perhaps to write a gospel or an epistle to be read by the godly to the end of time.

No one can foresee to what place in the kingdom the obedient soul may be assigned.

W. P. Breed

God calling yet! I cannot stay;
My heart I yield without delay.
Vain world, farewell! from thee I part;
The voice of God hath reached my heart.
Miss J. Borthwick *(Translation).*

March 31.

Believing, ye rejoice with joy unspeakable. — 1 PETER i. 8.

And ye now therefore have sorrow: but I will see you again, and your heart shall rejoice, and your joy no man taketh from you. — JOHN xvi. 22.

COMFORTING words for sorrowing souls. "In this world ye shall have tribulation." It is a common experience of the saints, and a necessary discipline. But sanctified sorrow is more than compensated.

Those words of Jesus, "I go away," together with an intimation of other trials, brought anguish to the disciples. How true, "Ye have sorrow now"! But "I will see you again" brought adequate consolation. The cross bore him from their sight, but he saw them again and they saw him; and though the clouds received him, yet in spirit he remained with them to the end, — a source of joy unspeakable.

So Jesus deals with all who love him. Their sorrows are many, but the sharpest pains come from a conscious separation from their Lord, — the communion interrupted by sin and unbelief. To them that mourn for him he will show himself again. "I *will* come to you." The severer the pangs, the greater the joy of deliverance. "Your *heart* shall rejoice." It is not surface-gladness, which is transitory, but a deep, solid, constant, lasting joy.

Goyn Talmage

> But see! the night is waning fast,
>   The breaking morn is near;
> And Jesus comes with voice of love,
>   Thy drooping heart to cheer.
> Then weep no more; 't is all thine own,
>   His crown, his joy divine;
> And sweeter far than all beside,
>   He, he himself is thine!
>
> SIR E. DENNY.

April 1.

Who through faith . . . obtained promises. — Heb. xi. 33.

. . . Believe ye that I am able to do this? . . . According to your faith be it unto you. — Matt. ix. 28, 29.

IN connecting as he does our faith with the exercise of his power and the benefits it confers, Christ's design is to produce a co-operation of human agency with the divine, so that we become co-workers with God in the reception and diffusion of the blessings he bestows. Thus, aside from the natural or physical effects of such co-operation, there springs up a moral or spiritual effect which enriches and ennobles the character of man. God honors us by making our faith the measure of his beneficence, and we honor him by attesting and acknowledging his power to do the things for which we pray. Hence the Scriptures say, "Without faith it is impossible to please him, for he that cometh to God must believe that he is, and that he is a rewarder of them that diligently seek him" (Heb. xi. 6).

But faith is likewise "the gift of God," and the concomitant of the divine "grace" which issues in salvation (Eph. ii. 8). So that it has been observed that duties are graces, and graces become duties. It is not therefore every state of mind in which the imagination — the faculty most akin to faith — is exercised. That constitutes the prescribed condition on which God will use his power and bestow his blessing. Many are liable to delusion just at this point. The best proof of a genuine faith in man is in the works wrought by divine energy and their results according to this faith. And so the believer may herewith prove God, if he "will not pour out a blessing that there shall not be room enough to receive it" (Mal. iii. 10).

B. Sunderland.

> Faith, mighty faith, the promise sees,
>   And looks to that alone,
> Laughs at impossibilities,
>   And cries, "It shall be done!"   C. Wesley.

April 2.

God also hath highly exalted him. — Phil. ii. 9.

For the Father judgeth no man, but hath committed all judgment unto the Son: that all men should honour the Son, even as they honour the Father. He that honoureth not the Son honoureth not the Father which hath sent him. — John v. 22, 23.

IN the language of nature, the Son is the reproduction of the Father. God is infinite. The finite cannot directly know the infinite; whatever it knows, it knows by finite measures. Yet man is related to the infinite Father. He seeks therefore to symbolize God, his conscience demands the infinite Judge, his heart the infinite Father; but his symbols and measurements are all imperfect, therefore God gives us his Son, — a perfect reproduction of himself, morally, spiritually, and affectionally. The Son stands on this side the chasm of the infinite, — a part of organic nature, able to reproduce himself in us, our very flesh and blood. God therefore makes him our Judge, because he is the Judge *in esse*, the true type, perfect in love, truth, sympathy. Also, because it is essential that the symbol of Deity should be authoritative; having given us his Son, so that we can come into clear practical relations with, and likeness to, himself, he will not have us dishonoring the Son, and so blurring the divine standard and belittling the infinite majesty that saves us morally. The perfect light has come, and God holds us responsible; we must be judged by the Son.

John H. Denison

All hail the power of Jesus' name!
 Let angels prostrate fall;
 Bring forth the royal diadem,
 And crown him Lord of all.
Edward Perronet.

April 3.

This is the promise . . . eternal life. — John ii. 25.

Verily, verily, I say unto you, If a man keep my saying, he shall never see death. — John viii. 51.

NOTICE what we may call the *majestic* simplicity of the words of Scripture. It has been said that the grandest and most pregnant sentence in our language is, "And God said, let there be light; and there was light." Yet in that sentence there is not a word of more than one syllable. Fully as pregnant, more mysterious in meaning, yet as simple in form, is our text. "*I* say unto you." Here, as so often when a mighty truth is to come, the personality of Christ stands forth. Not, "men say," "it is said," "you all know," but "*I* say." I who came down from heaven, I who am the truth, I who have the keys of death and hell, I who am the Resurrection and the Life, say, "If a man keep my saying he shall never see death." This stupendous contradiction to the natural mind becomes a mine of light and truth to him whose soul the Spirit of God illumines. He who spake was soon to die after the flesh. He was speaking to dying men. What did he mean, then? That he who faithfully keeps the saying of Christ shall not see that death from which Christ came to deliver man, — the death of the soul, the death of condemnation in hell, the death which comes from separation from God, the *only real* death. To the Christian, death is a sleep, a passage from earth to paradise, an unconscious journey whose end is light; but to the sinner it is an awful catastrophe, the close of hope, the beginning of the end. Abraham was not dead, though for centuries in his tomb. But many who heard Christ with beating hearts and flowing veins were dead even while they lived, because they neither knew nor obeyed him.

Edward L. Stoddard

Death, no longer now we die,
We but follow Christ on high.
         George Rawson.

April 4.

Faith, if it hath not works, is dead. — James ii. 17.

For whosoever shall do the will of my Father which is in heaven, the same is my brother, and sister, and mother. — Matt. xii. 50.

OUR Lord has made all the family relationships more sacred. The spirit which would dissolve them, which would dream of a holier life than that of the household, a discipline more sacred than that of a godly family, is contrary to the spirit of Christ. Through him we learn to love our kindred and friends with a nobler love. The Church is one great family, — sharers in the same parental care and heirs to a common inheritance. Jealousies may spring up between the fondest hearts, and the most passionate love may grow cool unless Christ purify it. He teaches us how to love brothers and sisters, and even our own children, aright. He bids the Church esteem men, not for rank or fashion, but because they belong to Christ.

Our Lord's dying words showed how dearly he loved his mother, and were a reflection of the love which she bestowed on his infant days. No mother was ever more tender and thoughtful; no child ever loved a mother so perfectly. There is no love like his; and he who possesses it will love his kindred better, and seek to win them to the brotherhood of Christ.

James Gardiner Vose

> Now I have found a friend
> Whose love shall never end;
>   Jesus is mine.
> Though earthly joys decrease,
> Though human friendships cease,
> Now I have lasting peace;
>   Jesus is mine.
>
>   Hope.

April 5.

Manifested to take away our sins. — 1 John iii. 5.

As the Father knoweth me, even so know I the Father: and I lay down my life for the sheep. — John x. 15.

THESE words illustrate the kind and quality of knowledge the good Shepherd has of his own, and they of him. Surely none but the eternal Son would or could use such a sublime comparison. This knowledge is not information concerning persons and their characters only; but it implies recognition, acknowledgment, approbation, confidence, and love. It indicates the close and affectionate intimacy of friends who know each other so well that there is a perfect understanding between them.

The import of these words of Jesus is that as between the Father and the Son, who are the same in nature, will, and purpose, this peculiar knowledge exists, so between Jesus and the believer, who are in a sense one in nature, will, and purpose, there is similar knowledge. And of this, the voluntary death of Christ is the grandest proof on his part, and the faithful imitation of his spirit and example is one of the best evidences on the part of the believer.

What a privilege is yours, O believer! — to know your Saviour, and to be known by him, as he knows the Father, and the Father knows him.

Let your life prove that you gratefully appreciate this sacred intimacy.

William Harvey

> So shall the world believe and know
>   That God hath sent thee from above,
> When thou art seen in us below,
>   And every soul displays thy love.
>
> C. Wesley.

April 6.

Behold, the Lord cometh. — Jude i. 14.

The Son of man shall send forth his angels, and they shall gather out of his kingdom all things that offend, and them which do iniquity; and shall cast them into a furnace of fire: there shall be wailing and gnashing of teeth. Then shall the righteous shine forth as the sun in the kingdom of their Father. Who hath ears to hear, let him hear. — Matt. xiii. 41–43.

THE same Son of man who was made "lower than the angels" that he might taste death for us appears here as the Lord of angels, and sends them forth to execute his decree, finally and irrevocably separating the wicked from among the just.

The same workers of iniquity who so often in this world increased in riches and glory and fared sumptuously every day, when the once despised and rejected Son of man comes to judgment are cast into the furnace of fire; and instead of pomp and self-indulgence, there is wailing and gnashing of teeth.

And the same humble followers of the Lamb (by divine grace accounted and made righteous) who here shared his tribulation and his reproach shall then "shine forth as the sun in the kingdom of their Father."

Well might our Lord, after these wonderful declarations, exclaim, "Who hath ears to hear, let him hear!" *Now* is the time to make our choice with which of these great throngs our portion shall be.

Elias Riggs.

> Among thy saints let me be found,
> Whene'er the archangel's trump shall sound,
>   To see thy smiling face;
> Then loudest of the throng I'll sing,
> While heaven's resounding mansions ring
>   With shouts of sovereign grace.
>   — Selina, Countess of Huntington *(probably)*.

April 7.

I will walk at liberty: for I seek thy precepts.
Psalm cxix. 45.

If ye continue in my word, then are ye my disciples indeed; and ye shall know the truth, and the truth shall make you free. — John viii. 31, 32.

LIKE genius in art, Christian genius comes not so much by endowment as by toil. He who continues in the word of the Master moves in an atmosphere of heavenly inspiration as well as of heavenly aspiration. Only by a faithful adherence to the teaching and example of Christ can one come to a full knowledge of spiritual truth.

Spiritual knowledge thus obtained touches all the powers as by a divine force, and each springs to highest activity along the lines of holy living. Yet not as a child learning to walk, nor as one lame, does a Christian move, nor do the rules of the art of Christian living harass the aspiring effort. Rather with free step and unhindered energy the disciple, trusting, loving, following Jesus, runs and is not weary, walks and faints not. The Christian worker reproduces the divine ideals, and brings forth results which alike are a blessing to humanity and a glory to the Master.

Dear fellow-disciple, it is your privilege to possess the great freedom with which Christ makes his people free, — free from the curse of sin, free from the restrictions of ignorance and weakness, — and in which he impresses on imperfect natures his own spirit, so that you may walk and work and live in the liberty of the sons of God.

J. M. Ellis.

Bondsman must each soul remain
Till the truth shall break his chain;
Truth of God, oh, make me free,
Set my soul at liberty.   R. M. Offord.

April 8.

𝔋𝔢 𝔱𝔥𝔞𝔱 𝔥𝔞𝔱𝔥 𝔪𝔢𝔯𝔠𝔶 ... 𝔥𝔞𝔭𝔭𝔶 𝔦𝔰 𝔥𝔢. — Prov. xiv. 21.

Blessed are the merciful: for they shall obtain mercy. — Matt. v. 7.

THIS text expresses a common truth, emphasized with countless illustrations. Kindness pays. Those who are considerate of others in trial are themselves generally remembered in their own times of need.

But our Lord here means more than this. He means that the merciful shall obtain mercy at the last day. Notice, —

1. That the Beatitudes present but one character. This character begins in humiliation and godly sorrow, is marked by spiritual meekness, longing after righteousness, and kindly feeling for others, and grows into purity of heart. Such a character cannot be a fruit of nature. It is that of an ideal child of God.

2. That our Lord does not teach that any man shall at last obtain mercy as pay for being merciful. What he says is that the man of these Beatitudes is blessed (happy), because he shall obtain mercy. He only states a fact, without giving a cause for it. We must look for the cause of all mercy at last in the free grace of God, and in our Lord's own atoning and saving work.

If we have, already begun in us, the character outlined in the Beatitudes, we have already entered into, and shall be ever growing in the blessedness of the blessed man.

David Cole

> Let grace our selfishness expel,
> Our earthliness refine;
> And kindness in our bosoms dwell
> As free and true as thine.
>
> John H. Gurney.

April 9.

Faith without works is dead. — JAMES ii. 26.

Not every one that saith unto me, Lord, Lord, shall enter into the kingdom of heaven; but he that doeth the will of my Father which is in heaven. — MATT. vii. 21.

THEY are false disciples who cry, "Lord, Lord," but who bear no fruit, who hold an orthodox creed and profess faith in Christ and attachment to him, while they fail to partake of his spirit or keep his commandments. They shall not enter into the kingdom of heaven. They may be outwardly in the membership of Christ's Church, but they are not of it; they do not understand its spirit; they are ignorant of its sacred joy; they have no part in its glorious destiny.

The true disciple is one who not only cries, "Lord, Lord," but also doeth the will of his Father which is in heaven. He is one who makes grateful and joyous confession of his dependence on and devotion to Christ, and who is entitled thus to do in virtue of the consistency between his profession and his experience and practice.

Obedience to the Father's will is the imperative condition of entrance into the kingdom of heaven. If eternal life is to be had, it must be had according to the principles of the divine law, and in no other way. Keeping God's commandments is the only life of the human soul. There is no opposition between the law and the gospel; they are two sides of the same thing, which is Love. The law prescribes duty, and the gospel brings light to see and strength to discharge that duty. The law urges obedience on penalty of death; the gospel comes, not to save us from that penalty *without* obedience, but to fill us with love, which is the spirit of obedience and the essence of eternal life.

R. R. Meredith.

Up, then, with speed, and work;
Fling ease and self away!
This is no time for thee to sleep,
Up, watch, and work, and pray!   H. BONAR.

April 10.

Let him ask in faith. — James i. 6.

Hitherto have ye asked nothing in my name: ask, and ye shall receive, that your joy may be full. — John xvi. 24.

THIS is one of Christ's words of farewell. It is a part of his legacy to his faithful people, — a blank checkbook on the bank of heaven, with our Lord's signature to it right through. Let us have faith to make a good use of it.

What encouragement and help it gives us! Our blessed Lord well knows how weak our faith is and how slowly it grows; that our hearts are likely to fail us in the presence-chamber of the Almighty, — and therefore for our stimulus and comfort he speaks to us these words: " Hitherto have ye asked nothing in my name, ask," — that is, as the word implies, go on asking, continue to ask, — "and ye shall receive."

Note finally the end proposed to be obtained by means of our prayer. It is that our joy may be completed; that we may be made truly happy. Our Lord desires that in this life we should have joy, and he points us to the only source of true blessedness, — to God. Let us then abound much in prayer; and with joyous hearts let us go about the work which God has given us to do.

Alex. Miller

Prayer makes the darkened cloud withdraw;
Prayer climbs the ladder Jacob saw,
Gives exercise to faith and love,
Brings every blessing from above.
                                            COWPER.

April 11.

His own received him not.—John i. 11.

And ye will not come to me, that ye might have life. — John v. 40.

AN undertone of tender pity and yearning love pervades these words. While in them our Lord fixes upon the unbelieving Jews the responsibility for their own spiritual ruin, he still speaks with the same sad regret as when he uttered his lament over Jerusalem.

In setting forth one purpose of his incarnation, Jesus said, " I am come that they might have life " (John x. 10). But those who would have life must come to him and receive from him the gift unspeakable which he is always ready to bestow. It is never forced upon unwilling recipients.

We wonder that any refused the loving invitations of our incarnate Saviour; that any could resist the pleadings of him whose voice hushed the storm-wind and calmed the angry billows and woke the dead to life. But how many now, with unwilling heart, turn away from the call of his love, and resist the Holy Spirit whom he hath sent! The intellect is convinced; the feelings are stirred; but the will remains obdurate. Men remain at a distance from Christ because they are *not willing* to come unto him. Are you among those of whom he is saying: " Ye are not willing to come to me, that ye might have life " ?

William K. Clark,

And when the sinner chooses wrath,
   God mourns his hapless lot;
Deep breathing from his heart of love,
   " I would, but ye would not."

ALEXANDER.

April 12.

The Lord is my shepherd; I shall not want.
PSALM xxiii. 1.

I have compassion on the multitude, because they have now been with me three days, and have nothing to eat. — MARK viii. 2.

CURIOUS ones have sought for a likeness of the face of Jesus the Christ, but the devout soul looks into the heart of him who reveals the Father and is glad. "I have compassion." His nature *compasses* our necessity. His heart enfolds us. Nor need one say, "I am left out," because it seems too hard to believe that on thee singly he fixes his love. With the multitude thou mayest stand and still be loved.

"There 's a wideness in God's mercy
Like the wideness of the sea."

Too much on our guard we cannot be against "the false limits of our own" by which "we make the love of God too narrow." "I have compassion on the multitude." Who has not found that "man's extremity is God's opportunity"? Blind unbelief asks, "Carest thou not?" Faith's triumph is that "he knows what we have need of." Only let us not misplace our necessities. The soul first — always first. "They have now been with me three days." What soul-feasting during that precious time! But the body has its place and must be cared for; so what he would not do for himself he did for the people, — he wrought a miracle to meet the extreme occasion. Is not every providence a miracle? Were our eyes but anointed with eye-salve, the commonest event of our lives would appear "big with mercy."

Alexander Grant

O little heart of mine! shall pain
Or sorrow make thee moan,
When all this God is all for thee,
A Father all thine own?   FABER.

The grace that should come unto you. — 1 Peter i. 10.

Blessed are your eyes, for they see: and your ears, for they hear. For verily I say unto you, That many prophets and righteous men have desired to see those things which ye see, and have not seen them; and to hear those things which ye hear, and have not heard them. — Matt. xiii. 16, 17.

THE superior blessedness of Christian privileges is manifold. For example, in respect to our knowledge of God, — his nature, character, purposes, methods; in respect to our knowledge of man, — his unity, fall, needs, moral capacities; in respect to our knowledge of duties, which comes to us through this knowledge of God and of man; in respect to our knowledge of a future life, — its certainty and possibilities; in respect to our knowledge of the promised Messiah, — his divinity, his humanity, his spirituality; in respect to our knowledge of the way of salvation, — the divinity of its mediation, the fulness of its scope, the completeness of its details, the freedom of its provisions; in respect to our knowledge of the nature of worship, — a spirit rather than a letter, a character rather than a formula, a life rather than a drill; in respect to the motives which Christianity in distinction from Mosaism sets before us, — motives inspired by the character of Jesus rather than by the sanctions of the law; in brief, in respect to all higher ranges of thought, experience, aspiration, possibility, — in all these the lowliest disciple under Jesus is greater than the greatest disciple under Moses, for the Christian as compared with the Jew has been translated from the realm of prophecy into the realm of fulfilment.

George Dana Boardman

How blessed are our eyes,
   That see this heavenly light!
Prophets and kings desired it long,
   But died without the sight.
                              WATTS.

April 14.

Who also maketh intercession for us. — ROMANS viii. 34.

Simon, Simon, behold, Satan hath desired to have you, that he may sift you as wheat: but I have prayed for thee, that thy faith fail not: and when thou art converted, strengthen thy brethren. — LUKE xxii. 31, 32.

THREE PERSONS, — Christ, Peter, and Satan, the Divine, the Human, and the Devilish, in one group.

1. *The Omniscient Lord*, reading the inmost soul of his disciple, seeing also the desires and movements of the Evil One, knowing to-morrow likewise and all things that are to be, solicitous for the disciple's safety, faithful to warn, quick to rescue and restore the tempted and fallen.

2. *Peter*, — sanguine, self-confident, boastful; so unaware of his own weakness, so ignorant of Satan's devices, and so unimpressed by his Master's words that though forewarned, he is not forearmed, but falls an easy prey to unexpected temptation, after which come shame, penitence, and merciful recovery.

3. *The Prince of Darkness*, — a deceiving spirit, prowling, stealthy, and seductive; audacious and subtle tempter of Christ and men; tireless, cunning, formidable; ensnaring sometimes the noblest, catching David through his passions, Judas through his covetousness, Peter through his fears, and making even Paul fear lest he become a castaway.

THREE LESSONS, — (1) Listen to the wise warnings of your tender Lord; (2) Be not self-confident, but humble; (3) Be watchful against the adversary.

William V. Kelley.

He lives, to bless me with his love;
He lives, to plead for me above;
He lives, my hungry soul to feed;
He lives, to help in time of need.
SAMUEL MEDLEY.

April 15.

I will open your graves. — Ezek. xxxvii. 12.

Lazarus, come forth. — John xi. 43.

THIS is the sublime conclusion of the touching story of the raising of Lazarus. It presents the estimate the Saviour had of prayer. He knew his power and how all things were subject to him; yet when he was about to perform this mighty work for the glory of God and the comfort of weeping hearts, he first prayed, and that prayer is full of confidence and trust. What a lesson to us to do everything with the same confident appeal to God (Phil. iv. 6)!

The text again shows the mighty power of Jesus. The greatest, the mightiest conqueror of man is death. The most mysterious and irrevocable state is that of the dead. None can conquer in that war. None ever attempt to revoke the decree that bids all to enter the grave. We may sorrow over the outward tomb, and weep at our own losses; but none dream of changing the result. Now the mighty power of Jesus is manifest, in that, standing at the dark door of this dread mystery and these helpless sleepers, he says, "Come forth;" and there is nothing can resist his call. Death, the grave, the unknown sleep, all respond; and he that was dead and buried stands again a living man, a loving brother. What joy and hope for those who trust in Jesus, not only for their loved ones gone before, but for their own glorious life beyond the death! "He has the keys of death and of hell."

J. M. Worrall

Asleep in Jesus! peaceful rest,
Whose waking is supremely blest.
No fear, no woe, shall dim that hour
That manifests the Saviour's power.
                               Mrs. Margaret Mackay.

April 16.

The washing of water by the word. — Eph. v. 26.

Now ye are clean through the word which I have spoken unto you. — John xv. 3.

IN how many ways do men seek to be clean *apart* from the Word, — by ceremonies, by reformations, by resolutions, by introspections, by feelings! All these ways how resultless! There is but one way, — " Now are ye clean through the Word." The Word gives us light upon our condition as sinners. The Word sets forth Christ. The Word assures us that believing in him, we are "accepted in the Beloved." We are "born again" by the Word. The Word sets us at liberty.

More than this, — we are "purged" by the Word. We are "*in* the Vine" by the Word; then, as the branches, we must be *pruned* by it. Our Saviour has in the thirteenth chapter marked this distinction, — " He that is washed needeth not save to wash his feet." The two words "washed," "wash," are not the same in the Greek. One is bathing the whole body; the other is washing or wiping the hands or the feet. One is regeneration; the other is restored communion. The whole man is washed from sin and washed at once and washed forever in the cleansing blood of Christ; but then the sandalled feet in life's journey may acquire a surface defilement. Hence we have need to look to our ways, to try to test them by the Word of God. Thus does the Word make us *consciously* clean. It gives us a conscience void of offence, — a great matter. "Wherewithal shall a young man cleanse his way? By taking heed thereto according to thy word."

George S. Bishop.

> Order my footsteps by thy Word
> And make my heart sincere;
> Let sin have no dominion, Lord,
> And keep my conscience clear. Watts.

April 17.

Keep yourselves in the love of God. — Jude i. 21.

As the Father hath loved me, so have I loved you: continue ye in my love. — John xv. 9.

THE very words of Christ have a peculiar charm. We especially prize those which declare his relations and his feeling toward us. The declaration that he loves us is an unspeakably comforting assurance, especially as we are conscious of our unworthiness and sinfulness even since we have believed. The mystery deepens, yet the thought becomes more definite and comforting when we hear, "I have loved you" "*as* my Father hath loved me," — the same in kind, measure, and duration of love. He desires our companionship and co-operation, as he has daily been the delight of his Father and associated in all his operations (Prov. viii. 30; John xvii. 4, 5, 24). He regards us with complaisance. There is in us no good thing, but he has already given us of his graces, and will change us into his image from glory to glory. He is the brightness of the Father's glory; and he delights in our obedience. It is very imperfect; but he notices our will and effort to do good, our resistance of temptation, and our patience under crosses and afflictions. His Father loved him because he was obedient unto death.

Nothing can separate us from this love of Christ. But we must be conscious of it and respond to it. "Continue ye in my love." Desire close intimacy with Christ. Seek conformity to his image, and crave his approbation in every act. "Well done, good and faithful servant, enter into the joy of your Lord."

J. Aspinwall Hodge

    Oh, the height of Jesus' love,
    Higher than the heavens above,
    Deeper than the depths of sea,
    Lasting as eternity!
    Love that found me — wondrous thought! —
    Found me when I sought him not!
                      William M'Comb.

April 18.

So shall we ever be with the Lord. — 1 Thess. iv. 17.

Father, I will that they also, whom thou hast given me, be with me where I am; that they may behold my glory, which thou hast given me: for thou lovedst me before the foundation of the world. — John xvii. 24.

THIS is the voice of man, and yet throughout its majestic rhythm we cannot but detect the accent of Deity. It is the word of a king. And where the word of a king is, there is power. When he pleaded for himself he said, "Not as I will." But now that he pleads for others, he does not hesitate to speak with authority, "Father, I will."

He came to be with us where we are, — amid the tears and sighs and graves of earth, — that we might go to be with him where he is forevermore. The one condition is whether we dare to include ourselves among those whom the Father gave unto him before the foundations of the earth were laid. And this we may do, for it is written, "All that the Father giveth me shall come to me." And the reverse is also true, " Those who come are those whom the Father has given."

Ah, immeasurable extent of love with which the Father has loved the Son! What glory will not that be with which he will crown him! Yet that love and that glory are also for us, if by faith we are forever one with him.

F B Meyer

"Forever with the Lord!"
Amen! so let it be!
Life from the dead is in that word,
And immortality.

J. Montgomery.

April 19.

Joint-heirs with Christ. — Romans viii. 17.

To him that overcometh will I grant to sit with me in my throne, even as I also overcame, and am set down with my Father in his throne. — Rev. iii. 21.

EACH of the epistles to the seven churches closes with a promise to "him that overcometh." Our text, which concludes the series and sums up the whole, contains the royal promise, — the Christian who perseveres to the end is to share in Christ's dominion. The believer receives the fulfilment of the promise in part in this world; already he is a member of the kingdom of God, and in virtue of his relation to Christ, himself a king. But this is only the potency and promise of what is to be.

The way to kingship is through conflict; the king is one who has overcome. Christ himself won his throne, though it was his by right. We must follow in his steps. Our foes are in many respects different from his. They are different from those of the Asiatic Christians to whom the promise was addressed; but they are none the less real. Satan appears in different guise in different ages, but the purpose of his warfare is the same. Our enemies are on every side, — in the sinful world about us, in the evil that lurks in our own hearts; but our Lord is mightier than Satan. Courage, friends! look onward and upward! The struggle is hard, but it is worth the pains. We are on the winning side. After the battle comes the crown. By and by we shall sit with Christ upon his throne.

Lewis F. Stearns

'T is God's all-animating voice
  That calls thee from on high;
'T is his own hand presents the prize
  To thine aspiring eye.

Philip Doddridge.

April 20.

Every one . . . when he looketh . . . shall live.
Numbers xxi. 8.

Verily, verily, I say unto you, He that believeth on me hath everlasting life. — John vi. 47.

WE speak of the mystery of life! No doubt obtained in the mind of Christ on this subject which so baffles and perplexes philosophy. To our eager questionings regarding the future he comes with positive teaching, giving us confidence and eliciting our faith. He, the life, out of his own infinite knowledge spoke of himself as the source of life. Life only produces life, and into the deadness of our hearts through the channel of faith pours the living stream in each member and through the whole Church, which is his body.

As Christians how little we realize the dignity of our present existence! "Hath everlasting life" saith our Lord. Even now by the new birth we have begun the heavenly life; and physical death is but the dropping of the leaf, in order to the entrance upon an everlasting spring-time. Christ establishes the unity and continuity of life unfolding from the germ of the present into the glorious fulness of eternity, — the Christian now endowed with all the infinite possibilities of the future only awaiting the development.

G. F. Hardin

> Rise, my soul, and stretch thy wings,
>   Thy better portion trace;
> Rise from transitory things
>   Toward heaven, thy native place.
>
> Robert Seagrave.

April 21.

Partakers of his promise in Christ. — Eph. iii. 6.

And I say unto you, That many shall come from the east and west, and shall sit down with Abraham, and Isaac, and Jacob, in the kingdom of heaven. But the children of the kingdom shall be cast out into outer darkness: there shall be weeping and gnashing of teeth. — Matt. viii. 11, 12.

THIS is a very important and most precious passage of the divine Word. It is a positive declaration by our Lord himself that there shall many come from all lands into the true Church of God, which was first established in the covenant with Abraham. In Luke xiii. 29, the words, "from the north and the south," make the expression more comprehensive of *all the world*. Jesus came to be the Saviour, not of the Jews only, but of *all who will call upon him*, of all nations and of all people. When he was on earth, the dispensation of the Gentiles had not come; yet he gave a gracious answer to the few Gentiles who approached him, as he did to this centurion, the woman of Canaan (Matt. xv. 22), the nobleman (John iv. 46), and the Samaritans (John iv. 40). He specially commended *the faith* of the centurion and the woman of Canaan. It is often seen now that heathen converts manifest strong faith which enables them to endure persecution and death for the name of Jesus. Church of Christ, to whom the blessed commission is given, "Go ye into all the world!" labor on, pray on, increase the agencies that this "multitude which no man can number" may be gathered in!

While the promise is thus full and precious to those that believe, the other alternative remains true: even "the children of the kingdom," if they believe not, "shall be cast out into outer darkness."

Andrew P. Happer.

Salvation, oh, salvation,
  The joyful sound proclaim,
Till earth's remotest nation
  Has learned Messiah's name. Heber.

April 22.

Wash me throughly from mine iniquity. — Psalm li. 2.

If I wash thee not, thou hast no part with me. — John xiii. 8.

EVERY act and every word of the Lord Jesus was an outward expression of his spiritual life, — a real, however minute part, of his sublime mission. In washing his disciples' feet, he at once revealed *himself*, and disclosed the social principle which lay at the foundation of his spiritual kingdom.

Long before this incident, Peter had openly accepted Christ as his Saviour, had confessed faith in him as his Messiah and Lord. It was therefore his duty cheerfully and unhesitatingly to submit to any and every expression of his Master's will. How could he have *part* in Jesus unless he practically recognized his authority? But in our Lord's words there was much more than this. His act was in itself the symbol of a higher truth. His word shed divine light on the symbol. That we may have a part in Jesus, we must not only embrace his atoning righteousness, we must be the willing subjects of his purifying grace. The feet, soiled by daily travel, must be washed, — washed, not by human hands, nor by our own, but by Christ's. The blood "in which we have redemption" is the blood by which we must be "cleansed from all sin."

K. M. Fenwick.

I look to my incarnate God
Till he his work begin,
And wait till his redeeming blood
Shall cleanse me from all sin.
TOPLADY.

April 23.

Let us watch and be sober. — 1 Thess. v. 6.

And unto the angel of the church in Sardis write; These things saith he that hath the seven Spirits of God, and the seven stars; I know thy works, that thou hast a name that thou livest, and art dead. — Rev. iii. 1.

HOW close and minute is the espionage of God! He knows our works, our words, our thoughts, the intents of the heart. He is quick to detect evil, and just as quick to discern good. He knew the heartlessness and formality of Sardis, and also the charity, the service, the faith, the patience, and the works of Thyatira. God is not a policeman, but an husbandman. He is more pleased to see a grain of corn sprout in the ground than to detect a worm gnawing at the root. He warns, he exhorts, he encourages, before he visits with scourge and ruin.

Sardis, opulent city of Lesser Asia, capital of ancient Lydia, mad with pleasures and with wealth, we do not wonder, knowing human nature, that the Church of God within thy walls and under thy influence became spiritually dead. And yet we may wonder, for he who founded thee could give the fulness of the Spirit, and also faithful pastors in the place of those who, dead themselves, were leading their people in the dance of death. There is no excuse for deadness when life can be had for the asking.

Even in Sardis there were those who had not defiled their garments. This is proof that spiritual life can be given and sustained in most trying conditions. This is proof that a man can be a Christian anywhere.

S B Rossiter

Come, let us to the Lord our God
  With contrite hearts return;
Our God is gracious, nor will leave
  The desolate to mourn.   John Morrison.

April 24.

Born again, not of corruptible seed. — 1 Peter i. 23.

Marvel not that I said unto thee, Ye must be born again. — John iii. 7.

AND yet men do marvel, as though it were a thing unreasonable that to live a new life we must be new-born. We may not understand how it is, but so it is. Christ has said it, and who shall gainsay his words?

The sinfulness of the carnal mind makes it needful. "Do men gather grapes of thorns, or figs of thistles?" Man's spiritual deadness makes it imperative. There must be new forces of spiritual life within. The Spirit of God, freely given, is "a well of water springing up into everlasting life." The nature of God and of his kingdom necessitates it, for without holiness "no man shall see the Lord." What fitness can there be for God's service and his kingdom in the natural man, which "receiveth not the things of the Spirit of God"? But, thank God! what *must* be *may* be. The new birth is from above, and of the Spirit, likened to water for its cleansing and to wind for its subtle, penetrating power; and God will give his Holy Spirit to them that ask him. Write this down, then, as an eternal law of the kingdom of grace, "Ye must be born again."

Robt Shindler

How helpless Nature lies,
 Unconscious of her load!
The heart unchanged can never rise
 To happiness and God.

Anne Steele.

April 25.

I will not fail thee. — Joshua i. 5.

I will not leave you comfortless: I will come to you. — John xiv. 18.

OUR blessed Lord will have his people to be a joyful people. He would not have them of sad countenances and heavy hearts, but wishes them to rejoice in him always, for the joy of the Lord is their strength. He was going away to prepare a place for them; he was coming to receive them to himself into those heavenly mansions in his Father's house especially fitted for their occupancy, and in the mean time he would not leave them without "another Comforter," even the Spirit of truth, who should not only bring to remembrance all that he had spoken to them, but mediate his perpetual presence and guide them into truth not yet revealed because they were not now able to bear it. Thus associated with and dwelling in them they would not be comfortless (Gr. orphans), but children of God, joint-heirs with Christ, and members of the blessed family of which Christ is the head.

All these precious assurances of Christ to be with his own are made to his people to-day. We need not wait for his coming for us, or rather our going to him, at death, or for his visible and personal appearance at the last day for the fulfilment of his promise, "I will come to you." We are sure he comes to all who will receive him here and now. He comes through the office and influence of the Comforter, the Spirit of truth, who takes the things of Christ and shows them unto us. May we open our hearts to receive him, and become fit temples for his holy indwelling!

Jael Swartz

Always with us, always with us, .
Words of cheer and words of love;
Thus the risen Saviour whispers,
From his dwelling-place above.   Edwin H. Nevin.

April 26.

Cast thy burden upon the Lord. — Psalm lv. 22.

If God then so clothe the grass, which is to-day in the field, and to-morrow is cast into the oven; how much more will he clothe you, O ye of little faith? — Luke xii. 28.

THIS is the Master's comforting conclusion from looking at a lily. Visible nature without, he teaches, is to illustrate the invisible nature within. Sight is to confirm faith, not to displace it. His doctrine is the direct opposite of that of some to-day who have been learning of the beauty and wonder of the natural world. These, seeing how much that is exquisite in structure perishes, reverse our Lord's saying, and would make it read, "If God so clothe the grass, which to-morrow is cast into the oven, shall he not also cast you into the oven, O ye of too presumptuous faith?" The Son, who knew the Father's heart, says, Nay. The lesson he reads us from the illuminated manuscript of the fields is in effect this: He who bestows his love on the least, shall he not lavish it upon the greatest? If he does so much to delight the eye, shall he not do more to comfort the soul? Consider that the lily, in all its beauty of color and perfection of form and delight of perfume, is simply to give you joy. The flower is neither useful for medicine nor good for food. It rises radiant at the Father's touch purely for your gratification. If your Father, then, so loves to make you happy, how truly must he love to make you good! His care for your enjoyment proves his tireless endeavor to transform you into his image.

C. C. Tiffany

> If our love were but more simple
> We should take him at his word;
> And our lives would be all sunshine
> In the gladness of the Lord.
>
> Faber.

April 27.

Who gave himself for us. — Titus ii. 14.

I am the good shepherd: the good shepherd giveth his life for the sheep. — John x. 11.

WHAT a precious truth is here presented! Like a sheep I am exposed to dangers; wandering about, I am sure to meet the roaring lion and be devoured by him. Jesus knew the danger I was in, and was so anxious about me that he would not send another, but came himself and brought me to his fold. Here I find him the best of shepherds, leading his flock to the green pastures of his love, and beside the still waters of comfort. While I follow him I know I am safe, whatever difficulties, trials, perplexities, or persecutions, I may meet, — for he hath said, "I will never leave thee, nor forsake thee;" yea, he giveth his life for his sheep. He loves me more than his own life, and has really died that I might live. There is therefore no good thing that he will withhold from me. There are, indeed, some things that I fancy are necessary and would like to have; but he knows best, and I am willing to trust in him, and say, Not my will, but thine be done. "The Lord is my shepherd; I shall not want."

D. Ferguson

Oh, for this love let rocks and hills
Their lasting silence break,
And all harmonious human tongues
The Saviour's praises speak!

WATTS.

April 28.

Woe unto them that are wise in their own eyes.
ISAIAH v. 21.

The light of the body is the eye : therefore when thine eye is single, thy whole body also is full of light; but when thine eye is evil, thy body also is full of darkness. Take heed therefore that the light which is in thee be not darkness. — LUKE xi. 34, 35.

JUST as the kingdom of nature bears the burden of the kingdom of grace, so the outer man bears the burden of the inner man. The freshness of the Saviour's teachings largely consists in his unfolding of these correspondences between the seen and the unseen. All the light which comes to the body and to every member of it comes through the eye. The eye is made for seeing. To be sure, when there is no sight through the eye, even the ears may become eyes, even the fingers. A blind man walks, guided by the echoes of his own footfalls, guided by the touch of material objects, reads the printed page with his own fingers. But it is nevertheless true that the light-organ of the body is the eye. So light comes to the inner man through the conscience. This is the light that is in us which is so often darkness ; that is, holds darkness.

The eye is evil, or untrustworthy, when the light from objects seen comes at different angles. A man with spectacles who looks over them is uncertain in his descent of the stairs. He has a double vision of distances, and is likely to trip and fall. It is so with a man who tries to walk in part by the light he gets from earth, and in part by the light he gets from heaven.

J. E. Rankin.

Guide me, O thou great Jehovah,
　Pilgrim through this barren land.
I am weak, but thou art mighty;
　Hold me with thy powerful hand.
WILLIAM WILLIAMS.

April 29.

It shall not return unto me void. — Isaiah lv. 11.

Let both grow together until the harvest: and in the time of harvest I will say to the reapers, Gather ye together first the tares, and bind them in bundles to burn them: but gather the wheat into my barn. — Matt. xiii. 30.

IT is God's way to let "both grow together." Here are lessons of patience and of charity. If God can wait, his servants can. If the Master of the harvest can bear with the tares, the children need not be anxious about them. The wheat and the tares in their early growth are alike; the best farmer cannot distinguish them. God sees the difference; man cannot, but the "day will declare it." There is no tareless wheat-field, there is no pure Church on earth. The tares will not always be hidden, but when God's sickle is thrust in, they will be given to the fire. The wheat will all be gathered in due time, — not one of God's children will be lost. When we see the tares, let us be patient; we would have cast Judas out long before Jesus did. He may try the faith, the charity, and the patience of his people now, by leaving Judas in the Church as he did then.

Be charitable. What you think to be tares may be God's wheat. What if they walk not with us? they may be for us. Bear with human frailty and sin; you also are frail and sinful. It is safe to leave the results with God.

Henry Harris Jessup

> Thou canst not toil in vain;
> Cold, heat, and moist and dry
> Shall foster and mature the grain
> For garners in the sky.
>
> J. Montgomery.

April 30.

This house which is called by my name. — JER. vii. 11.

Take these things hence; make not my Father's house an house of merchandise. — JOHN ii. 16.
It is written, My house shall be called the house of prayer; but ye have made it a den of thieves. — MATT. xxi. 13.

OUR Lord was in his holy temple. From the context we learn that he was there for a threefold purpose, — to receive worship (Matt. xxi. 15); to promote righteousness (John ii. 14, 15); and to do mercy (Matt. xxi. 14). These are the only legitimate objects for which churches can be used, — as houses of prayer and praise; as schools for teaching and applying the Word, which is able alike to save the soul and sanctify the life (James i. 21; Acts xx. 32); and as centres of evangelizing and charitable work.

We learn equally what uses of a church are *not* legitimate, and which yet are in danger of insinuating and establishing themselves within its sacred courts. We are not likely to make it "a den of thieves," as those Jewish sharpers did, but we may degrade it into a "house of merchandise" by conducting it too much in the commercial spirit and method; and it is a serious question whether many a church is not desecrated by the side uses to which it is put for the purpose of raising money. Let us learn to look upon a church with the eyes of Jesus, as our "Father's house," and to love and reverence it for his sake.

Francis N. Zabriskie

    How lovely are thy dwellings fair,
      O Lord of hosts! how dear
    The pleasant tabernacles are,
      Where thou dost dwell so near!
                         JOHN MILTON.

May 1.

Unto him shall the gathering of the people be.
GEN. xlix. 10.

And I, if I be lifted up from the earth, will draw all men unto me. — JOHN xii. 32.

THROUGH his crucifixion the Saviour saw his triumph. "For the joy that was set before him," he would endure the cross, "despising the shame," that so he might "sit down at the right hand of the throne of God," and there draw all men unto him. His crucifixion conditioned the reach and power of his attraction as the Redeemer of men. He must suffer if he would save. His lifting up was the beginning of his eternal exaltation. From that exaltation his influence reaches the lowest depths of human degradation. It is a mighty, a universal gravitation, of which multitudes are indeed quite unconscious, and which other multitudes are resisting. Christ does not drive any, but he does draw all, as the sun draws all. The redeeming power is personal influence; it is moral and spiritual attraction. It centres in the uplifted Christ; but each believer may, and therefore must help draw men to Christ. Slowly but surely this great prophecy is securing realization. "He shall see of the travail of his soul, and be satisfied." Satan shall not have the real harvest of the world. That belongs to the uplifted Christ.

Thos. S. Hastings.

Christ for the world, we sing;
The world to Christ we bring
   With one accord;
With us the work to share,
With us reproach to dare,
With us the cross to bear,
   For Christ our God.

SAMUEL WOLCOTT.

May 2.

Thou rulest the raging of the sea. — Psalm lxxxix. 9.

Peace, be still. — Mark iv. 39.

IT was eventide. The setting sun perchance smiled a farewell, flooding the waters with golden light. The sky was cloudless. Gennesareth reposed in quiet loveliness, like Lucerne in Switzerland or beautiful Loch Lomond among the Scottish hills. The disciples were not afraid as they embarked. Suddenly the storm swept down upon them. The angry waves smote the little ship. Skilful hands plied the oars in vain. They were in jeopardy. Then, in answer to their cry, the Christ arose. It needed but a word: "Peace, be still." "There was a great calm."

And this is life. One hour all is bright and peaceful; the next the billows break over us, the desire of our hearts dies, human help avails nought. Within the soul itself are all the elements of unrest. When conscience convinces of sin, and memory recalls our selfishness and ingratitude, our own unworthiness is revealed. We are in despair.

Blessed be God, we have a sure refuge! He who calmed the troubled waters speaks peace to human hearts. His blood atones for every sin; his grace supplies every need. Begin, my soul, this day with a penitent, trustful prayer to him, and through its toilsome or suffering hours shall come the cheering refrain, "Peace, be still."

Edward A. Rees.

> The wild winds hushed; the angry deep
> Sank, like a little child, to sleep;
> The sullen billows ceased to leap,
>   At thy will.
>
> So, when our life is clouded o'er,
> And storm-winds drift us from the shore,
> Say, lest we sink to rise no more,
>   "Peace, be still."
>
> GODFREY THRING.

May 3.

They that will be rich fall into temptation. — 1 Tim. vi. 9.

And again I say unto you, It is easier for a camel to go through the eye of a needle, than for a rich man to enter into the kingdom of God. — Matt. xix. 24.

THESE words condemn, not wealth, but the love of it. They put not a premium on worldly poverty, but on poverty of spirit. They warn against the possible influence of riches. Human nature seeks ease and honor, and mostly through earthly possessions; the subtle tendency of such possession, or the desire of it, is to wean the soul from the contemplation of the eternal Creator to the worship of the perishing creature. Giving way to this tendency makes these words terribly significant. The young ruler's inordinate love of wealth suggested them, yet Christ's thought comprises not merely those who have "great possessions," but those, be they never so poor, whose hearts are engrossed in that desire. God enriched the earth for man's good; the possession and enjoyment of its bounties may very legitimately subserve man's chief end. But forget not that the grand, noble, and sublime aim of life is the possession and enjoyment of the riches of the grace of God our Saviour. He looks on the heart, and demands from all followers true consecration of heart and possession. Be your worldly state in poverty or riches, remember this eternal truth, "Blessed are the poor in spirit: for theirs is the kingdom of heaven."

William N. Chambers.

The dearest idol I have known,
 Whate'er that idol be,
Help me to tear it from thy throne,
 And worship only thee.

COWPER.

MAY 4.

From me is thy fruit found. — HOSEA xiv. 8.

I am the true vine, and my Father is the husbandman. — JOHN xv. 1.

THE union between Christ and his Church is the closest and tenderest in the universe of God, except the union between the three persons of the Godhead. The world of nature and the most endearing relations of human life are laid under contribution in the Scriptures, and are combined, and thus combined are inadequate to express the intimacy of this union and the deep unutterable love of Christ for his Church. The fundamental idea suggested by the emblem of the vine and its branches is the vital union between Christ the true vine and the members of his mystical body. Without this union there can be no spiritual life and no good fruit. The decisive test of this union is to be Christ-like. Our spiritual growth is organic, like the vine, and not mechanical, like the building of a wall. It is an organic development by the mighty power of faith, which works from within outward, and brings the soul under the operation of the great doctrines of grace, and into the closest sympathy with Christ and his cause. The creator of this union is the Father. He engrafts the branches into the true Vine. As the vine-dresser uses the pruning-knife to increase the fruitfulness of the vine, so our heavenly Father corrects his children, and often makes their hearts bleed to increase their Christian graces.

J. J. Bullock

> Lord Christ, we humbly ask
> Of thee, the power and will,
> With fear and meekness, every task
> Of duty to fulfil.
>
> J. MONTGOMERY.

May 5.

I die daily. — 1 Cor. xv. 31.

If any man will come after me, let him deny himself, and take up his cross daily, and follow me. — Luke ix. 23.

WE are wont to say that Christ died that we might not die. We should speak more truly if we affirmed that he died that we might die. He died *for* sin that we might die *to* sin; he bore our guilt in his own body, that we might bear about his dying in our bodies. Hence it is written in the Scripture: " Forasmuch, then, as Christ hath suffered for us in the flesh, arm yourselves likewise with the same mind." " With the same mind," not with the same instrument! The jewelled cross or the marble crucifix can do nothing to enable us "fill up that which is behind of the afflictions of Christ." Not the image of his crucifixion laid upon us, but the fellowship of his crucifixion wrought within us, is what he requires. " *Let this mind* be in you which was also in Christ Jesus." Our wills surrendered to Christ's even as his will was surrendered to the Father's; our self-pleasing daily foregone for his sake who "pleased not himself;" our ease surrendered day by day in order that we may endure hardness as good soldiers of Jesus Christ, — these are the crucial tests of discipleship. Our souls are saved only by Christ's outward cross of atonement; they are sanctified by his inward cross of self-abnegation.

A. J. Gordon.

> Take up thy cross, and follow Christ,
>   Nor think till death to lay it down, —
> For only he who bears the cross
>   May hope to wear the glorious crown.
>
> C. W. Everest.

MAY 6.

With such sacrifices God is well pleased. — HEB. xiii. 16.

But when thou makest a feast, call the poor, the maimed, the lame, the blind; and thou shalt be blessed; for they cannot recompense thee: for thou shalt be recompensed at the resurrection of the just. — LUKE xiv. 13, 14.

WHAT the poor and the afflicted cannot do, he who has made such sufferers his representatives will not fail to do. Jesus links the day of final judgment and award with service given on earth to earth's neediest children. We may not always with wisdom copy to-day the Oriental habit of feast-giving to miscellaneous companies of the blind, maimed, and poor. But the celestial spirit of helpfulness and loving hospitality to all who are in physical or spiritual need is the one immortal duty and glory of Christly hearts. Charity to-day should mean not only alms, but Christian friendship. Putting aside social schemes that would turn the masses of men into shiftless and brutalized parasites of the State, there is demanded the bringing to bear on men's lives of all remedial, educating, preventive, and regenerating influences in the spirit of the Golden Rule. When Lowell's Sir Launfal shared with the beggar his crust of bread and gave him to drink from the icy stream, a heavenly light suffused that feast of the Holy Grail, till suddenly the leper rose up before him, "shining and tall," in the awful splendor of the Crucified and the Crowned. He who with a brother's heart shares with the needy brother the bread and water of eternal life, sits down to a holy banquet with his Lord and shall be welcomed to the marriage supper of the Lamb.

John Henry Barrows.

                    I behold in thee
An image of him who died on the tree.
Thou also hast had thy crown of thorns;
Thou also hast had the world's buffets and scorns;
And to thy life were not denied
The wounds in the hands and feet and side.

May 7.

Be ye doers of the word.—James i. 22.

Hear ye therefore the parable of the sower. When any one heareth the word of the kingdom, and understandeth it not, then cometh the wicked one, and catcheth away that which was sown in his heart. This is he which received seed by the wayside.—Matt. xiii. 18, 19.

IN the parable of the sower, our Lord strikingly presents the method and results of the ministry of truth in his divine kingdom. The seed is sown broadcast. The field, with its diversified conditions of soil, represents human hearts. Some hearts are hard, like the beaten track which can yield no fruit. They are not receptive of the truth. In their case, the seed simply lies on the surface. Dew, rain, and sun are of no use to it. Moreover, it is not allowed to remain. "The birds came and devoured it." In other words, "Satan cometh and snatcheth away that which has been sown in the heart." Want of interest, inattention, and speedy forgetfulness characterize a large mass of the hearers of the gospel, hence the disastrous failure which is here depicted.

But even the hardened wayside was once soft loam. Hearts that were once tender and susceptible of good impressions become gradually hardened. Wasted opportunities, the riotous revel of sins, the action of worldly pleasures, the tramp of business, all or any of these may render the heart impervious to the truth, and consequently unfruitful.

Souls, however, are not helpless and irresponsible. The wayside may be converted into fertile soil. God can change the hardened heart into "an honest and good heart," which shall yield precious and abundant fruit.

Happy they who seek and obtain this grace that "they may believe and be saved."

Tho. Davies.

Lord, by thy grace, to me impart
An honest, understanding heart,
For gracious seed a fitting soil;
Nor let the foe of truth despoil.

R. M. Offord.

MAY 8.

Now are we the sons of God. — 1 JOHN iii. 2.

And the glory which thou gavest me I have given them ; that they may be one, even as we are one : I in them, and thou in me, that they may be made perfect in one ; and that the world may know that thou hast sent me, and hast loved them, as thou hast loved me. — JOHN xvii. 22, 23.

WONDERFUL is the relationship which Christ Jesus has established by his obedience unto death between God and his disciples. "The Spirit itself beareth witness with our spirit, that we are the children of God; and if children, then heirs; heirs of God, and joint-heirs with Christ" (Romans viii. 16, 17), writes Paul. "Ye are a chosen generation, a royal priesthood, a holy nation, a peculiar people" (1 Peter ii. 9), writes Peter. "Beloved, now are we the sons of God, and it doth not yet appear what we shall be: but we know that when he shall appear we shall be like him; for we shall see him as he is" (1 John iii. 2), writes John. But more wonderful than the words of Paul or Peter or John are the words of our Lord himself, quoted above. In heaven alone can we hope fully to understand their meaning.

"*The glory which thou gavest me*" — not the glory which belonged to me as the eternal Son, but the glory which thou gavest me as "the Word made flesh;" the glory of a spotless righteousness which as "the Son of man" I have wrought out for my people; the glory of free access to God, and communion with him; the glory arising from the indwelling of the Spirit, through which sinful man becomes "a temple of the Holy Ghost;" the glory of being "workers together with me" in the salvation of a lost world. For all this there can be but one reason given: "God has loved us, even as he loved Christ."

Geo. D. Armstrong

Lord Jesus, are we one with thee?
O height, O depth of love !
Thou one with us upon the tree,
We one with thee above.

J. G. DECK.

MAY 9.

Ye do shew the Lord's death. — 1 Cor. xi. 26.
This do in remembrance of me. — Luke xxii. 19.

WHO is there of all the dwellers on earth that has not felt a desire to be remembered? To fulfil this wish monuments have been raised and colleges founded and hospitals endowed and brave exploits performed. To this object the miser has devoted his savings, the student his stores of learning, the painter his skill. Eulogiums have been pronounced by living orators, and inscriptions engraved upon lasting brass and marble. Poems have been written, statues sculptured, and bodies embalmed, that the names of men and some record of their lives might be perpetuated. Men have left legacies to be expended in celebrating with mournful obsequies the anniversary of their death, and annual feasts have been established for the purpose of remembering the departed.

So Jesus Christ, in instituting the Holy Supper, expresses a wish to which every human heart responds. By this ordinance shall his death, so ignominious in its circumstances, but so glorious in its results, be remembered in the repeated celebration of this prelude to the scene on Calvary, by the whole world of believers whom the power of his love and the preaching of his cross is to subdue to his beneficent control and make sweetly obedient to his blessed commands. Thus shall he be loved and trusted, and his memory be honored by sinners saved and sanctified to the end of time.

Charles Augustus Stoddard.

According to thy gracious word,
  In meek humility,
This will I do, my dying Lord,
  I will remember thee.

And when these failing lips grow dumb,
  And mind and memory flee,
When thou shalt in thy kingdom come,
  Jesus, remember me.   J. Montgomery.

May 10.

He hath made him to be sin for us. — 2 Cor. v. 21.

As Moses lifted up the serpent in the wilderness, even so must the Son of man be lifted up: that whosoever believeth in him, should not perish, but have eternal life. — John iii. 14, 15.

MEN are bitten by fiery serpents, and they die because human skill can furnish no antidote. By divine command a brazen image of the fiery serpent is "lifted up" among them, and every bitten one who looks up to that serpent-likeness finds the death-current checked and life again coursing through his veins (Numbers xxi. 6-9). Thus sin is a virulent poison, caused by the bite of that "old serpent ... the devil." Physicians have ever been studying the case and prescribing remedies. But *nature* furnishes no antidote; therefore all their panaceas fail, and the poison spreads, working death, physical, spiritual, eternal. Is there then no hope? Plainly there can be none except it come from God himself. Such is the suggestion of that strange transaction "in the wilderness," and the direct teaching of these words of our Lord. God himself has undertaken the case. "His own Son," having been made "in the likeness of sinful flesh," has been "lifted up," first on the cross, that he might make expiation, "bearing our sins" — as it were, receiving the poison for us — "in his own body;" then to "the right hand of power," that he might send "the Spirit of grace" and thus make "the preaching of the cross" effectual in inducing the perishing to look unto him and live.

> He left his starry crown,
>   And laid his robes aside,
> On wings of love came down,
>   And wept and bled and died;
> What he endured, oh, who can tell,
> To save our souls from death and hell!   S. STENNETT.

May 11.

I will pour my spirit upon thy seed. — Isaiah xliv. 3.

And, behold, I send the promise of my Father upon you: but tarry ye in the city of Jerusalem, until ye be endued with power from on high. — Luke xxiv. 49.

AFTER Christ had risen from the dead for our justification, and was ready for ascension and for coronation on his mediatorial throne, he appears to the apostles assembled in Jerusalem, gives them a charge and the promise of the Holy Ghost — "the promise of my Father," "power from on high" — to come upon them while they tarry in the city. In obedience to this promise, early on the second Lord's day after the ascension, "they were all filled with the Holy Ghost." Here began the new dispensation of the Holy Ghost, and here the Church starts off with one hundred and twenty spiritually baptized souls. Since Pentecost, his personal presence is the agent by whom all gracious and divine influences are communicated to man. He is omnipresent, and we cannot withdraw from his influence. He produces all internal religious experience, enlightens the understanding, purifies the purpose, influences the will, exalts the affections. All right feeling in the human heart is traceable directly or indirectly to the Holy Spirit. Our personal salvation and our personal usefulness depend upon heeding the Saviour's injunction to tarry in the place of his appointment until we be "endued with power from on high."

James M. King.

Grant this, O holy God and true,
   The ancient seers thou didst inspire,
To us perform the promise due,
   Descend, and crown us now with fire.

Henry More *(altered)*

MAY 12.

Having received of the Father the promise of the Holy Ghost. — ACTS ii. 33.

Nevertheless I tell you the truth; It is expedient for you that I go away: for if I go not away, the Comforter will not come unto you; but if I depart, I will send him unto you. — JOHN xvi. 7.

SORROW filled the disciples' hearts as they heard their Lord speak of his imminent departure. What will become of his little flock, what of his work, scarcely begun, if now the Head should depart from them, and on such a route, through the shame of the cross! But whether they grasp it or not, nevertheless he tells them the truth. It is their salvation that he goes away. "If I go not away, the Comforter" — that is, the Paraclete, the Advocate — "will not come unto you." What an awful thought! *No Comforter!* no testimony of Christ; no reproving of the world; no guiding of the disciples into all truth; no knowledge and confession of Jesus the Lord; no assurance to the heart of the believer that he is the child of God; no assistance and intercession for the saints in their infirmities; no peace and joy in the Holy Ghost; no fruits of the Spirit, — in short, no Pentecost! But thanks be to God, Christ went away through the darkness of Gethsemane and Calvary to the glory of Easter-morning and Pentecost. Of a truth, it is expedient for us that he went away.

Adolph Spaeth

    And his that gentle voice we hear
      Soft as the breath of even,
    That checks each fault, calms every fear,
      And whispers us of heaven.
                        HARRIET AUBER.

MAY 13.

We have an advocate with the Father. — 1 JOHN ii. 1.

I pray not that thou shouldest take them out of the world, but that thou shouldest keep them from the evil. — JOHN xvii. 15.

THE Redeemer's intercession for his people comprehends all that is essential to their welfare and happiness. They might be taken directly to heaven, but he does not ask this, because it is better for them to reach the harbor of rest after the storms of life are ended. The disciple is not above his Master, who was "made perfect through sufferings." He, who knew the power of temptation and the blessedness of enduring it, prays that his followers may be preserved from the corruption that is in the world, and from the overcoming subtlety of the Evil One. It is an error to suppose that there is safety in the seclusion of monastic life. A Christian's place is in the world. We have no need to go out of the world for work, for here it is; or for comfort, for God sends it to us here. Christian graces are polished by daily use, and character is developed by friction with the world. While we are working for the Master, he is praying for us. Where duty calls us to go we are safe. If Vanity Fair lies in the way to the Celestial City, he will guide us through without harm; and then the Redeemer's other prayer will be answered, " Father, I will that they also whom thou hast given me be with me where I am."

    Clothed with our nature, still he knows
      The weakness of our frame,
    And how to shield us from the foes
      Which he himself o'ercame.

ALEXANDER PIVIE.

MAY 14.

I live by the faith of the Son of God.—GAL. ii. 20.

As the living Father hath sent me, and I live by the Father: so he that eateth me, even he shall live by me. This is that bread which came down from heaven: not as your fathers did eat manna, and are dead: he that eateth of this bread shall live for ever.—JOHN vi. 57, 58.

A WONDERFUL passage upon which the soul can feed for hours. It teaches that God is a living God manifesting himself in both the natural and spiritual world. It teaches that as Christ lives in God and God in him, and as he gains all his life and power from God, so the Christian lives in Christ and Christ in him, and he gains all his spiritual life and power from Christ; through Christ the disciple is in union with God, and the divine life abides in his soul. Notice the conditions. As our bodies through the natural organs appropriate of nature's strength to their own vitality, so the soul by faith eats of Christ and appropriates of his atoning death to its own spiritual life, receiving of his personal love, grace, and spirit, as its food, strength, and life; and as long as we daily feed upon Christ's words, love, and death, we have not only our own powers, but the power of Christ in God to overcome, endure, be, and do all that is required of us. This fact in the darkest hours makes us brave, patient, and cheerful, for we know that as children of the King we shall be more than conquerors through him that loved us and gave himself for us.

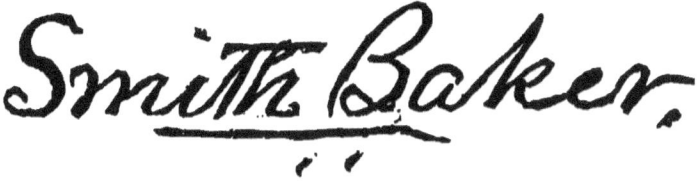

I feed by faith on Christ; my bread,
His body broken on the tree.
I live in him, my living Head,
Who died, and rose again for me.
J. MONTGOMERY.

May 15.

Whom the Lord loveth he chasteneth. — Heb. xii. 6.

As many as I love, I rebuke and chasten: be zealous therefore, and repent. — Rev. iii. 19.

LOVE and discipline, tenderness and fidelity, God our Father and God our Teacher, these two are the supreme facts of religion. Our Lord here defines his own action in his relation to the chosen. He is carrying forward two processes in us, and the command which follows in the same text has two parts, each of them in correspondence. Chastisement should bring the soul to repentance, and love ought to stimulate to a zeal in due proportion. The double declaration is the basis on which the double precept rests.

The orbit of a planet is determined by the play of balanced forces, centrifugal and centripetal, so the development of spiritual life will be regulated by the two principles here defined. By chastisement we are made to see the awful depth of sin, and by love, the sublime height of the divine holiness. In chastisement we come to know self, the creature, and in love we come to have some notion of him, the Creator. The two aspects of redemption are not hostile, but each is the complement of the other, — discipline and privilege, two messengers of the same king, two pages of the same lesson, two facts making up together the one supreme truth. He loves, and therefore he educates. Loving us, he makes to us a wonderful offer; he offers to give us himself, and chastening us, he makes it possible that we should accept such an offer. The affection is wonderful, the discipline is severe, but the vital link, uniting the two, is the Lord Jesus himself.

James I. Riggs

> I thank thee for both smile and frown,
>   And for the gain and loss;
> I praise thee for the future crown
>   And for the present cross.
>
> Mrs. Jane Crewdson.

May 16.

Upon the wicked he shall rain . . . an horrible tempest.
PSALM xi. 6.

The lord of that servant shall come in a day when he looketh not for him, and in an hour that he is not aware of, and shall cut him asunder, and appoint him his portion with the hypocrites: there shall be weeping and gnashing of teeth. — MATT. xxiv. 50, 51.

THE faithless servant shall be stung with deepest remorse when he shall see his Lord. In the face of the triumphant Saviour he shall read the disappointment which his indifference has wrought, and how great the loss has been to him by neglecting those duties which would have brought in their train eternal blessedness. He shall be surprised in his indifference. His brightest hopes shall prove a cloud without rain. Though planted by a heavenly husbandman in a garden on a fruitful hillside, tended with all the love that can well up from the heart of an infinite Saviour, and watered by the dews of the Spirit, he shall be cut asunder. The vine laden with sour grapes shall be torn from its trellis-work, and the fruitless tree shall be rooted up. He shall find his portion, but without, among the hypocrites. Instead of the wedding march, heralding the approach of the bridegroom, his stupid ear shall be shocked by the groans of those who obeyed not the call. Instead of the flutter of angels' wings to bear him up, he shall hear the gnashing of teeth. O Spirit of life, whisper again thy loving *come*, that we may not fall into this death!

Conrad Clever

Have I long in sin been sleeping,
Long been slighting, grieving thee?
Has the world my heart been keeping?
Oh, forgive and rescue me, — even me.
MRS. E. CODNER.

May 17.

𝔍 press toward the mark. — Phil. iii. 14.

No man, having put his hand to the plough, and looking back, is fit for the kingdom of God. — Luke ix. 62.

A SERVANT has undertaken to guide the plough. His feet are in the furrow, his grasp is upon the handle; but his face is turned backward. He will make a bad job of ploughing. The furrow will be spoiled. That servant is not "well placed" with regard to the work before him.

Christians, above all other people in the world, ought to be decided, whole-hearted, enthusiastic. There is no service on earth where enthusiastic devotedness is so reasonable as in the service of Christ.

Men are not usually indifferent where their affections are enlisted, or where they believe that any great interest is at stake. If I hear of one who loved me in my ruin, — so loved me that he left his throne and came to my level, not only to teach me but to die for me, — and still I feel no awakening of affection for him, and am not aroused to any warmth or earnestness in my service to him, it must be that I do not believe the story that tells of his sacrifice of himself for me. I do not give him my heart because I do not give him my faith, and therefore *I am not fit for the kingdom of God.*

> Were the whole realm of nature mine,
>   That were a present far too small;
> Love so amazing, so divine,
>   Demands my soul, my life, my all.
>
> Watts.

May 18.

Christ must needs have suffered, and risen again.
Acts xvii. 3.

Ought not Christ to have suffered these things, and to enter into his glory? — Luke xxiv. 26.

HE certainly did, and therefore certainly he *ought*, for he made no mistakes. Not that our Saviour deserved any punishment, nor that he was under any obligation to become our sacrifice and substitute. But when he took on himself the office of our Redeemer it became necessary and indispensable that he must suffer and bear the penalty of our sins. The disciples were astounded at his arrest, condemnation, and death, and all their hopes in him as the promised Deliverer seemed taken away. But ought not these things to have happened? Should not these very sufferings have strengthened their faith and convinced them he was the Messiah? Had he not repeatedly foretold these things, and had not all their prophets testified beforehand of the sufferings of Christ and the glory that should follow? It is in this sense he uses the word "ought." The very thing at which they stumbled was the most convincing proof and demonstration of what they hoped.

Yes; he ought and he did. He drew not back, but paid the dreadful penalty of our transgressions. What he undertook he accomplished, and having borne the cross now wears the crown.

Jacob Fry.

There was no other good enough
To pay the price of sin;
He only could unlock the gate
Of heaven, and let us in.
Mrs. C. F. Alexander.

May 19.

They shall reign for ever and ever. — Rev. xxii. 5.

If any man serve me, let him follow me; and where I am, there shall also my servant be: if any man serve me, him will my Father honour. — John xii. 26.

IN following Christ we have the advantage of being in the light (John viii. 12) and thus knowing where we are, and rendering him a more intelligent service. No wonder he links following and serving together. I suppose service rendered to him is really fruitful only when he is followed implicitly and trustingly, in the sense of taking him as infallible teacher and absolute master. Efforts, and sincere ones too, are often made to serve him when this condition is not carried out. The world or self is too often master.

It were natural to be where the Master is, if we *follow* him; and yet sometimes we are surprised, and not quite pleased, to find ourselves there. So far from honor being our lot, we meet with shame.

There may not be this, there may be even no trial at all, in confessing Christ. Thrown among Christians, we may have a kindly welcome and sympathy. But does not the absence of trial sometimes lead to a too easy-going and complacent sort of living, which ends in a forfeiture of the honor we had hoped for? God grant, dear reader, that when those who *follow* him shall appear with Christ in glory we may be among them!

F. Janvier Newton.

> Glories upon glories
> Hath our God prepared,
> By the souls that love him
> One day to be shared.
>
> DEAN ALFORD.

May 20.

The friendship of the world is enmity with God.
JAMES iv. 4.

No man can serve two masters: for either he will hate the one, and love the other; or else he will hold to the one, and despise the other. Ye cannot serve God and mammon. — MATT. vi. 24.

HERE are two masters, God and Mammon, or the things of God and the things of this world. There are only these two masters. The choice is made more easily when it is seen to lie between two things or individuals only; and the choice is not only of an individual, but for a service. The person chooses to serve, and to serve in the service of one of these two masters. Both of these masters cannot be chosen; both of these services cannot be given. From its nature and working, the one necessarily excludes the other.

In choosing God as master, we choose his service; we choose to serve. "For me to live is Christ;" to live is blessed. "For me to die is gain;" to die is blessed. But this service must be prompted by love, not performed as duty. It must be a service given in a holding to and a loving of God. A person may do the godly and yet not be godly; love determines the true service. Love must lead to labor, and labor will increase love.

Jesus, Master, whose I am,
  Purchased thine alone to be
By thy blood, O spotless Lamb,
  Shed so willingly for me,
Let my heart be all thine own,
Let me live to thee alone.

F. R. HAVERGAL.

May 21.

Do it with thy might. — ECCL. ix. 10.

I must work the works of him that sent me, while it is day: the night cometh, when no man can work. — JOHN ix. 4.

IN saying " I must," as he did more than once, our Lord associated himself with those whom he came to teach and save, as being, in common with them, under the law of duty. In saying, " I must work," he showed that he was under the law of labor. In saying, " I must work the works of him that sent me," he implied that for him duty was not the mere satisfaction of his own moral sense, but subjection to the will of one by whom his task was assigned and to whom he owed obedience. In speaking of the approaching night, he represented himself as under the law of death.

In each of these particulars he is an example for us. If we are not free from the law of duty, neither was the Son of God. If we are often obliged to say " I must," it is a comfort to remember that Jesus also said it. If he had a definite work to do, so too have we. Duty, for us as for him, is obedience to the will of God. As the Father sent him, so has he sent us. To us also the night is drawing nigh. The secret of his peace was his identification of his own will with that of God. It is still the secret of peace.

Edward B. Coe

O Master, let me walk with thee,
In lowly paths of service free.
Tell me thy secret; help me bear
The strain of toil, the fret of care.

WASHINGTON GLADDEN.

May 22.

Whoever will not hearken, ... I will require it of him.
Deut. xviii. 19.

He that rejecteth me, and receiveth not my words, hath one that judgeth him: the word that I have spoken, the same shall judge him in the last day.— John xii. 48.

LET me confront my soul with this solemn truth. The word of Jesus is to be my judge. In a court of justice the judge pronounces the sentence, but it is the law that condemns the criminal. In the same way the Lord Jesus, as the final judge, will pronounce my sentence; but it is the word which judges and condemns.

How solemn then is the relation in which we stand to the words of Jesus! We have been familiar with them from childhood; they will remain in our memory and will rise up to witness against us at the judgment. They would carry their own condemnation with them even though the judge were silent; but the words which Christ spoke were words of mercy. Oh, how dreadful to be condemned by the very words which Christ spoke in mercy and for our salvation!

Think, O my soul, have I declined his words of warning, have I rejected his words of promise, have I perverted his words of mercy into words of judgment?

But the Christian who believes and obeys Christ's words need have no apprehension. "There is no condemnation to them that are in Christ Jesus." Christ himself will witness for them, saying, "I gave them my words and they received them, for they are thine, and all thine are mine, and I am glorified in them."

William M. Paxton

Lord, in this thy mercy's day
Ere from us it pass away
On our knees we fall and pray.

. . . . . .

Judge and Saviour of our race,
Grant us when we see thy face
With thy ransomed ones a place.   Isaac Williams.

May 23.

In him verily is the love of God perfected. — 1 John ii. 5.

He that hath my commandments, and keepeth them, he it is that loveth me: and he that loveth me shall be loved of my Father, and I will love him, and will manifest myself to him. — John xiv. 21.

WHO will fathom the depth of this wonderful saying of Jesus? It contains words of direction and words of promise for all Christians.

Here we find the true test of spiritual life. We often torture ourselves with questions like these, "Am I indeed a Christian? Do I really love Jesus?" We fear that our feelings for him have not the warmth and rapture that should be found in his followers. But Jesus tells us that obedience — "keeping his commandments" — is the only trustworthy evidence of love. Let us not be disheartened because we know little of the inward raptures which some other Christians enjoy. If we are striving for Christ's sake to do the good and right unto all men, we really love him who "went about doing good." If we are striving for Christ's sake to forgive our persecutors and slanderers, we really love him who prayed on the cross, "Father, forgive them, they know not what they do." An obedient life is the sure token of a loving heart.

How precious and inspiring are the privileges here assured to those whose obedience proves them to be "the lovers of Jesus." They become in a special sense the beloved of the Father. The Saviour feels that they are linked to him by the tenderest ties. They enjoy continual and increasing revelations of the glory and power and beauty of Christ.

S. M. Hamilton.

> Abide in me! there have been moments blest
>   When I have heard thy voice and felt thy power;
> When evil lost its grasp; and passion hushed,
>   Owned the divine enchantment of the hour.
>
> Mrs. H. B. Stowe.

MAY 24.

We love him, because he first loved us. — 1 JOHN iv. 19.

Her sins, which are many, are forgiven, for she loved much ; but to whom little is forgiven, the same loveth little. — LUKE vii. 47.

PURITY and gentleness incarnate have crossed the path of sin and shame. Had either been alone, the purity had made her cower away blinded by excessive light, while gentleness alone could convey no promise of help, but together they have inspired a faith which enables her to face the Pharisee's proud scorn ; and lo! she finds them linked to a Power which can forgive sins also. Humbled and melted she will unobtrusively pour out the wealth of her heart upon the feet of that One who alone "hath power on earth to forgive sins." Her love and gratitude are proportioned to her sense of former guilt and ill-desert, while both enhance the value of that grace "unmerited and free" which has brought to her the consciousness of pardon. It was not that in the eyes of the Master her guilt was intrinsically greater than that of the cold, hard Pharisee, but that in her consciousness of sin her perception of all the sins of others lost itself. To affirm that she was forgiven because she loved much would be to misrepresent the whole teaching of the parable, for the love was not the spring but the evidence of the forgiveness, — the strength of the one indicating the extent of the other.

It is when we know how much we have owed and how much we have been forgiven that the measure of love and gratitude overflow.

Merrett Hulbrund

Nought can I bring, dear Lord, for all I owe;
Yet let my full heart what it can bestow.
Like Mary's gift, let my devotion prove,
Forgiven greatly, how I greatly love.   S. J. STONE.

May 25.

God . . . hath . . . spoken unto us by his Son.
HEB. i. 1, 2.

He that loveth me not keepeth not my sayings: and the word that ye hear is not mine, but the Father's which sent me. — JOHN xiv. 24.

THE highest test of love to Christ is obedience at the cost of any self-denial or sacrifice, and the most essential qualification for receiving the manifestations of his love. When Jesus said, "It is my meat and drink to do the will of him that sent me," he disclosed the secret of his perfect union and communion with the Father; and when we can say from the heart that we delight to do the will of Christ as revealed in the word of the Father, then do we enter into fellowship with him, and he "manifests himself unto us as he does not unto the world." Disobedience closes every avenue of the soul against the manifestations of Christ's love, as shutting the blinds and drawing the curtains excludes the warm light of the sun. Just to the extent we feel that the commands of Christ are grievous and irksome, imposing unreasonable self-denials, do we disqualify ourselves for receiving and reciprocating the tokens of his love.

Blessed is the disciple who can say, "Thy statutes are the rejoicing of my heart; more to be desired are they than gold, yea, than much fine gold; sweeter also than honey and the honeycomb: thy precepts are my songs in the house of my pilgrimage;" heavenly visions and moments of transfiguration are awaiting him in the closet, the sanctuary, and at the sacramental table.

Gilbert R. Brackett

Let us obey; we then shall know,
Shall feel our sins forgiven,
Anticipate our heaven below,
And own that love is heaven.

C. WESLEY.

May 26.

Not by works of righteousness which we have done.
TITUS iii. 5.

Verily, verily, I say unto thee, Except a man be born again he cannot see the kingdom of God.... Except a man be born of water and of the Spirit, he cannot enter into the kingdom of God. — JOHN iii. 3, 5.

THESE wonderful words of the Lord Jesus were spoken to Nicodemus, a Jewish gentleman, a Pharisee, and a ruler and master in Israel, who "came to Jesus at the first by night." Observe closely the four "Amens" which are translated by as many "Verilys" in our English New Testament, "Amen! Amen! I say unto thee." The great Teacher speaks with authority as "the Amen, the faithful and true Witness." Mark *the new birth* of which he testifies. "Except a man [Nicodemus, or any other man] be born again," — or from above, as the margin reads, — "born of water and the Spirit," whose chosen emblem is the cleansing water. This is God's way of making a sinful man over again, "a new creature in Christ Jesus," with a new heart and a new spirit, "by the washing of regeneration and the renewing of the Holy Ghost. Note again the two "cannots:" "Except a man be born again, he *cannot see* the kingdom of God;" "he *cannot enter* the kingdom of God." But by the new birth he becomes the child of a king, "a king and a priest unto God," "an heir of God and a joint-heir with Jesus Christ" to "the kingdom prepared for him from the foundation of the world."

William J. R. Taylor.

Nor alms, nor deeds, that I have done
Can for a single sin atone;
To Calvary alone I flee.
O God, be merciful to me!

CORNELIUS ELVEN.

May 27.

In me is thine help. — HOSEA xiii. 9.

I counsel thee to buy of me gold tried in the fire, that thou mayest be rich; and white raiment, that thou mayest be clothed; and that the shame of thy nakedness do not appear; and anoint thine eyes with eye-salve, that thou mayest see. — REV. iii. 18.

HERE we have a letter from heaven, the last letter from Jesus addressed to men. Every soul has an interest in it. The Laodiceans still live, though their city and church have perished. Observe: 1. He discovers the sad state of the church, "lukewarm," — the worst of the seven, nothing good is said of it. 2. He reveals its ignorance of its miserable condition, supposing itself rich when it was poor and blind and naked. 3. He announces the ignominious fate of such a church, "spewed out" with disgust, as a nauseating lotion.

Let men take warning. Jesus then mercifully offers them the sovereign remedy for all their ills: 1. He counsels them to buy fire-tried gold which will make them "rich toward God." This buying is "without money," for it is the riches of Christ, the gift of God. 2. He counsels them to buy white raiment of him to clothe their nakedness. That is the blood-washed robe of his own righteousness. No other garment will admit us to the marriage-supper. Only such can ever "enter through the gate into the city." 3. Finally, he counsels them to anoint their blind eyes with eye-salve, with the illumination of the Holy Spirit, that they may see God and live.

Edw. O. Guerrant

My heart lies dead; and no increase
  Doth my dull husbandry improve.
Oh, let thy graces, without cease,
  Drop from above.
                              GEORGE HERBERT.

MAY 28.

Rich unto all that call upon him. — ROMANS x. 12.

O woman, great is thy faith: be it unto thee even as thou wilt. — MATT. xv. 28.

WHAT a wonderful concession this, of the grace of Jesus Christ! It suggests the omnipotence of determined faith. It illustrates what we may regard as a law in the higher realm of spiritual relations and results. In it there would seem to be not only no conflict between sovereignty and free agency, but the sovereignty of God would seem, by his gracious permission, to have passed over into the agency of his child, — the child a sovereign of grace. We may call it one of the great moral equations of the Bible, the "Be it unto thee" of the Master being in exact equipoise with the "As thou wilt" of the believer. The woman's faith was "great" in kind, — by virtue of the vital energy, the courage to face discouraging conditions, the skill in pleading, which it embodied. Such a faith as this, though seeming "as a grain of mustard seed," shall avail great things. That faith is always great which admits no element of unbelief, and so, great in degree.

In particular, why should we not believe that Christ is as willing to save men from their sins as he was to heal the Syrophœnician woman's daughter? And why may we not suppose it a certainty that when we present our appeal for the salvation of sinners with as much earnestness and dexterity as this woman used, — their grievous condition resting with equal heaviness on the heart, — the blessing will in his own time be granted?

George A. Tewksbury.

Thou art coming to a king,
Large petitions with thee bring;
For his grace and power are such,
None can ever ask too much.
JOHN NEWTON.

May 29.

𝔈 will give you pastors according to mine heart.
JER. iii. 15.

The harvest truly is plenteous, but the labourers are few; pray ye therefore the Lord of the harvest, that he will send forth labourers into his harvest. — MATT. ix. 37, 38.

SUCH is the duty enjoined by Christ upon his disciples. It indicates both the object and the plan of his work. He was a missionary sent to save sinners. Every pulsation of his heart throbs in sympathy with sinners; every utterance of his lips, every act of his life, his dying agonies, and all his appointments, contemplate the salvation of sinners.

In the accomplishment of his purposes Jesus employs human agency. His Church is a grand missionary organization, — the light of the world and the salt of the earth, the repository and the source of saving influences. The living ministry is the grand leading instrumentality which he employs in the execution of his work. Its business is to reap and garner the harvest. In view of the magnitude of the work, the vastness of the harvest, and the inadequacy of the laborers, Jesus still as emphatically commands his followers, as he did his disciples while upon earth, to pray for an increase of laborers; and they, prompted by the yearnings of their own hearts, cheerfully obey his command. And while they thus pray, they freely give of their means, their time, and influence to secure an answer to their prayers. Effectual prayer and the use of the means necessary to obtain the blessing sought, like living faith and works, are always conjoined.

Abel J. Brown.

Saints of God! the dawn is brightening,
  Token of our coming Lord;
O'er the earth the field is whitening;
  Louder rings the Master's word, —
    "Pray for reapers
  In the harvest of the Lord." MRS. MAXWELL.

MAY 30.

If we say that we have no sin, we deceive ourselves.
1 JOHN i. 8.

If ye were blind, ye should have no sin: but now ye say, We see; therefore your sin remaineth. — JOHN ix. 41.

OUR Lord means by these words that if those who were rejecting his moral allegiance were really blind they would not incur sin. But since they were rejoicing in their light, the fact of their sin remained. Where there is no law there is no sin, and where there is no light there is no shadow. So then whenever we see a law of God and act regardless of it, or wherever we recognize a sin and yet indulge in it, we bring our consciousness to be our own judge, we make our very light the revelation of our moral darkness.

Wm Wilberforce Newton

Blame not the times in which you live,
Nor fortune frail and fugitive;
Blame not thy parents, nor the rule
Of vice or wrong once learned at school;
But blame thyself, O man!
Although both heaven and earth combined
To mould thy flesh and form thy mind,
Though every thought, word, action, will,
Were framed by powers beyond thee; still
Thou art thyself, O man!
And self to take or leave is free,
Feeling its own sufficiency;
In spite of science, spite of fate,
The judge within thee soon or late
Will blame but thee, O man!
Say not, I would, but could not; he
Should bear the blame who fashioned me.
Call you mere change of motive, choice?
Scorning such pleas, the inner voice
Cries, "Thine the deed, O man!"

May 31.

Bless the Lord, O my soul. — Psalm civ. 2.

Were there not ten cleansed? but where are the nine? — Luke xvii. 17.

WE have here an example of ingratitude so base as to call forth from our Saviour the above exclamation. When we consider the persons (lepers), their need, their helplessness, their prayer, and what was done for them, the very deed witnessing and declaring who it was that thus gave them life, — snatching them by a word out of the jaws of a living death, — and furthermore when we consider their ingratitude as shown by their conduct, who can help wondering? But let us ask ourselves if our treatment of our Saviour is any less wonderful? The disease which afflicted them affected the body; it could not destroy the soul. Ours affects both soul and body.

Moved by his love for us, our Saviour left his throne, came to earth, became a man, paid the penalty for our sins, ransoming us by his own blood, thereby becoming our Redeemer. And he now offers us without money and without price, peace, pardon, a sonship in heaven; he offers us all this, waits to bestow it upon us, if we will but accept. And we, what is our conduct?

W. E. Locke

Oh, bless the Lord, my soul!
Nor let his mercies lie
Forgotten in unthankfulness,
And without praises die.

WATTS.

June 1.

We also should walk in newness of life. — Romans vi. 4.

Follow me; and let the dead bury their dead. — Matt. viii. 22.

HE who spoke these words "bare our sicknesses," and wept at a grave side. There was, then, in this startling injunction no lack of sympathy with human sorrow, but rather a holy impatience of conventional customs which engross his servants at the expense of their work. The Lord here speaks not only to a man likely to be detained during long-protracted funeral ceremonies, but through him to all in all ages who might be liable to yield unduly to this world's fashion and custom. "The king's business requireth haste!" "Seek ye *first* the kingdom of God." How it would simplify all our life if we who claim to be Christians would obey the Lord in this, and would trust that "all these things shall be added," whether it be the burial of a dead father, or the supply of daily needs! Surely the few who live unto God in this world may more and more leave the conventionalisms of the world to those who, living in worldly pleasure, "are dead while they live," and be single-eyed in the service of the Master! And surely he who says, "I come quickly," if he felt a sharp word was needed to be given to this candidate for discipleship, would speak a far more solemn word to many called by his name to-day, whose Christianity is little more than an inheritance, not a personal conviction, and whose lagging footsteps are so easily clogged by their very culture and the resources of civilization, whose "loins" are *not* "girded," whose "lights" are *not* "burning," and who, calling themselves servants, do not "wait for their Lord."

Ernest Graham Ingham

Jesus calls us o'er the tumult
Of our life's wild, restless sea;
Day by day his sweet voice soundeth,
Saying, Christian, follow me!

Mrs. C. F. Alexander.

June 2.

Other foundation can no man lay. — 1 Cor. iii. 11.

Therefore whosoever heareth these sayings of mine, and doeth them, I will liken him unto a wise man, which built his house upon a rock: and the rain descended, and the floods came, and the winds blew, and beat upon that house; and it fell not: for it was founded upon a rock. — Matt. vii. 24, 25.

THEREFORE, — because "many in that day" who in this life "work iniquity," Jesus will bid "depart."
These sayings of mine, — the sermon, enjoining a religion of the heart, a life of prayer, and penitent seeking after God; the sermon too, as expanded and explained in his future teachings, — for example, prayer, answered only for Christ's sake, "Ask in my name;" forgiveness, given only through Christ's death, "My blood, shed for the remission of sins." *Doeth them,* — yielding to Christ as God, for he gives the law and will judge the world. "*I* say unto you," "Then will *I* profess unto them;" submission to God, "Thy will be done;" loving and trusting God, "Seek first his kingdom and righteousness." A renowned editor wrote, "My creed is the Sermon on the Mount. Live by that and you will be saved." "Yes," replied a college president, "but no one ever did; and if that is the only way of life, none can hope." Yet none build on the rock but those who do these sayings of Christ: that is, who have *in some degree* the *kind of spirit* he here describes, and which for his sake is accepted, whether the penitent knows it or not, instead of perfect obedience.

Albert H. Plumb

> My hope is built on nothing less
> Than Jesus' blood and righteousness;
> On Christ, the solid Rock, I stand,
> All other ground is sinking sand.
>
> Edward Mote.

JUNE 3.

Thy face, Lord, will I seek. — PSALM xxvii. 8.

If ye then, being evil, know how to give good gifts unto your children, how much more shall your Father which is in heaven give good things to them that ask him? — MATT. vii. 11.

HOW wonderful it seems, God plying men with considerations why they shall pray, arguing to make them bold! This is the nature of all his promises, pledges addressed to our faith. "Put me in remembrance; let us plead together." For himself he would not have us say, "for Christ's sake," as a ground for our acceptance before we can be heard, but because the repetition will assure us of our power in the all-prevailing Name. Our want of faith is the occasion for the argument. The persuasion is to be of ourselves. "If ye, being evil, etc.," The "being evil" is a shadow; but it can only modify, it cannot restrain the generous impulses of parental love. But divine love is the clear shining of a cloudless sky, the glad melody of an unimpeded stream. Two arguments are addressed to our faith: First, God shall give more *abundantly*, according to the incomparable fulness of his grace. Second, he shall give more *appropriately*, according to his infinitely wise comprehension of our want. Our human love is borne up to its loftiest round that it may perceive the love of God stretching illimitably beyond it.

And dost thou say, "Ask what thou wilt"?
Lord, I would seize the golden hour;
I pray to be released from guilt
And freed from sin and Satan's power.

JOHN NEWTON.

June 4.

Who gave himself for our sins. — GAL. i. 4.

Behold, we go up to Jerusalem; and the Son of man shall be betrayed unto the chief priests and unto the scribes, and they shall condemn him to death, and shall deliver him to the Gentiles to mock, and to scourge, and to crucify him; and the third day he shall rise again. — MATT. xx. 18, 19.

NEVER had there been such a going up to Jerusalem as that which Jesus here proposes to his disciples. Jesus goes up voluntarily. The act was not enforced by any external compulsion. Jerusalem might at this time have been avoided. It was deliberately sought. Jesus was hereby fulfilling the Father's will, executing the mission upon which he had been sent. It was after this journey that he said, "I have finished the work thou gavest me to do." His going up was a part of that work. Hence it was right for him to go up, although he knew that betrayal, arrest, condemnation, and crucifixion awaited him. It was a going up to a triumph to be reached through defeat, a coronation to be attained through ignominy and humiliation (Heb. ii. 9).

O believer, in your walk through the world to-day, be strengthened, be comforted, be inspired, by the spectacle of the Captain of your salvation thus going up to Jerusalem! And remember in all those apparently *downward* passages of life where sorrow, and it may be death, lie before you, that all such descents made or endured in the spirit of Jesus are really *upgoings*, steps leading you to the mount of God and the resurrection-glory.

Joseph B. Stratton

E'en though it be a cross
That raiseth me!
Still all my song shall be,
Nearer, my God, to thee,
Nearer to thee! MRS. S. F. ADAMS.

JUNE 5.

Hath given himself for us an offering. — EPH. v. 2.

Therefore doth my Father love me, because I lay down my life, that I might take it again. No man taketh it from me, but I lay it down of myself. I have power to lay it down, and I have power to take it again. This commandment have I received of my Father. — JOHN x. 17, 18.

CHRIST here asserts his own absolute freedom and voluntariness in dying. No act of self-sacrifice can be conceived of as more unforced. It is the model and warrant, as it has been the inspiration of every noble act of self-devotion from that time till now. He was under no obligation in the first place to throw his own body across the track along which remorseless death was rushing upon mankind. Every step on the road to Calvary he took shrinking yet resolved. His innocent, sensitive nature appreciated the torture, the shame, the horror of the death-pang; but he went forward to meet them. The betrayal, the arrest, the consent of Pilate, the rude violence of the Roman soldiery were only prearranged parts of the process by which his voluntary sacrifice was to be consummated. There was no power in the universe less than God's that could have reft his life without his own consent. Up to the last expiring cry, all was free; the most stupendous act of self-sacrifice the world has ever seen.

Do you love him as you ought, O man, for such a shame, for such a death endured for you; and will you learn from such an example to make some sacrifice at least for the good of others?

Samuel M. Hopkins

> This was compassion, like a God,
> That when the Saviour knew
> The price of pardon was his blood
> His pity ne'er withdrew.   WATTS.

June 6.

He hath filled the hungry with good things. — Luke i. 53.

Blessed are they which do hunger and thirst after righteousness: for they shall be filled. — Matt. v. 6.

IF we would take these words by the heart we must make sure of these vital truths concerning them, —

First, as to their character. They are not a promise; they are not a law. A promise is founded on conditions; a law is subject to repeal and amendment. They are the fourth article in the constitution of the kingdom of heaven on earth. John had declared that the kingdom was at hand. Jesus began his reign in the new kingdom by announcing to the world its constitution, — the Beatitudes. The constitution is the eternal, unchangeable truth back of all promises and laws. Make sure of these Beatitudes, and you are at home in all worlds, in time and in eternity. These truths have reigned in the mind and heart of God from the beginning.

In the second place, be sure to note that the Beatitude is pronounced upon *hunger* and *thirst*, — our symbols of unrest and pain and poverty. To be cursed is to be full and contented and lodged in a nest. To be blessed is to be shaken out of our nest and compelled to develop both our wits and our wings in the endless quest of spiritual food.

In the third place, do not fail to notice that it is that very simple, fundamental thing, righteousness, which we are to seek with consuming desire. Rightness, not spiritual peace, not grace, not soul power, but first and last rightness with God and men. When Rightness is enthroned in the holy of holies her train of joys and graces will fill the temple.

James H. Ecob

> He leads me to the place
>   Where heavenly pasture grows,
> Where living waters gently pass,
>   And full salvation flows.   Watts.

June 7.

The upright shall have dominion. — Psalm xlix. 14.

And he that overcometh, and keepeth my works unto the end, to him will I give power over the nations: and he shall rule them with a rod of iron; as the vessels of a potter shall they be broken to shivers: even as I received of my Father. And I will give him the morning star. — Rev. ii. 26-28.

THE promise given to conquering fidelity is here expressed in most striking and impressive terms. It is nothing less than complete and unbroken dominion over the nations.

In his ideal republic, Plato dreamed of a golden age when all kings should be philosophers, and all philosophers should be kings; how transcendently does the heavenly kingdom surpass that of the philosophical dreamer, for there all kings shall be saints, and all saints shall be kings.

The morning star is here the image of the glory of the kingdom. It is frequently associated with the sceptre, as the star of Jacob in the prophecy of Balaam (Numbers xxiv. 17).

This destined inheritance, so unspeakably great, is for him that overcometh, and keepeth Christ's works. True religion is not spasmodic, it is not a thing of times and seasons. Victory and its rewards are for him only who continues in well-doing, who keeps the faith. Hold fast, then; let no man take thy crown.

Harvey Glass

Onward, ever onward,
  Journeying o'er the road
Worn by saints before us,
  Journeying on to God.

Leaving all behind us
  May we hasten on;
Backward never looking
  Till the prize is won.
        GODFREY THRING.

JUNE 8.

I have given him for a witness to the people.
ISAIAH lv. 4.

Thou sayest that I am a king. To this end was I born, and for this cause came I into the world, that I should bear witness unto the truth. Every one that is of the truth heareth my voice. — JOHN xviii. 37.

JESUS elsewhere calls himself the truth. Here he states it to be the purpose not only of his birth as a man but of his coming into the world as the pre-existent Son of God to bear witness to the truth. Never was such testimony given by such a being to such a fact, as was rendered by him who at the last before Pontius Pilate witnessed a good confession. The glad tidings were attested not only by Jesus, the Truth, but by the Father, in the works he wrought through his holy Son, and in the word he spoke from heaven. Yet even such testimony may be disregarded, rejected. Those who had not God's word abiding in them refused to believe him whom God sent. For effectual hearing, there must be a congruity in the recipient; he must be "of the truth," — one who is eager to know and ready to do God's will. To him God makes himself known; and he believes, not because of the words of others, but because he has himself heard Jesus, and knows that this is indeed the Christ, the Saviour of the world.

Henry M. Baird.

Oh, for a strong, a lasting faith
To credit what the Almighty saith;
To embrace the message of his Son,
And call the joys of heaven our own.
WATTS.

June 9.

That ye put on the new man. — Eph. iv. 24.

Either make the tree good, and his fruit good; or else make the tree corrupt, and his fruit corrupt: for the tree is known by his fruit. — Matt. xii. 33.

IN this world of "vain shows," shams, semblances, and self-deceptions, we need every hour some certain test by which to distinguish the true from the false. Such a touchstone the Master here furnishes us in his inimitable nature-teaching manner in the tree. "The tree is known by its fruit." The fruit is the only true thing about the tree. All things else are mere accidents and appendages, preludes, preparations, and promises; that upon which the tree expends all its labors and exhausts all its nature, and into which it pours its whole life, is its fruit. Its leaves and blossoms fade and fall, its branches wither, itself dies; but its fruit, enwrapping a living seed, springs up it may be in another garden on a distant continent, and lives on and on, reproducing itself forever, the only immortal thing of earth. So character, the expression of the whole nature, the product of the whole life's activities, the one reality which abides amid all changes, the only immortal thing about man, is the only infallible touchstone by which we can test ourselves and others. Professions and promises, however fair, are worthless as the faded leaves and blossoms of summer where they do not ripen into the fruits of holiness; and the fruitless tree is fit only for the burning. Reader, let me beseech you to try yourself by this test, and remember it is for your life.

Joseph J. Smith

So let our lips and lives express
The holy gospel we profess;
So let our works and virtues shine,
To prove the doctrine all divine. WATTS.

June 10.

Chosen ... in him before the foundation of the world.
Eph. i. 4.

Then shall the King say unto them on his right hand, Come, ye blessed of my Father, inherit the kingdom prepared for you from the foundation of the world. — Matt. xxv. 34.

IT is the great and notable day of the Lord. He who came "in weakness clad" to be, as the Son of man, the Saviour of the world, by offering himself once for all an atoning expiation for sin upon the cross, has come in the power and majesty of heavenly glory to judge the world in righteousness and mete out to men their eternal doom. See how his lowly, faithful followers fare! On earth it cost them self-crucifixion and the bitter contempt of men to confess the Lord and follow him; now they are recognized, welcomed by the King of kings, and greeted as sharers of his glory. For his sake and the gospel's they had become poor, naked outcasts; now for the trashy perishable tinsel and trinkets they had dropped, they receive treasures pure and true which shall endure forever. They had counted all things but loss so they might win Christ; through abounding grace they had won Christ and heaven and shall rejoice eternally in the full possession of that "inheritance which is incorruptible, undefiled, and shall endure forever." Were they deceived in their trust, hope, and obedience? Does the reward equal the promise? Ask them! Nay, rather, "be followers of them who through faith and patience inherit the promises;" then shall their exceeding joy be yours.

J.H.A.Bomberger

Judge and Saviour of our race,
Grant us, when we see thy face,
With thy ransomed ones a place.
I. Williams.

June 11.

God hath revealed them unto us by his Spirit.
1 Cor. ii. 10.

Howbeit when he, the Spirit of truth, is come, he will guide you into all truth: for he shall not speak of himself; but whatsoever he shall hear, that shall he speak: and he will shew you things to come. He shall glorify me: for he shall receive of mine, and shall shew it unto you. — John xvi. 13, 14.

WHEN Jesus went back to heaven, he sent another divine Person, the Spirit of truth, to take his place, carry forward his work, and to abide with his followers. On the day of Pentecost that Spirit came from heaven in mighty power and filled the disciples, and has been here ever since as a teacher and a guide. Unless he reveals them unto us, we cannot understand the things of God. Every believer needs to be taught by him out of the Scriptures. With the words of Christ in our hands and this Spirit in our hearts, we are led into true and blessed knowledge of God, which is life eternal. The weakest believer thus taught may know far more of God than the wisest man of this world.

This divine Teacher reveals to the believer the glories of Christ Jesus as they shine in the written Word. He is the Advocate of an absent Christ and pleads his cause. He enables us to see the matchless beauty of the character and life of our Redeemer, and makes him *glorious* in the eyes of all them that believe. If we open wide our hearts to this blessed person and do not grieve him by our sins, he will guide us into the fulness of the knowledge and joy of our Lord.

A. W. Pitzer.

He teaches us the Father's grace,
Reveals to us the Saviour's face,
And doth to all our hearts declare
The glory it is ours to share.
Mrs. M. J. Walker.

June 12.

Godliness with contentment is great gain. — 1 Tim. vi. 6.

Take heed, and beware of covetousness: for a man's life consisteth not in the abundance of the things which he possesseth. — Luke xii. 15.

HERE we have a solemn command evoked by a striking incident and backed up by a pertinent reason. The command itself is cumulative in form. "Take heed *and* beware." If we carefully consider what covetousness is in its nature and tendencies, we will diligently avoid it. "Take heed." Meditate upon the tenth commandment as well as repeat it; revolve in mind how discontent with our lot dishonors God, how envy of the apparent happiness of others destroys brotherly sympathy, how covetousness kills generosity, stifles good impulses, and stands in the way of that charity which "suffereth long and is kind" because it "envieth not." And having taken heed, "beware!" Set a watch on every thought and motive that tends toward envy. Be strict with yourself and generous with others. Covetousness creeps in unnoticed, and you will be startled to find it appearing in heart and life. Hence the need of being "wary," vigilant.

The incident out of which this command grew is very striking (v. 13). The dividing of inheritances has been in all the ages a fruitful source of covetousness. Envy is "as rottenness in the bones." How soon envy entered into the world! The first sin was Adam's pride; and the second, perhaps, was Cain's envy.

J. M. Harsha

> The Lord my shepherd is;
> I shall be well supplied.
> Since he is mine, and I am his,
> What can I want beside?   Watts.

June 13.

The fire shall try every man's work. — 1 Cor. iii. 13.

Every plant, which my heavenly Father hath not planted, shall be rooted up. — Matt. xv. 13.

THIS is one of our Lord's enigmatical replies. His disciples had informed him that the Pharisees had taken offence at certain of his remarks. Without commenting on their conduct, he points his followers to a future when all error and malice will be brought to nought. He thought it better to impress a truth on his friends than to confute his enemies.

We are taught by Christ's words that we are not always to take the responsibility of opposing openly that which we disapprove, but that we may at times leave it to the providence of God to thwart and defeat the evil practices and false opinions of others. We are taught also that our own characteristics and cherished habits are to be estimated in view of the source from which they came. The question respecting our plans and occupations is not, Are they attractive? Do they comport with our pride or our place in the world? but, Are they of God? They will be surely rooted up unless they derive their support from him. Most cheering of all is the truth that what God has planted will abide forever. The seeds which Christ sows in the heart will spring up and bear fruit unless we permit them to be snatched away or to be choked by weeds of which an enemy has sown the seed. The fruits of the Spirit will always be cherished by the heavenly Father.

Geo. Nye Boardman

  O Master, point thou out the way,
  Nor suffer thou our steps to stray;
  Then in that path that leads to day,
    We follow thee.
           H. Bonar.

June 14.

The kingdom of God is ... joy in the Holy Ghost.
ROMANS xiv. 17.

These things have I spoken unto you, that my joy might remain in you, and that your joy might be full. — JOHN xv. 11.

THESE things are all the words of Christ, but especially those spoken in the two preceding verses, where his joy is traced directly to his Father's love, resting on him in the keeping of his commandments, as our joy comes from his love while doing his will. My joy and your joy are fruits of the Vine mentioned a little while before. Indeed, this joy is the very wine of the Christian life. It is not so much one of the fruits of the Spirit as the resultant of them all. The joy of Christ here is not the blessedness he had with the Father before the worlds were, but the joy that was set before him for enduring the cross and despising the shame. So the joy of his people when full will far transcend the happiness of primeval man.

How amazing is the absence of joy in the average Christian experience, seeing it is not only the logical result of salvation, but that Christ has made special provision for it in his continued communion with his people! He bears the thought with him a little while afterward into the holy of holies, and prays, "And now I come to thee, and these things I speak in the world that they might have my joy fulfilled in themselves."

John. W. Neil.

My merry heart is springing,
   And knows not how to pine;
'T is full of joy and singing
   And radiancy divine.
The sun whose smiles so cheer me
   Is Jesus Christ alone;
To have him always near me,
   Is heaven itself begun.
              RICHARD MASSIE *(Translation).*

JUNE 15.

Put on … as the elect of God … bowels of mercies.
COL. iii. 12.

Be ye therefore merciful, as your Father also is merciful. —
LUKE vi. 36.

THE Pagan philosophers, who spake as men, taught that justice is a duty required of all men. Our divine Master, who spake as never man spake, goes farther and enjoins upon his disciples mercy as a Christian duty. Mercy consists of kindness that goes beyond all the requirements of justice, and does for men more and better than their merits deserve. We have no merit in the sight of God; therefore all his goodness toward us is the gift of his mercy. Our God is the Father of mercies, and he is kind unto the unthankful and to the evil. Therefore, saith our Saviour, we should be merciful and love our enemies, and do good to those who would do us evil. This is an original and peculiar law of our Christianity, and it proves that it is not of the earth, but from heaven. Mercy in the heart of man is a grace that is all divine, and one which makes the man more manful and more than a man, — it makes him a Christian. "The meek shall inherit the earth." The merciful shall obtain mercy, and with Christ shall inherit all things.

John M. P. Otts

> Come, thou Spirit of pure love,
>   Who didst forth from God proceed,
> Never from my heart remove,
>   Let me all thy impulse heed;
> Let my heart hence forward be
> Moved, controlled, inspired by thee.
>
> CATHARINE WINKWORTH *(Translation)*.

June 16.

Labourers together with God. — 1 Cor. iii. 9.

And he that reapeth receiveth wages, and gathereth fruit unto life eternal: that both he that soweth and he that reapeth may rejoice together. — John iv. 36.

THE cheering lesson of this verse is that immediate results often follow Christian work. Usually seed-time and harvest are divided by a considerable interval of time; but here we learn that they may follow in quick succession. This cheering truth is impressed by our Lord's experience, when, as the result of his wayside sowing in his words to the woman of Samaria, a rich harvest was reaped on the selfsame day. So it was on the day of Pentecost, and so it has been in many other instances when the Spirit of God has given the truth immediate power, and the sower and the reaper have rejoiced together.

An insight is also given us into the nature of Christian service. It is a co-operative system, and God is a liberal master. He gives those who work for him a share in the profits that accrue, — that is, the blessings and results that follow such work. "He that reapeth receiveth wages." The Master here distinctly encourages us to expect immediate results in Christian work at home and abroad, and happy are they who midst the tears of sowing hear the joyous shout of the reapers.

B. C. Henry

> The harvest dawn is near,
> The year delays not long;
> And he who sows with many a tear,
> Shall reap with many a song.
> George Burgess

June 17.

He first findeth his own brother. — JOHN i. 41.

Go home to thy friends, and tell them how great things the Lord hath done for thee, and hath had compassion on thee. — MARK v. 19.

THE command had peculiar significance as given to the man out of whom Christ had sent the unclean spirits. In the case of the leper at Capernaum, or the deaf and dumb sufferer subsequently in Decapolis, the excitement was already so great about the miracle-worker that Christ's work was in danger of serious obstruction. But here and now in accord with the wishes and entreaties of their unbelief, Christ was already on board the vessel that was to take him across the lake, and his cause must suffer. So this healed demoniac from the tombs, a signal monument of his mercy, must go to places from which Christ in his own person was debarred, to testify of Christ's power. And he *did* go among his friends at home, and subsequently to the south in Decapolis proclaiming the wonder-working power of Jesus with blessed results. It was a far nobler work, too, for him thus to go where those who knew him before and dreaded him before could now see the great change and hear him tell what Christ had done than to go where he was unknown. The man himself where he was known of old was a monument now of Christ's healing mercy. So, too, Christ's direction to the man thus healed is one of significance for every one of us who has felt spiritually Christ's healing power.

Our first and best testimony as to any change Christ has wrought in us is always given at home, among our friends and those who know us best.

A piety that cannot stand such a test, a piety that languishes at home, is to be suspected.

Michael Beanham,

Thanks we give, and adoration,
For thy gospel's joyful sound.
May the fruits of thy salvation
In our hearts and lives abound ! ROBERT HAWKER.

JUNE 18.

That no flesh should glory in his presence. — 1 COR. i. 29.

Yea; have ye never read, Out of the mouth of babes and sucklings thou hast perfected praise? — MATT. xxi. 16.

HOW beautiful the hosannas of childhood offered to him who said, "Suffer little children, and forbid them not, to come unto me"! Cold formalism and pharisaic holiness would rebuke the approach of children to Jesus, and silence their songs in the temple. But the blessed Jesus welcomes their presence, and listens well-pleased to their hymns of praise. He indeed spoke words of hope to the dying thief, and graciously regards the penitential tears of the hoary-headed sinner; but still more is he pleased to receive into his favor and to his service those of early years. He would have their character early moulded into his likeness, and imbued with his spirit. He would have all from their earliest years devoted to his service in works of benevolence and piety. He would have the entire life.

Yes, let the children come to Jesus. He waits to welcome them. To them is extended a special promise, "Those that seek me early shall find me." Let parents as they love their children, strive to bring them to Jesus. Let Sabbath-school teachers seek to lead those under their care to a saving knowledge of his truth. Let pastors remember the words of the Master, "Feed my lambs." Yes, dear children, come to Jesus.

Frederick Merrick.

All glory, laud, and honor
  To thee, Redeemer, King,
To whom the lips of children
  Made sweet hosannas ring.
. . . . . .
Thou didst accept their praises;
  Accept the prayers we bring,
Who in all good delightest,
  Thou good and gracious King.
             J. NEALE *(Translation).*

JUNE 19.

Godliness is profitable unto all things. — 1 TIM. iv. 8.

But seek ye first the kingdom of God, and his righteousness; and all these things shall be added unto you. — MATT. vi. 33.

SEEK *first*, not exclusively; this is no rebuke to intensest business devotion. Nor does "first" mean merely in order of time, — say prayers in the morning, serve God on Sunday, the first day of the week, get religion in early life. "First" means chiefly, — serve God supremely, even in secular matters.

This does not imply that one shall be most of the time thinking about religious things. Our supreme secular purpose in going to business is to provide comfort for our families; yet we hardly think of a loved face in business hours, except as in leisure moments it peers in through the window of the heart. But however absorbed in the scramble of trade, there is always over us a delightful, though vague, impression of home and its loves; just as there is always an impression of the sky over our heads, though we do not look up at it incessantly. So may the delightful sense of the kingdom of God environ us, the sceptre-shadow of his righteousness be always upon our consciences, the benediction of his love upon our hearts! This feeling will add all good things to us, in that it will make all things good. It will mark everything we possess as a souvenir of infinite affection.

James M. Ludlow.

    Saviour, happy would I be,
    If I could but trust in thee, —
    Trust thy wisdom me to guide;
    Trust thy goodness to provide;
    Trust thy saving love and power;
    Trust thee every day and hour.
                      EDWIN H. NEVIN.

JUNE 20.

His wife looked back. — GEN. xix. 26.

Remember Lot's wife. — LUKE xvii. 32.

OUR Lord was depicting scenes of the judgment day, and points to the shore of the Dead Sea, where Lot's wife built herself a monument, a piece of statuary, making a complete picture in itself.

Why this injunction? She was the type of the worldly-minded. "Remember," then, "the friends of the world are the enemies of God;" that Christ died "to deliver us from this present evil world," therefore, "he that forsaketh not all that he hath cannot be my disciple." "Remember," the time hastens when the world must be abandoned, love it as we may. We can carry nothing away; the things of Sodom taken to Zoar would make a Sodom there, necessitating the fire that burns the world and the worldling.

We must not only leave Sodom, but "linger not in the plain." Remember, if the separation from the world be not complete, it must soon be final, from God, home, friends, all. "Two shall be in the field, one shall be taken and the other left."

"Remember," the love of the world perpetuates itself in the generations that follow; the "lovers of pleasure, more than lovers of God," are seen in her daughters and descendants down through Moab and Ammon.

J. W. Lupton.

> Once earthly joy I craved,
>   Sought peace and rest;
> Now thee alone I seek,
>   Give what is best.
> This all my prayer shall be,
> More love, O Christ, to thee,
>   More love to thee!

MRS. E. P. PRENTISS.

JUNE 21.

The Lord is . . . plenteous in mercy. — PSALM ciii. 8.

And he arose, and came to his father. But when he was yet a great way off, his father saw him, and had compassion, and ran, and fell on his neck, and kissed him. — LUKE xv. 20.

A PICTURE of divine pity, forgiveness, and love more affecting than this it would be impossible to find! In this parable we see not only to what degradation sin has brought a human soul, but we see also what divine compassion is felt for it, and what grace and love are lavished upon it. The instant the prodigal turns toward his father, that instant the father runs to meet him. Contrast the slow approach of the son with the eager haste of the father running to meet him, the shame and fear of the one with the love and joy of the other. And though still in rags, his father fell on his neck and kissed him, not only forgiving the wanderer, but restoring to him fully the possession and enjoyment of his forfeited filial rights. Such welcome awaits every returning prodigal. How return? In King's College, Cambridge, was once a young man anxious about his soul. He read and pondered Lev. xvi. 20–22. The gospel interpreted the passage. His heart was touched; he said, "If the Lamb of God has borne and carried away my sins, I will not bear them another hour." This was Charles Simeon. Like him yield to the drawings of the Saviour's love.

George C. Noyes.

Spread for thee the festal board,
See, with richest bounty stored;
To thy Father's bosom pressed,
Thou shalt be a child confessed,
Never from his house to roam;
Come and welcome, sinner, come!

THOMAS HAWEIS.

June 22.

The wicked shall be turned into hell. — Psalm ix. 17.

Then shall he say also unto them on the left hand, Depart from me, ye cursed, into everlasting fire, prepared for the devil and his angels. — Matt. xxv. 41.

TWO characters only are to be found among all the millions of this earth. In the hour of judgment two characters only will appear before the Judge. Throughout eternity but two characters will remain. There are two and only two characters delineated in the Word of God. These characters are distinct, antagonistic, eternally separated, — the righteous and the unrighteous. The smile of God is upon them that do well, his frown upon them that do evil. The present state of the godly is happiness and prosperity; the ungodly are not so. The reward of the righteous is eternal union with God, the end of the wicked banishment from his presence. Heaven is a being with God, hell a being without him.

Our Lord depicts the final separation of the righteous and the unrighteous. To those on his left hand the King exclaims, "Depart!" Unwilling to come to him that they might have life, they are now to be deprived of the joy and glory of his face. Union with him is no longer possible, and separation brings torment. This punishment is not prepared for human souls; but sharing with the Devil and his angels here, they are sharers with them also hereafter, cursed because they refused to be blessed, lost because unwilling to be saved. Which will you be? What character are you making for yourself now?

O just Judge, to whom belongs
Vengeance for all earthly wrongs,
Grant forgiveness, Lord, at last,
Ere the dread account be past!
Dean Stanley *(Translation).*

June 23.

If we suffer, we shall also reign with him.
2 Tim. ii. 12.

Verily I say unto you, There is no man that hath left house, or parents, or brethren, or wife, or children, for the kingdom of God's sake, who shall not receive manifold more in this present time, and in the world to come life everlasting. — Luke xviii. 29, 30.

THE light and power of this text is in the phrase, "For the kingdom of God's sake." Fearful calamities have befallen the Church from errors concerning the principle of true evangelical sacrifice and service. Christ is not making a bargain nor appealing to our self-interest, but stating a fact verified in the experience of millions who have joyfully sung, "For thy sake we are killed all the day long." The mother who rushes through the flames to save her child, the soldier who counts not his possessions or life dear that he may serve his king, do not speak or think of sacrifice. Jesus Christ gains men by his attractive power. When the kingdom of God and the beauties of its King are revealed to the soul, it enters at once upon its glorious inheritance of everlasting life, and asks no other reward. We have long possessed a picture of a saint of the Middle Ages kneeling at the feet of Christ. The Lord is saying to him, "Thou hast done much for me, what shall I give thee?" And Saint Thomas Aquinas is answering, "Lord, nothing but thyself."

J. M. Woodbridge

Jesus, I my cross have taken
  All to leave, and follow thee;
Naked, poor, despised, forsaken,
  Thou from hence my all shalt be!
Perish every fond ambition,
  All I've sought, or hoped, or known;
Yet how rich is my condition,
  God and heaven are still my own!   Lyte.

June 24.

Him hath God exalted . . . to give repentance . . . and forgiveness. — Acts v. 31.

Except ye repent, ye shall all likewise perish. — Luke xiii. 3.

TWICE does this declaration come from the lips of Jesus Christ in one brief discourse. He speaks with the authority of a king and a judge. It is at our peril if we disregard or remain inattentive to what he says. And this sure word comes to all — to me! No judgments falling upon others can justify me in believing that I am without guilt. Perchance my brother's guilt may be greater than mine, but still repentance is not more indispensable to him than to me. Failing to give it, there lies before the sinner that doom expressed in the word "perish," — a doom so great, so unspeakably awful to a human soul, that no language can adequately describe it.

Repentance is the escape of the soul from the dominion of sin; it is enlightenment of the mind, so that the sinner sees the danger and folly of his course. It is the renewal of the heart, so that it separates itself from the sin that was destroying it. It is the beginning of a new and glorious life. Should it then be a hard thing to repent? True, repentance has its tears, but they are indeed blessed tears. It has its lamentations, but they soon turn to joy and praise. It has its humiliations, but it leads to a glorious exaltation.

Samuel Nicholls

With broken heart and contrite sigh,
A trembling sinner, Lord, I cry:
Thy pardoning grace is rich and free,
O God, be merciful to me!

Cornelius Elven.

JUNE 25.

God, who quickeneth the dead. — ROMANS iv. 17.

For as the Father raiseth up the dead, and quickeneth them; even so the Son quickeneth whom he will. — JOHN v. 21.

LIFE is the prerogative and gift of God, alike of Father and Son. So declare these words of Saint John; and all life is essentially one. But to the conscious recipient is there not a difference in the gift suggested by these same words corresponding to the person of the giver? Surely to such a recipient a gift carries with it the personality, the touch, of the hand from which it comes. And it is this personality which gives it most often its highest value and influence. "The gift without the giver is bare." But what is true of our smaller earthly tokens is vastly truer of the high gifts of heaven, and this highest gift of all. Grateful, happy, is it to the devout soul, to recognize in every heart-throb, every function, physical or spiritual, the Father's forethought and provision for his children. But an element of even deeper tenderness and love, as well as responsibility, is added to the gift, as coming from the wounded human hand of Jesus. It glows and breathes with the very spirit of his life and redeeming work.

And this is the gift, this life, which he gives to every earnest seeking heart; for "whom he will," is after all only another expression, according to the gospel, for "whosoever will."

W. M. McVickar

> Thou art the life; the rending tomb
> Proclaims thy conquering arm;
> And those who put their trust in thee
> Nor death nor hell shall harm.
>
> BISHOP DOANE.

June 26.

We have redemption through his blood. — Eph. i. 7.

Take, eat; this is my body. . . . Drink ye all of it; for this is my blood of the new testament, which is shed for many for the remission of sins. — Matt. xxvi. 26-28.

PRECIOUS words of Jesus! Our Lord here institutes the sacrament or feast which should ever commemorate his love and delivering mercy to his believing people, "Take, eat," etc. This feast is "meat indeed, and drink indeed" to those who have faith to discern the Lord's body and blood, and love to feed upon his grace. "Do this in remembrance of me" is his tender loving command to his Church and people of all ages, "till he come." Can we refuse to obey, and not "deny him before men"?

This supper is not a sacrifice, it is a feast commemorating a sacrifice; we should observe it with thankful hearts. It tells us, in mute eloquence, of the victory he achieved, and of the life and liberty he purchased for us. It breathes the love of Christ; it is fragrant with the mercy of our God, who is now ready to welcome the weakest believer who comes trusting and resting the soul upon the righteousness of Jesus only. In this feast of love, there is food for hungry souls, refreshment for weary spirits, and heavenly comfort for those that mourn. It brings the believer into closer union with Christ, it strengthens faith, brightens hope, and cheers the Christian along the way.

L. S. Handley.

> Bread of the world, in mercy broken,
>   Wine of the soul, in mercy shed,
> By whom the words of life were spoken,
>   And in whose death our sins are dead,
> Look on the hearts by sorrow broken;
>   Look on the tears by sinners shed;
> And be this feast to us the token
>   That by thy love our souls are fed.   Heber.

June 27.

What things were gain to me, those I counted loss for Christ. — PHIL. iii. 7.

For what is a man profited, if he shall gain the whole world, and lose his own soul? or what shall a man give in exchange for his soul?
— MATT. xvi. 26.

THERE can be no true discipleship without sacrifice. To follow the Master is "to take up his cross." It may require the surrender of friends, of chosen pursuits, of opportunities for securing wealth, and in obeying the calls of his spirit and providence, even of life itself. It is for Christ against the world that the sincere, well-considered, loving choice is to be made. But what if it should not be made? What compensation does the world offer, even at its best estate? How uncertain and short-lived earthly friendships! How disappointing the gratifications of taste and worldly honors! How evanescent, how unsatisfying, how limited at best the period of its enjoyment! And all this to be balanced by the irremediable loss of the soul!

But what if the better alternative is elected? There may, indeed, be heavy sacrifices required, and human tears. But in all this we follow and enjoy the presence of our divine Leader. We are supported by his promised aid. We are filled with joy amid our sufferings, "we glory in tribulations also," and in the end receive the crown of an immortal life.

Bradford K. Peirce

Jesus, thy boundless love to me
  No thought can reach, no tongue declare;
Oh, knit my thankful heart to thee,
  And reign without a rival there.
Thine wholly, thine alone, I am;
Be thou alone my constant flame.
                 · J. WESLEY *(Translation).*

June 28.

Let patience have her perfect work. — James i. 4.

In your patience possess ye your souls. — Luke xxi. 19.

A glance at our Revised Version, "In your patience ye shall win your souls," shows us that this text is a promise, not a command, a blessed hope, not a stern ordinance. What is the spirit of this promise? "Souls" is rendered in the margin "lives;" and the thought of winning one's life is of accomplishing the highest end of life, and of realizing its highest possibility of power and of peace. Regarded in this light, how sweet is the promise for those who are compelled to live in this impetuous, harassing generation! By patience we shall win our lives! Impatience in our work; the chafing of the spirit against providential restrictions; the wild haste to be rich; the intolerant and consuming ambition, which to satisfy itself will crush a path over the rights of others, — these are characteristic types of world-life to be seen around us every day. But the servant of the Lord must not, will not abandon himself to this impatient, selfish strife. He will maintain the bright example of the patient Jesus. He will discern by the light of the Holy Spirit's teaching that the highest end of our life on earth cannot be won by the selfish and by the impatient; he will receive the strength to remember that impatience is waste and loss, the strength to live in the hourly atmosphere of that blessed prayer for every busy and every earnest life.

Chas Cuthbert Hall

> Calm me, my God, and keep me calm;
> Let thine outstretchèd wing
> Be like the shade of Elim's palm
> Beside her desert spring.
>
> H. Bonar.

June 29.

Take heed therefore unto yourselves. — ACTS xx. 28.

The men of Nineveh shall rise in judgment with this generation, and shall condemn it: because they repented at the preaching of Jonas; and, behold, a greater than Jonas is here. — MATT. xii. 41.

THESE words of the Master teach that light measures responsibility, that obligation is commensurate with opportunity.

We of this generation may find a solemn joy in the fact that our opportunities and our obligations are unequalled. Not only is this the formative and decisive period in that portion of our country which is to determine the national destiny, but there is the quickening of a new intellectual life among the churchless multitude, which needs the moulding hand of the Church. Moreover, the door of opportunity, "great and effectual," is as wide as the world, for this is the first generation in man's history that has seen the whole world open to the gospel. The highways of commerce have been opened; channels of benefaction have been established; wealth has been amassed; and an intellectual revolution which seems to follow the touch of the nineteenth century is shattering traditional beliefs and preparing heathen nations, like the Ninevites, to receive the preachers of righteousness. We can now stretch out our hands in benediction over Asia and Africa.

The men of Christ's generation sinned above others in refusing to accept light. We of this generation shall sin above others if we refuse to give it.

Josiah Strong.

> Be this my one great business here,
> With serious industry and fear,
>   Eternal bliss to insure;
> Thine utmost counsel to fulfil,
> And suffer all thy righteous will,
>   And to the end endure.   C. WESLEY.

June 30.

We have peace with God. — Romans v. 1.

Peace be unto you. — John xx. 19.

THE natal song of Christ sung by prophetic angels was "peace" and "glory," — "glory in the highest, and on earth peace." Yet when Jesus began his ministry, he said, "I came not to send peace, but a sword." Are these statements and others like them contradictions? No! sweet paradoxes. By nature, man is at peace with the world and at war with God. Christ came to reverse this, and by his atonement to establish a peace between God and man which involves war with the world. The Christian, then, is called to fight his way to eternal peace. But has he no peace until the end? Yes, blessed peace; war without, and peace within, — "the peace of God that passeth all understanding." His turbulent passions are stilled; his soul's great anxieties are laid to rest; his sin is forgiven; he is cleansed in the blood of the Lamb; he has promises of final salvation, "a place" in the "house of many mansions," and "a crown of glory that fadeth not away." With a consciousness of all these in the Christian's soul, time, death, and eternity cannot mar his imperturbable repose.

Robert P. Kerr

Grant us thy peace throughout our earthly life,
Our balm in sorrow, and our stay in strife;
Then, when thy voice shall bid our conflict cease,
Call us, O Lord, to thine eternal peace.

John Ellerton.

JULY 1.

Spiritual sacrifices, acceptable to God by Jesus Christ.
1 PETER ii. 5.

But the hour cometh, and now is, when the true worshippers shall worship the Father in spirit and in truth : for the Father seeketh such to worship him. God is a Spirit: and they that worship him must worship him in spirit and in truth. — JOHN iv. 23, 24.

ALAS, how sad that the Hebrews had forgotten the God of Israel as he revealed himself to their fathers, and had fallen into formalism ! But our Lord had come to bring in a better state of things and to prepare a people over all the earth, diverse from one another in many things, but one in this, that they aim at worship which is true to the truth of things, and which is spiritual. We live in the time contemplated. Let us be profoundly thankful for what we witness, still more for what we have been taught of the Holy Ghost to join in rendering to the Father.

For the Father, combining love which looks to the good of his creatures with law which comes from his own nature, seeks spiritual worshippers. Let us be fellow-workers with him and try to teach men his nature that, forsaking idols and errors, they may worship him in spirit and in truth.

The nature of God determines the kind of worship. He is holy. He calls for holiness in them that come nigh him. He is omniscient. He sees and hates evil in the heart no less than in the life. He requires heart purity in his worshippers. He is not like the gods of the heathen, and he will not accept what blinded men carry to them. He has made known his nature and his attributes to men with clearness enough to show them what they ought to be and to offer.

John Hall.

> The holy Church throughout the world,
> O Lord, confesses thee,
> That thou the eternal Father art,
> Of boundless majesty.
>
> TATE *(Translation)*.

July 2.

That Christ may dwell in your hearts by faith.
Eph. iii. 17.

Yet a little while, and the world seeth me no more; but ye see me: because I live, ye shall live also. At that day ye shall know that I am in my Father, and ye in me, and I in you. — John xiv. 19, 20.

THE above words were uttered by the Saviour on the eve of his crucifixion, at a time when the most painful scenes of his life were crowding one upon another and sorely pressing him on all sides. They were given to comfort the hearts of his disciples, who were overwhelmed with grief. Thus soon their Lord and Master was to be taken from their midst. And as we read and re-read this valedictory, we exclaim, How beautiful! how fitting to the occasion! how comforting! Surely the disciples, though stricken with grief, must have felt, to some degree at least, their hearts burn within them at the announcement of these exceeding great and precious promises.

"Yet a little while," says the Saviour. He had but a few hours to live. Judas at that very hour, perhaps moment, was consummating his treason. And before the morrow's sun appeared over the hills of Judea the Saviour was in the hands of his betrayers and murderers. "And the world seeth me no more." No, not till the morning of the resurrection, when every eye shall see him, but not as a man of sorrows and acquainted with grief, but as a conqueror amid the splendors and soldiery of heaven. "But ye see me." Between the time of his resurrection and ascension, for the space of forty days he appeared to his apostles, and on one occasion was seen of above five hundred brethren at once. Yes, and his followers ever see him by the eye of faith, and at last will see him as he is.

Prince of light, to thee I cry!
By thy glorious majesty,
Lord, thy presence let me see;
Manifest thyself to me!   Richard Mant.

July 3.

So shall we ever be with the Lord. — 1 Thess. iv. 17.

In my Father's house are many mansions: if it were not so, I would have told you. I go to prepare a place for you. And if I go and prepare a place for you, I will come again, and receive you unto myself; that where I am, there ye may be also. And whither I go ye know, and the way ye know. — John xiv. 2-4.

HOW clear and satisfying a view of the life to come is presented in these words of our Saviour's! So positive an affirmation of its reality from the lips of one who came forth from God puts to silence the denials of unbelief. All speculations respecting the future state are valueless to those who have looked upon this picture of home life beyond the grave. How cheering in view of earthly conflicts, and what a stimulus to untiring activity in Christian work!

Into this land of many mansions, or abiding places, the Lord has gone as the head and representative of ransomed humanity. Our hope, as an anchor of the soul, is sure and steadfast, entering into that which is within the veil, whither the forerunner has for us entered, even Jesus. There he reigns for the overthrow of sin; and when he has accomplished his purpose of mercy in the hearts and through the agency of his faithful followers, he receives them to himself that they may share his glory.

Nor need any one go astray. Christ is the way. Trustful reliance upon him and his finished work will secure all the blessings that are wrapped up in the terms, Home and Father.

R. M. Sommerville,

Well, the delightful day will come,
When my dear Lord will bring me home,
   And I shall see his face.
Then with my Saviour, brother, friend,
A blest eternity I'll spend,
   Triumphant in his grace.

Samuel Medley.

July 4.

A very present help in trouble. — Psalm xlvi. 1.
Be of good cheer ; it is I ; be not afraid. — Matt. xiv. 27.

"JESUS constrained his disciples to get into a ship and go to the other side" away from influences which tended only to the carnal and temporal; and "he himself went up into a mountain apart to pray." If we would escape temptation, we must flee from it and draw nigh unto God. And sometimes it may seem that in escaping temptation we fall into dire calamities. The winds may be contrary, the waves may be rough and boisterous, the night may come on dark and starless, and yet it were better to be overwhelmed in such a sea than to be engulfed in sin and error. But Jesus does not forget his disciples. High on the mountain-top he prays, and in the hour of need comes with almighty help to convert our calamities into blessings.

We are sailing to the other shore. Sometimes the sea is wild and raging; sometimes the heart is troubled like the sea, but Jesus comes walking on the angry waters, and over the roar of the tempest, within and without, we hear his voice, "Be of good cheer; it is I: be not afraid;" and that voice brings a calm to the sea and the soul. And when he bids us come to his side, we can look to Jesus, and walk, like Peter, on the angry flood. But if we look away from Jesus to the threatening tide and storm, our faith will weaken, our courage will fail, our feet will sink. But happy for us even then if there yet remaineth faith to cry, "Lord, save, or I perish;" for in that hour Jesus will stretch forth his hand to save, and to bring the peace which the soul needs.

Robert Moffett

Ridge of the mountain-wave, lower thy crest!
Wail of the tempest-wind, be thou at rest!
Sorrow can never be, darkness must fly,
Where saith the Light of light, "Peace! it is I!"

J. Neale *(Translation).*

JULY 5.

Thy words were found, and I did eat them. — JER. xv. 16.

Verily, verily, I say unto you, Ye seek me, not because ye saw the miracles, but because ye did eat of the loaves, and were filled. — JOHN vi. 26.

THE miracles should have convinced the Galileans that Jesus of Nazareth is the Saviour of the world. This was their design. After he had seen a few of them, Nicodemus of Jerusalem made a distinct confession. But these Galileans were gross and sensual in their desires. Food without work was an attraction. Curiosity was aroused. The material advantages of our Lord's ministry were welcome. Like the Roman soldiers who crucified him and then divided his garments, they were glad to accept all that he would give, while they were unwilling to accept *him*. Thus they announced their own condemnation. In refusing salvation they ultimately lost every blessing.

Their mistake is constantly repeated. Men "eat of the loaves" and still reject the Saviour. Freedom, civilization, home, the Sabbath, — these are all the miracles of our Lord. No one would wish to live away from them. Life is not worth much if it is not within sound of the church bell. But these things cannot save; they are evidences of a Saviour's presence. They are not the Saviour; he, and he alone, can save, and the silent appeal of these precious blessings is an urgent entreaty to accept his salvation. Have you found the Saviour, or are you satisfied to "eat of the loaves"?

Henry M. Booth —

Break thou the bread of life, dear Lord, to me,
As thou didst break the loaves beside the sea.
Beyond the sacred page I seek thee, Lord,
My spirit pants for thee, O living Word!
                                    MARY A. LATHBURY.

July 6.

In nothing terrified by your adversaries. — Phil. i. 28.

But there shall not a hair of your head perish. — Luke xxi. 18.

IN terms proverbial and figurative Jesus here signifies the immunity of his servants; adversity cannot hinder what he promises them. The family ties of a believer may be rent, but not the union of his soul with his Saviour, once it has in good faith been established. No slander of adversaries can diminish our inheritance with the saints in glory. Tribulations endured on earth shall only enhance "the rest that remaineth," and add zest to the more active joys of each guest arriving with angels to welcome him at the celestial home. The very defeats suffered by the servants of the Lord shall set forward and build up the kingdom they labor for. Stephen in his death was defeated, but the end of the victory he then achieved, in bringing converts to Christ, is not seen yet. His body was bruised; his head was fractured, and yet not a hair of it perished. Sustained, honored, saved he was. Heaven he saw opened, and Jesus standing there by the throne, who received his spirit.

Our Lord has not promised exemption from all violence of evil men, on the contrary has bidden us look for it; but he promises his blessed presence and a safety higher and more enduring. They that suffer with him shall succeed. His tried ones shall triumph. His slain shall survive. Followers of the Lamb shall reign forever with him.

David Trumbull.

How are thy servants blest, O Lord!
How sure is their defence!
Eternal wisdom is their guide,
Their help, omnipotence.

Joseph Addison.

July 7.

The Lord hath laid on him the iniquity of us all.
Isaiah liii. 6.

All ye shall be offended because of me this night: for it is written, I will smite the Shepherd, and the sheep of the flock shall be scattered abroad. — Matt. xxvi. 31.

THESE touching words of our most holy Lord must have made a deep impression on his disciples; and so they should on us. The occasion and the surroundings were sad; and in the tones of his voice and in his words there was sadness. They reveal the loneliness of Christ, on the one hand, and on the other, the weakness of even his own chosen and best disciples. When troubles come, friends forsake us. Many people will shrink from standing by their friends or the Church when in trouble, even if good is to come out of the troubles. The good appear to disadvantage and are at a discount in this world, and people last of all help a good man because he is good, or suffers for the good.

All the disciples were "offended" because of Christ that night, and all forsook him, and were like sheep without a shepherd. Oh, that we may never from fear or shame allow our Master's cause to suffer, or forsake it when dangers surround it or threaten it! Although all were "offended" and forsook Christ, he still fulfilled his high and holy mission, and so let each one of us, even if all alone and forsaken, live, labor, and suffer for God, his cause, and his children.

F. W. E. Peschau.

Ashamed of Jesus! — empty pride;
I'll boast a Saviour crucified,
And, oh, may this my portion be,
My Saviour not ashamed of me!
Joseph Grigg.

July 8.

Render . . . to all their dues. — Romans xiii. 7.

Render therefore unto Cæsar the things which are Cæsar's; and unto God the things that are God's. — Matt. xxii. 21.

THIS answer of our Lord evokes our admiration of his wisdom in dealing with his hypocritical adversaries. But now that eighteen centuries have passed, it remains one of the most convincing proofs of his wonderful wisdom as a teacher of men. Sadly enough it happens that those bearing his name have not profited by this plain discrimination. A large proportion of the public troubles in Christendom may be traced to our practical ignoring of the distinction between duties to God and duties to the government. The first Christian emperors sought to subordinate the Church to the State, and this error still prevails. The Papacy seeks to subordinate the State to the Church, while Puritanism sought to make Church and State identical. All these efforts have failed. In our country the correct principle prevails. But how many Protestants err in one or the other of the ways just indicated! In a free country more than in any other safety depends on following closely this principle laid down by our Master.

M. B. Riddle

> May we thy bounties thus
> As stewards true receive,
> And gladly, as thou blessest us,
> To thee our first fruits give!
> — W. W. How.

July 9.

Clothed with white robes, and palms in their hands.
Rev. vii. 9.

He that overcometh, the same shall be clothed in white raiment; and I will not blot out his name out of the book of life, but I will confess his name before my Father, and before his angels. — Rev. iii. 5.

WHAT earnestness there must be in the life of a Christian if we either look upon how much he has to overcome, or how much he is in danger of losing! We, as Christians, have before us difficulties and temptations, enemies within and without, especially that dreadful and deadly disease, self-confidence, when we are pleased with what we are and therefore do not press on toward the goal unto the prize of the high calling of God in Christ Jesus. But no matter what is in our way it ought not to discourage, still less deject us, as if it would be almost hopeless to think of overcoming. The last words in our text not only show us the glorious things we may lose, but they at the same time hold up before our eyes what we will gain by continuing the fight till the last enemy is overcome; yea, they are properly promises that ought to give us courage and strength to hold out to the end. Then what a victory, — white raiment, having our names in the book of life as members of the heavenly commonwealth, and confessed by our Saviour as being his before God and the world!

T. N. Hasselquist

Ten thousand times ten thousand,
In sparkling raiment bright,
The armies of the ransomed saints
Throng up the steeps of light.

'T is finished, all is finished,
Their fight with death and sin!
Fling open wide the golden gates
And let the victors in!

Dean Alford.

July 10.

He shall come to be glorified in his saints.—2 Thess. i. 10.

Ye have heard how I said unto you, I go away, and come again unto you. If ye loved me, ye would rejoice, because I said, I go unto the Father: for my Father is greater than I.—John xiv. 28.

NO wonder the disciples were grieved at the thought of losing the familiar presence of their Lord. But whither was he going? To the Father. And would he return? Assuredly, and soon. In this twofold fact, therefore, they were to rejoice, if their love for the Master was intelligent and true: (1) They would be glad of his *ascension* to the place of his glory both for his sake and their own,—for his, because the humiliation he was enduring was thus about to be replaced by a corresponding exaltation; for their own, because in this same exaltation the assurance was to be found that the great salvation was at last achieved. (2) The final step is thus about to be taken for his *speedy return* in the person of another and better Comforter than himself,—that of the Holy Spirit. In all this Christ exults in the superiority of his Father who is now recalling him,—superiority in view of that stupendous method of grace which originated with the Father, and who, having sent his Son to mediate it in his name and as his willing servant, promised to reward so signal a service by peopling heaven with those multitudes of the redeemed who shall forever make that abode of bliss resound with the rapturous acclaim: "Salvation unto our God which sitteth on the throne, and unto the Lamb."

Joseph R. Wilson.

    Hark, those bursts of acclamation!
    Hark, those loud triumphant chords!
    Jesus takes the highest station;
      Oh, what joy the sight affords!
    Crown him, crown him,
      "King of kings and Lord of lords."
                              Kelly.

𝕷𝖔𝖗𝖉, is it 𝕴? — Matt. xxvi. 22.

Verily, verily, I say unto you, that one of you shall betray me. — John xiii. 21.

FROM the foreknowledge here displayed it results that so shocking an event as the betrayal of Christ by a disciple, which some might allege as grounding at least a suspicion against Christianity, is rescued from even a seeming support of such an objection, and becomes itself a "true yoke-fellow" in the grand array of Christian evidences (v. 19). Judas revolted from the Master; but the Master had foretold it. The shock was broken, his Messiahship was confirmed.

2. Judas heard the prediction, and therein his own characterization at the lips of the Son of God, and also those concurrent words, "It had been good for that man if he had not been born." Thus a rehearsal of the judgment day, an earnest of future punishment.

3. The betrayer, said Jesus, shall be one of you. This emphatic word brings home the question, Am I treacherous to him? Is there no Judas-way in me?

4. Jesus was "troubled in spirit." What compassion toward the traitor, although justice must take its course! How great an evil to his eye is sin! And that trouble of his spirit was but as the twilight to the then fast-coming darkness of Gethsemane and Calvary. Amazing love to sinners!

Wm. R. Nicholson

Blest Jesus, come and rule my heart,
And make me wholly thine,
That I may never more depart,
Nor grieve thy love divine.
Benjamin Cleveland.

July 12.

Feed the flock of God.—1 Peter v. 2.

Who then is a faithful and wise servant, whom his Lord hath made ruler over his household, to give them meat in due season? Blessed is that servant, whom his Lord when he cometh shall find so doing. Verily I say unto you, That he shall make him ruler over all his goods.—Matt. xxiv. 45–47.

A FAITHFUL and wise servant, or steward, as Luke calls him, watches — that is, cares for — the interests of his Lord. This is one of those striking parabolic pictures for which our Lord's teachings are distinguished. It is here in the form of a question which each of us must put to his own soul: "Am I this faithful and wise servant or steward?" The main characteristics of such a servant are that he should be faithful and wise. Paul writes, "It is required of a steward that a man be found faithful." The proof of his faithfulness is his watchfulness. The punishment of a sentinel who sleeps on his post has in all ages been death. An unwatchful steward who allows his master's goods to be stolen has his portion with the hypocrites; but let us be watchful, faithful, and wise, and we shall hear the Lord saying, "Blessed is that servant."

Especially are our Lord's words addressed to ministers, who are "stewards of the mysteries of God," which demands fidelity to Christ as servants, fidelity to the people as dispensers of his Word. To be thus faithful we must be full of faith. And then as to the blessedness, the reward of faithful stewardship, we can only say in the words of the beloved John, "It doth not yet appear what we shall be, but we know that when he shall appear we shall be like him: for we shall see him as he is."

S. D. Alexander

> 'T is not a cause of small import
>   The pastor's care demands,
> But what might fill an angel's heart,
>   And filled a Saviour's hands.
>
> Philip Doddridge.

July 13.

Thy testimonies also are my delight. — Psalm cxix. 24.

It is written, Man shall not live by bread alone, but by every word that proceedeth out of the mouth of God. — Matt. iv. 4.

JESUS meets temptation as a man. Had he used divine power to destroy the Tempter, his victory could neither guide our conduct nor inspire our hope. He fought as we may fight; he won as we may win. He never performed miracles for his own comfort. "It is written," — by this weapon he conquered Satan in each conflict. "The sword of the Spirit, which is the Word of God," was his weapon. On each occasion he cites words from Deuteronomy. He found in this book, against which the critics are hurling their poisoned arrows, an armory of defence. In opposing this book rationalism tilts with divinity. Moses taught the people that God in giving manna was able to feed them with something other than bread; so Jesus teaches us faith in God's power to help us by whatever he appoints. Jesus was a profound thinker; he went to the heart of truth. The man who tries to live on bread alone, dies. A soul cannot eat wheat; earthly food feeds earthly life. But man is made to be a son of God; he is a child of eternity, a possible heir of heaven. His spiritual nature, as truly as his physical, must have its appropriate food. The heart is made for God; it cries out for him. A living soul needs a living God. A "thing" may be satisfied with things; a true man needs and must have as his portion the true and living God. This great truth is man's highest glory. Happy they who turn from that which is not bread to eat of the true and "living bread which came down out of heaven."

R. S. MacArthur.

Oh, grant us grace, almighty Lord,
To read and mark thy holy Word,
Its truth with meekness to receive,
And by its holy precepts live!

Benjamin Beddome.

July 14.

God hath given to us eternal life. — 1 John v. 11.

This is the bread which cometh down from heaven, that a man may eat thereof, and not die. — John vi. 50.

WHAT was the lesson of the manna to the Israelites? Moses explained it thus: "That he might make thee know that man doth not live by bread only, but by every word that proceedeth out of the mouth of God."

To the saints of the Old Testament the Word of God was the food of the soul. With how much greater ardor and gratitude should we receive this heavenly food! The Word of God has now become incarnate, has dwelt among us in his ineffable purity and holiness, pitied us, loved us, taught us, healed us, suffered and died for us, risen again on our behalf, and promised to come in glory to receive us to himself, in the mean time offering himself to us in the depths of his love, and by the most simple rite, as the true bread from heaven, the food of our souls.

Let us feed on Christ, feed on him daily and constantly. When we approach his table, let us not busy ourselves with curious questions about the nature of the mystery we celebrate, but make it our one concern to receive into our hearts our crucified Saviour. So we shall know what it is to dwell in him, and have him dwelling in us, — to be made like Christ, having within us that new and endless life which comes from Christ and from God, and which bears in it the promise of a glorious resurrection at the last day.

Henry Blodget

True Bread of life, in pitying mercy given,
   Long famished souls to strengthen and to feed,
Christ Jesus, Son of God, true Bread of heaven,
   Thy flesh is meat, thy blood is drink indeed.

H. Bonar.

July 15.

Lest haply ye be found even to fight against God.
ACTS V. 39.

Forbid him not: for there is no man which shall do a miracle in my name, that can lightly speak evil of me. For he that is not against us is on our part. — MARK ix. 39, 40.

WE are taught that *working for* and with Christ is the way to church union.

Opposition to deceit and violence, to wrong acts or opinions, is opposition to evil spirits, and real alliance with "the Son of God," who "was manifested that he might destroy the works of the Devil."

What work is so "mighty" as that which dispossesses the Devil of his captives and victims? Can it be done except by the truth and authority inseparable from the "Name which is above every name?" It *may* be done without the sanction for the moment of habitual association with professed followers of the Lord. Nevertheless, whenever with the weapons of truth one fights against the spirits of evil, he is already on the way to full fellowship with all the disciples. The work needs no authority beyond the power to do it received from the Master; but the doer needs for himself the support and comfort of those who are "like minded." The disciples are forbidden to hinder those who are resisting evils in Christ's name, since they will at length come into open unity with all the brethren.

Wm. V. V. Mabon

Work, for the night is coming,
　Work through the sunny noon;
Fill brightest hours with labor,
　Rest comes sure and soon.
　　　　　　　ANNIE L. WALKER.

July 16.

The liberal soul shall be made fat. — Prov. xi. 25.

Give, and it shall be given unto you; good measure, pressed down, and shaken together, and running over, shall men give into your bosom. For with the same measure that ye mete withal it shall be measured to you again. — Luke vi. 38.

GIVE not stintedly, but freely, liberally, cheerfully, not as if driven by a need, except the need of a heart which must satisfy its own motions of love. It is therefore not simply a command from the Master by the authority of the Lord, but it is the challenge of one who is the believer's friend, and who by his wisdom knows how the exercise of this grace will enrich the giver with an abundance of all that is best. It is the voice of him whose love for his is ever actively desiring that his followers shall rejoice and be glad in the enjoyment of all that is enduring.

These words of our Saviour bear to us the thought which the apostle refers to when he says, "It is more blessed to give than to receive." Now while it is true that God's goodness is fullest in a spiritual sense, we do hurt to his truth and we fail to reach the intention of the words of Jesus in this text when we refer their application either to the world to come, or to the sphere of purely spiritual things. It is this life which is to be enriched by the free and loving emulation of the example of Jesus. It is here and now that the seed we sow with ungrudging spirit and an open hand shall bring us the promised return. Because " God *loveth* a cheerful giver," therefore it is that "he which soweth bountifully shall reap bountifully" (see 2 Cor. ix. 6–13). Thus, then, giving with loving heart and hand for Jesus' sake is the surest way of refreshing, beautifying, and enriching most abundantly our own life. Thus will his disciples be more like the Master both in spirit and deed.

D. Earnest Klopsh

Who sparingly his seed bestows,
  He sparingly shall also reap;
But whoso plentifully sows,
  The plenteous sheaves his hand shall heap.
THOMAS COTTERILL.

July 17.

Yet will I trust in him. — Job xiii. 15.

And blessed is he, whosoever shall not be offended in me. — Matt. xi. 6.

THE occasions of offence in the Christian life are many, and come from every side. John the Baptist was offended because he was imprisoned. The sisters Mary and Martha were offended when their brother, whom Jesus loved, languished and died. So it is still, and so it will be always. What Christ does we know not now. His conduct toward his dearest friends is often apparently very strange; they know disappointment, disaster, and death. As with Jacob of old, all things seem to be against them. Nevertheless it is Christ who gives sight to the blind and preaches the gospel to the poor. He it is who, though he was rich, for our sakes became poor. In the multitude of our thoughts within us these comforts should delight our souls. Come what may, the love of the cross can never fail; Jesus Christ is the same yesterday, to-day, and forever. Blessed indeed is it, though nature faints and fails, to look beyond the clouds into his face and say, "Though he slay me, yet will I trust him," then heaven comes down our souls to greet, and we have songs in the night, in the assurance that the same hand that was pierced for us is leading us by the right way to the city of habitation.

Chas. H. Mason Cox.

> Far, far above thy thought
> His counsel shall appear,
> When fully he the work has wrought
> That caused thy needless fear.
>
> J. Wesley *(Translation).*

July 18.

They were all filled with the Holy Ghost. — Acts ii. 4.

Receive ye the Holy Ghost. — John xx. 22.

IT is the peculiar excellence and glory of our religion that it is spiritual; that the soul of man is quickened, enlightened, sanctified, and consoled by the indwelling presence of the spirit of the eternal God. To his disciples, in view of the great work to which he had called them, — the evangelization of the world, — Jesus said, " Receive ye the Holy Ghost." The gift of the Holy Spirit was not peculiar to the chosen ambassadors of the Christ. The same gift is expressly promised " to them that obey him." The saints in Ephesus trusted in Jesus after they heard the word of truth, the gospel of their salvation, and after they believed they were sealed with the Holy Spirit which had been promised. Saint Paul exhorts his brethren to pray "always with all prayer and supplication in the Spirit;" and assures them that he prays to our Lord Jesus Christ, of whom the whole family in heaven and earth is named, that he would grant them according to the riches of his glory to be strengthened with might by his spirit in the inner man. This blessing is needed by Christians now; and it may be possessed and enjoyed by faith, love, obedience, and prayer. Be assured that " our Father which art in heaven " will freely " give the Holy Spirit to them that ask him."

B. B. Tyler.

  O Holy Spirit, now descend on me
   As showers of rain upon the thirsty ground!
  Cause me to flourish as a spreading tree;
   May all thy precious fruits in me be found!
            C. Forsyth.

July 19.

𝔜e have known the 𝔉ather. — 1 John ii. 13.

O righteous Father, the world hath not known thee: but I have known thee, and these have known that thou hast sent me. And I have declared unto them thy name, and will declare it: that the love wherewith thou hast loved me may be in them, and I in them. — John xvii. 25, 26.

SO ends the tender intercessory prayer of our Lord. First it was the " Father," then the " holy Father," and now it is the "righteous Father" to whom the appeal is made, — righteous to condemn the faithless and to justify the believer, — ready to impute his righteousness to those who rely on the atonement of his Son, and to implant that righteousness in those who seek conformity to his image.

But the unbelieving world knows not God as the fountain of forgiving love. This knowledge can be communicated only by one who knows the Father as the Son knows him, in the riches of his grace and glory. Christ comes bearing a royal commission, and what he is sent to do he will surely accomplish. To all who receive him he will make immediate and continued revelations of what is implied in the Father's saving, sanctifying, glorifying name, — once a name which the trembling worshipper scarcely dared to pronounce, but now a name inspiring confidence, love, and joy; once a name expressive of eternal being only, but now of eternal love. God, therefore, may be known, not as " the power without us that works for righteousness," but as a personal Father, revealing himself to our consciousness and to our affection.

Moses D. Hoge

> Regard thine own eternal prayer,
>   And send a peaceful answer down.
> To us thy Father's name declare;
>   Unite and perfect us in one.
>
> C. Wesley.

July 20.

There is but one ... Lord Jesus Christ. — 1 Cor. viii. 6.

But be not ye called Rabbi: for one is your Master, even Christ; and all ye are brethren. — Matt. xxiii. 8.

BOTH by precept and example our blessed Saviour teaches us the greatness and the glory of a meek and lowly spirit, — that superiority comes by subjection; that mastership goes hand in hand with ministration; that the only true greatness is the greatness of him that serves. He washed his disciples' feet, and said, "I am among you as he that serveth." He declares of himself that he came "not to be ministered unto, but to minister," and says, "Whosoever will be chief among you let him be your servant." How often he said, "He that exalteth himself shall be abased, and he that humbleth himself shall be exalted"! The teaching of his entire ministry, and especially the teaching of his cross, is against the desire to be called "Rabbi."

One is our Master, even Christ. How deep a want of our being is answered here! We must have a master; we were formed for reverencing and loving, for learning, following, and obeying. Such a master we have in Jesus Christ our Lord; and upon him we may expend those feelings of boundless admiration and passionate attachment and devotion which we may cherish for no earthly master. Let us sit at his feet and learn of him. Let us take our orders from him. Let us be loyal to him.

J. Spangler Kieffer

O Master, let me walk with thee
In lowly paths of service free.
Tell me thy secret; help me bear
The strain of toil, the fret of care.
Washington Gladden.

July 21.

Shewed toward his name, in that ye have ministered to the saints. — Heb. vi. 10.

For ye have the poor always with you; but me ye have not always. — Matt. xxvi. 11.

"THE poor shall never cease out of the land." Opportunities to relieve the needy will never be wanting; but the opportunity to anoint Christ for his burial came but once in the history of the world. A few days later he was to be nailed to the cross. The Christ as we have him on that day in the house of Simon, under the shadow of Calvary, will never in this way come precisely over this same path of sorrow again. As he there is, he will not always be with them. This sort of anointing was possible only then. It was Mary's great opportunity, and with what an enthusiasm of self-forgetting zeal did she seize upon and improve it! The poorest offerings of love, of grateful love, are well pleasing to our Saviour. With our bodies no less than with our spirits, with our mite no less than with our millions we can acceptably glorify him.

We belong to Christ. This is our only comfort, living and dying. Ourselves we must consecrate to him as a living sacrifice. But do not fail to break the alabaster box, else the sweet-scented spikenard will not anoint his body, nor its pleasant fragrance fill his house.

[signature]

> In them thou mayst be clothed and fed,
> And visited and cheered,
> And in their accents of distress,
> Our Saviour's voice is heard.
>
> Philip Doddridge.

July 22.

God, which always causeth us to triumph in Christ.
2 Cor. ii. 14.

In the world ye shall have tribulation: but be of good cheer; I have overcome the world. — John xvi. 33.

WITH what frankness Christ tells that the vessel of the Church shall not move over smooth seas, with favoring breezes filling her sails till she reaches the desired haven. No, not thus, but on the contrary, wind and wave shall often threaten shipwreck and disaster, though all shall be well at last. Listen to these words of the Lord Jesus, you who, like Baruch (Jer. xlv. 3), are moaning, "Woe is me now, for the Lord hath added grief to my sorrow!" Listen to the Lord's words you who, like David (1 Sam. xxvii. 1), are saying, "I shall one day perish by the hand of Saul!"

Perhaps your desponding heart replies, "This is tantalizing me, not helping. For he may well overcome, but that is not the same as my overcoming!" Is it not? Think again, — think better of the Lord's most gracious words. Did he not say (John xiv. 19), "Because I live, ye shall live also"? Every branch in the Vine is one with the Vine. Every believing sinner is a branch in the Vine. You were united to Christ the first moment you leaned on him. The Holy Spirit who led you to Christ did also unite you to him; and that union stands fast, however great be your trials and tribulations.

It was in your feeble nature ("The flesh is weak!" — Matt. xxvi. 41) that he overcame tribulation, — tribulation ten thousand times more terrible than yours, — and he is following up his victory when from day to day the feeblest disciple, simply leaning on him, is shown to be mightier than all hell, and stronger than the world. He would lose his fame as conqueror if you, a member of his body, were to fail.

Andrew A. Bonar.

Thou dost conduct thy people
  Through torrents of temptation;
Nor will we fear, while thou art near,
  The fire of tribulation.   C. Wesley.

July 23.

I will bless thee . . . because thou hast obeyed my voice.
GEN. xxii. 17, 18.

Stretch forth thine hand. — MATT. xii. 13.

PICTURE to yourself the scene at the moment when this command broke forth from the lips of our Lord: there is the hand, feeling, motion all gone, its executive power utterly lost; there is Jesus, the divine healer, able to restore it whole as the other. We see these; but is that all? Nay, but between these two figures — this divine Person and this withered hand — there is a channel through which the almighty energy of the one flows with life-giving, curative virtue into the dry and shrunken form of the other. What is that channel? The man believed Jesus could heal him. Was it that? In part, but not all. When Jesus said, Stretch forth thine hand, the man's faith prompted him to instant obedience; although he had tried to do this a thousand times before, and had not been able, yet such was his belief in Jesus that without a moment's hesitation he again makes the effort, and it was just in the act of making this effort that he felt the healing vigor given to him. What then is the lesson that this incident has for us? Surely this, — that when Volition is wedded to Faith, Omnipotence will bless the banns. Here lies the secret of all strength. Apply it to whatever emergency or requirement, and it will never fail. Are you enslaved to some habit which Christ bids you put off? Look to him and make an effort at freedom, and the bonds will be burst. Is a hard task imposed upon you, and do you feel inadequate to it? Trust in him and make the effort, and you will find that what is impossible with man is possible with God.

W. F. V. Bartlett

My highest hope to be where, Lord, thou art,
    To lose myself in thee my richest gain ;
To do thy will the habit of my heart,
    To grieve the Spirit my severest pain.
MONSELL.

His own reward according to his own labour. — 1 Cor. iii. 8.

For the Son of man shall come in the glory of his Father with his angels; and then he shall reward every man according to his works. — MATT. xvi. 27.

THESE words of our Saviour immediately follow the announcement of his impending death in Jerusalem, and the call to all his disciples to a life of self-sacrifice for him. They present a powerful incentive to duty by showing us that the rewards of the future will more than compensate for all the trials of the present, however severe.

As our blessed Lord, in view of his baptism of suffering, in the true spirit of trustful obedience nerved himself for the dread conflict by looking forward to the "joy that was set before him," so he would stimulate our faith and courage by directing our thoughts to that great day of assize when those who have suffered with him shall also be glorified with him. When he comes in the glory of his Father with his angels, when the judgment is set and the race of man is judged by the "Son of man," who will not rejoice to have lived for Christ, like Christ, and if God has so ordered it, suffered for Christ?

John L. Nevius

Stand up! stand up for Jesus!
 The strife will not be long;
This day, the noise of battle,
 The next, the victor's song:
To him that overcometh,
 A crown of life shall be;
He with the King of glory
 Shall reign eternally.

S. DUFFIELD.

July 25.

He knoweth the way that I take.—JOB xxiii. 10.

I know thy works, that thou art neither cold nor hot: I would thou wert cold or hot. So then because thou art lukewarm, and neither cold nor hot, I will spue thee out of my mouth.—REV. iii. 15, 16.

HOW searching are the eyes of God, "discerning the thoughts and intents of the heart"! How naked our souls "to him with whom we have to do"! His vision is both telescopic and microscopic, seeing us afar off and magnifying our actions in their true light. Where art thou? he asks us as he did Adam. What doest thou here? he asks as he did Elijah. We are to examine ourselves to see whether we are in the faith or not. In the light of eternity where do I stand? Am I a Laodicean, and lukewarm? Once my faith was bright and warm; now but a few dying embers left. Have I just enough religion to lull my conscience into a false security? Lukewarm; he wants me to be either cold or hot (boiling, fervent) rather than lukewarm; yes, even cold (ice cold), rather than lukewarm. Does our text mean he would rather have me no Christian than a lukewarm professor? No, it does not question the state as much as the *tendency* of my heart. Lukewarmness, if I am going from cold to hot, is desirable; but if I am passing from hot to cold, it is worse than coldness. What says the thermometer; which way points the barometer of my heart? Am I inclining to evil or to good,—growing in grace or in evil? Lord, help me to return to thee! "The peaceful hours I once enjoyed," may they return with richer, fuller peace! "Oh, for a closer walk with God!" Take a coal from off thine altar, dearest Lord, and warm my heart with holy fire.

> Low at thy feet my soul would lie;
> Here safety dwells, and peace divine.
> Still let me live beneath thine eye,
> For life, eternal life is thine.
>
> ANNE STEELE.

July 26.

Children are a heritage of the Lord. — Psalm cxxvii. 3.

Whosoever shall receive one of such children in my name, receiveth me. — Mark ix. 37.

THIS is not a charter for an orphan asylum, but an index to individual duty. Every home ought at some time to have a child, and every child a home. If God denies us the boon, there are forlorn hearts of other parentage, and wistful faces in plenty that appeal for a father's love and a mother's care.

But whether the children come to us by birth or by adoption, we are to receive them in Jesus' name, — not merely for the love they bring us, still less for any help they may give, but for what we can do for them in the name of Christ. We are to make our embrace like the very arms of Jesus, and the putting forth of our hands a benediction on their lives; and great shall be our reward. Christ says to us as did Pharaoh's daughter to the mother of Moses, "Take this child and nurse it for me and I will give thee thy wages." Our wages are himself. In entertaining strangers we may find an angel unawares. But in receiving and training a child for Christ, Jesus is sure to be our guest. He has joint interest with us in the work, and considers himself welcomed in the welcome which we give his helpless wards.

Joseph F. Elder.

> Lord, we tremble, for we know
> How the fierce malicious foe,
> Wheeling round his watchful flight,
> Keeps them ever in his sight;
> Spread thy pinions, King of kings,
> Hide them safe beneath thy wings,
> Lest the ravenous bird of prey
> Stoop, and bear the brood away!
>
> COWPER.

Now to appear in the presence of God for us. — HEB. ix. 24.

And for their sakes I sanctify myself, that they also might be sanctified through the truth. — JOHN xvii. 19.

JESUS lived and died for the benefit of others; he pleased not himself, did nothing for himself. All was done to honor God and to save mankind. About to go unto the Father, he prays for his apostles. He had given them his Father's words, and would, when just ready to ascend to heaven, give them the gospel and his law of pardon for the whole world. Anxious to have them filled with the spirit of truth, and their entire energies devoted to the work of making the truth known to others, he prays the Father to set them apart, or "sanctify them through the truth," on the plea that it was for their sakes and to this end he had given up everything else and sanctified himself.

In this prayer Jesus includes with the apostles *all who believe on him through their word*, and all such can learn from it how he intercedes for them in heaven. While praying to their Father to sanctify them through his Word, and striving to follow Jesus, this text will assure them of a union with him in action, in prayer, and in truth, — a union soon to be consummated in eternal glory.

Donald Crawford

Lord, in all thy power and glory,
   Still thy thoughts and eyes are here,
Watching o'er thy ransomed people,
   To thy gracious heart so dear.
Thou for us art interceding,
   Everlasting is thy love,
And a blessed rest preparing
   In our Father's house above.

J. G. DECK.

July 28.

For not the hearers of the law are just before God, but the doers. — Romans ii. 13.

Take heed therefore how ye hear. — Luke viii. 18.

THE gift of hearing is properly one of the valued endowments of life. How intricate and delicate is the structure of the ear, and how great the loss when by disease, accident, or advancing age our hearing is impaired or destroyed! This faculty is frequently mentioned in Scripture, usually in connection with serious counsel or warning.

The free use of any favor always implies the possibility of its abuse, and our Saviour evidently had an eye to this danger when he said, "Take heed therefore how ye hear!" In the parable of the sower he has just said, "The seed is the Word of God." This may fall upon the fickle heart, like the thin soil on a ledge of barren rock, or upon the pathway of a worldly life, to be snatched away by greedy fowl of adventure, or where thorns of cares, riches, and pleasures of this life will surely choke its growth.

The "therefore" is to be emphasized. There is danger that our hearing of gospel truth will not be appreciative, receptive, and of the assimilating kind, not as good ground bringing forth thirty, sixty, and a hundred fold (Matt. xiii. 8). *Therefore take heed how ye hear!*

David Van Horne.

> My soul rejoices to pursue
> The steps of him I love,
> Till glory breaks upon my view
> In brighter worlds above.
>
> Cowper.

July 29.

Wounded in the house of my friends. — Zech. xiii. 6.

Verily I say unto you, One of you which eateth with me shall betray me. — Mark xiv 18.

WE are appalled at the sin of Judas. Yet, as when Jesus said this word the other disciples asked, "Lord, is it I?" we may well consider whether we ourselves are not in danger of such sin.

It is not, indeed, wise to exaggerate our faults as though every failure were a betrayal. Some who followed Jesus after awhile "went back, and walked no more with him," and some in his hour of trial "forsook him and fled," and Peter "denied" him; but only Judas betrayed him.

When one called a Christian lives in such open sin as to bring dishonor upon Christ, so that "the name of God is blasphemed through" him, is it not betraying Christ? Or if one misleads and perverts those younger, "offending the little ones which believe" in Jesus, of which sort of offenders our Lord said, "It were better for him that a millstone were hanged about his neck and he were cast into the sea," is not this to betray Christ?

Seeing that such sins have not ceased, let us fear, and pray that no temptation without, or weakness within, may make us false to the Lord at whose table we have eaten.

Andrew Longacre

Oh, to grace how great a debtor
  Daily I'm constrained to be!
Let thy goodness, like a fetter,
  Bind my wandering heart to thee.
Prone to wander, Lord, I feel it,
  Prone to leave the God I love.
Here's my heart; oh, take and seal it,
  Seal it for thy courts above.
                        Robert Robinson.

July 30.

And mercy rejoiceth against judgment. — JAMES ii. 13.

O Jerusalem, Jerusalem, thou that killest the prophets, and stonest them which are sent unto thee, how often would I have gathered thy children together, even as a hen gathereth her chickens under her wings, and ye would not! Behold, your house is left unto you desolate. — MATT. xxiii. 37, 38.

JESUS uttered this intense cry of love, grief, and warning at sight of the doomed city. Jerusalem then represented the Church and chosen nation; and in her external glory she vied with the proudest cities of earth. But the Saviour bewailed her moral and spiritual decline, for it had filled the measure of iniquity, and justice waited on mercy. The people formed rival sects, persecuted God's messengers of grace, and welcomed false prophets and false Christs. The rulers believed not in Jesus, and "gathered together against the Lord and against his Christ," purposing to kill him and seize his inheritance. In them the Saviour saw sin in its most damning features; yet "straitened" to cleanse them by his blood, he makes this melting appeal. Surely, "waters cannot quench nor floods drown" the love of Jesus for perishing sinners. But if we refuse him, nothing can "hide us from the wrath of the Lamb."

Our Lord Jesus has "all power in heaven and in earth," that he may save the lost. The Church is the recipient, depositary, and dispenser of his saving grace. Does she own her King? Is she united in the love of truth? Do her ministry and members co-operate with him? Let us beware of the blood of precious souls. Join not in the prevalent cry, "We will not have this man to reign over us." Be ready and eager to "bring forth the royal diadem and crown him Lord of all." Jerusalem's desolations still speak to each one.

J. C. K. Milligan.

Our day of grace is sunk in night; thy noon is in its prime.
Oh, turn and see thy Saviour's face in this accepted time!
So, Gentile, may Jerusalem a lesson prove to thee,
And in the New Jerusalem thy home forever be.   HEBER.

July 31.

𝔓repare to meet thy God. — Amos iv. 12.

They that were foolish took their lamps, and took no oil with them; but the wise took oil in their vessels with their lamps. — Matt. xxv. 3, 4.

LAMPS, but no oil! There was preparation to meet the bridegroom, and confidence, but a vain confidence, in an insufficient preparation. When the bridegroom came, the foolish virgins were left behind and the door was shut. We who call ourselves Christians have made our preparation and are waiting for Christ to come. We all have lamps, which represent what is external in our Christianity, whether it be rites, or creed, or works of charity, or morality, or zeal for our church. But have we oil, that true spiritual consecration of the soul which alone can fill outward acts with light and life?

The lamps may be of various shapes and patterns, but the oil must be the same in all. Whether, in burning, it shines out as repentance or faith or good works or worship, its essence is love, pure unselfish love to God and man. Where this love is wanting, there is no true spiritual life and no sufficient preparation to meet our Lord when he comes.

George Washburn

Beware, my soul, take thou good heed lest thou in slumber lie,
And, like the five, remain without, and knock, and vainly cry;
But watch, and bear thy lamp undimmed, and Christ shall gird thee on
His own bright wedding-robe of light, the glory of the Son.

G. Moultrie.

August 1.

That also he should gather together in one the children of God. — JOHN xi. 52.

And other sheep I have, which are not of this fold: them also I must bring, and they shall hear my voice; and there shall be one fold, and one shepherd. — JOHN x. 16.

OUR blessed Master, looking around upon his followers, looked also beyond the few who were before him, beyond the walls of the sacred city, beyond the boundaries of the Holy Land, to the whole world; and among people of every age, of every clime, he recognized his own and claimed them as his. As Christ said "other sheep," he saw you and me; he saw his own, his chosen ones, among the rich and poor, the abhorred and the despised, the savage Africans and humble Koreans asking to be taught, and even the gospel-hardened of our own land turning a deaf ear to the divine call; and as he saw these "others," he said, "Them also I must bring." They are his; he *must* bring them. And he has left those who love him to take his place and "in his name" to bring them. He knows *them* and they will know *him*; they will heed God's call.

And *all* these shall be one. A sweet promise is ours, a glorious fulfilment awaits us. There shall be one flock, one shepherd. We shall all be "like him." We shall all be of the Shepherd's heart and mind. No difference, — kings and beggars, rich and poor, civilized and heathen, "barbarian, Scythian, bond and free," *all* one in the full enjoyment of the freedom, the wealth, the knowledge, and the kingship that has come to us as joint-heirs with Christ!

Then there will be no "other sheep," for all shall have been made "perfect in one," — "one flock, one shepherd."

H. G. Underwood.

> We all shall think and speak the same
>   Delightful lesson of thy grace,
> One undivided Christ proclaim,
>   And jointly glory in thy praise.   C. WESLEY.

AUGUST 2.

Whosoever doeth not righteousness is not of God.
1 JOHN iii. 10.

That which is born of the flesh is flesh; and that which is born of the Spirit is spirit. — JOHN iii. 6.

"A GREAT and universal proposition, — that which is begotten carries within itself the nature of that which begat it." Christ is teaching Nicodemus the necessity of the new birth. He had been born of the flesh, physically and intellectually developed, socially and even religiously cultivated; but the life he now sought came from another and higher germ. As we cannot cultivate the vegetable into animal, so the physical cannot grow into the spiritual. Each has its own seed and fruit. Christ is the seed of the kingdom. " In him was life; and the life was the light of men." " He that hath the Son hath life; and he that hath not the Son of God hath not life."

True piety is more than sentiment or creed; it is life. " Christ in you the hope of glory." Reader, have *you* been born of the Spirit? " Except a man be born again, he cannot see the kingdom of God."

Samuel H. Greene,

> Light immortal, Light divine,
> Visit thou these hearts of thine,
> And our inmost being fill.
> If thou take thy grace away,
> Nothing pure in man will stay,
> All his good is turned to ill.
>
> CASWALL *(translated)*.

August 3.

𝕷𝖊𝖙 𝖙𝖍𝖊 𝖕𝖊𝖆𝖈𝖊 𝖔𝖋 𝕲𝖔𝖉 𝖗𝖚𝖑𝖊 𝖎𝖓 𝖞𝖔𝖚𝖗 𝖍𝖊𝖆𝖗𝖙𝖘. — COL. iii. 15.

Peace be unto you. — JOHN xx. 21.

MAN is naturally at war with himself and with his Maker. Christ came to transform his heart, give him peace of conscience, and reconcile him to God. This he accomplished by submitting to death, through which he became the herald and dispenser of peace; and his parting benediction, "Peace be unto you," becomes, therefore, efficacious to believers during all time.

This peace is not the work of man, but the gift of God and the fruit of the Spirit, through "the truth as it is in Jesus." In its source, nature, and blessedness, it is supernatural, and transcends all human comprehension. It takes away the sting of guilt, silences the alarm of conscience, and gives assurance of pardon, reconciliation, and salvation. In all these respects the peace of Christ differs from that of this world, which can neither give nor take it away. It is real and self-evidencing, abides and comforts in prosperity and adversity, and lifts the soul of the believer so far above earth that he has his "conversation in heaven." And now, reader, may the peace of the Lord Jesus Christ, "which passeth all understanding," keep your heart and mind in the true faith unto everlasting life!

F. W. Conrad

Peace, perfect peace, in this dark world of sin?
The blood of Jesus whispers peace within.
Peace, perfect peace, by thronging duties pressed?
To do the will of Jesus, this is rest.
BICKERSTETH.

August 4.

Sorrow not, even as others which have no hope.
1 Thess. iv. 13.

Let not your heart be troubled: ye believe in God, believe also in me.
— John xiv. 1.

ALL Scripture is profitable, and given "that we through comfort of the Scriptures might have hope;" but some texts are specially precious, short, easily understood and remembered, full of meaning, of wide application, and specifics in all circumstances. These words, breathing kindness and comfort, were spoken by our Lord when his own spirit was sorely troubled, the gloom of Gethsemane and the shadow of the cross gathering thickly upon his soul; yet unmindful of his own great sorrow, his tender sympathy went out to his disconsolate and desponding disciples, who were filled with perplexity, anxiety, fear, and grief. Heart-trouble is an old, universal malady. How cheering to the sons of sorrow and daughters of distress are these words of the great Consoler! They are a sovereign balm for every wounded heart and a perfect panacea for all earthly trouble. Heard first in the upper room in Jerusalem, they have echoed ever since in the chambers of suffering and in the ears of the sorrowful. Faith in God as a living, loving Father is an antidote to all troubles arising from without.

Trust in the Lord, forever trust, and banish all your fears;
Strength in the Lord Jehovah dwells, eternal as his years.
WATTS.

August 5.

He that is spiritual judgeth all things. — 1 Cor. ii. 15.

Are ye also yet without understanding? — Matt. xv. 16.

THE question was asked his disciples by our Lord. Why should he have occasion to ask it? They had the sublimest and most comprehensive Teacher the world has ever seen, — he who is the Light of the world and who is made unto all his people wisdom as well as righteousness was their instructor. And yet they were without understanding, for the question implies the fact. Alas! it is equally true of all souls without divine illumination. A man may "understand all mysteries" in relation to the material universe, may weigh the gravity of the stars, tell their numbers, and measure their distances, and yet in the high sense in which the text suggests, may be without understanding. There are men whose names have reached the utmost bounds of civilization, who sit in the cabinets of princes and guide the destiny of nations, "wise men," "learned men," "influential men," as they are called, and yet they are without understanding, if they are without the indwelling and abiding presence of the Holy Spirit. For "the fear of the Lord is the beginning of wisdom: and the knowledge of the Holy is understanding."

William Adams

    Come, Light serene and still,
    Our inmost bosoms fill!
      Dwell in each breast;
    We know no dawn but thine.
    Send forth thy beams divine,
    On our dark souls to shine,
      And make us blest.

Ray Palmer *(Translation).*

AUGUST 6.

Whatsoever we ask, we receive of him. — 1 JOHN iii. 22.

Receive thy sight: thy faith hath saved thee. — LUKE xviii. 42.

IT was a blind man and a beggar to whom these gracious words were spoken. Only one said anything so kind to him. The multitude counted him a nuisance with his importunity, and angrily told him to keep still. The disciples gave him no encouragement. As in the case of the children brought to Jesus, they were cold, while their Lord was ardent with compassion. But the character of the "Son of David" was exactly drawn in the Psalms of David: "He shall deliver the needy when he crieth; the poor also, and him that hath no helper" (Psalm lxxii. 12). The more lonely, wretched, needy, and friendless any man was, the more sure was he of hearing and help from the great Deliverer.

The cry of need and of faith was the one thing the Master could never resist. "O woman, great is thy faith; be it unto thee even as thou wilt." "If ye have faith as a grain of mustard, . . . *nothing* shall be *impossible* to you."

Bartimæus went away with his eyes opened. That was his petition and request. What is yours? The Lord is just the "same Jesus" that he was that day. "What wilt thou?" "According to your faith be it unto you."

[signature: P. H. Marling]

   Look down in pity, Lord, we pray,
    On eyes oppressed by moral night,
   And touch the darkened lids, and say
    The gracious words, "Receive thy sight."
   Then in clear daylight shall we see
    Where walked the sinless Son of God,
   And aided by new strength from thee,
    Press onward in the path he trod.
           W. C. BRYANT.

August 7.

Whom have I in heaven but thee? — Psalm lxxiii. 25.

Simon, son of Jonas, lovest thou me more than these? — John xxi. 15.

JESUS in tender compassion thus addressed Simon Peter, who had thrice denied him, but who afterward "went out and wept bitterly." The avenue by which he approached him was love. "*Lovest* thou me?" The probe was gently inserted into the depths of his affections to prepare him for the sweet assurance of pardon, and for a wider and higher mission. The question was intensely personal, — "Lovest *thou me?*" Thus did the Saviour draw the sinner to himself "with cords of a man, with bands of love."

"Lovest thou me *more than these*" — thy brethren — love me? Wilt thou again protest, "Though *all men* shall be offended because of thee, yet will *I* never be offended"? In the school of experience he has learned so well the lessons of humility and self-distrust that he now avows his love most earnestly indeed, but without invidious and boastful comparisons.

We, too, should love Jesus with all our heart, mind, soul, and strength, — far more than we love our possessions, employments, friends, and relatives, yea, more than life itself (Luke xiv. 26, 33). We should with holy emulation ever strive to love him more than others love him, and to prove our love by an earnest and consecrated service, in obedience to the divine injunctions, — "Feed my lambs," "Feed my sheep," and "If ye love me, keep my commandments."

Robt. H. Nall.

> Thou art the sea of love,
> Where all my pleasures roll;
> The circle where my passions move,
> And centre of my soul.
>
> Watts.

AUGUST 8.

Prove all things. — 1 THESS. v. 21.

Take heed that no man deceive you. For many shall come in my name, saying, I am Christ; and shall deceive many. — MATT. xxiv. 4, 5.

THE Christ sat within a circle of disciples. They had just crossed "black Kidron." They had turned their backs on the city doomed to be "left desolate." "Day was dying in the west" as they ascended Olivet, and they found themselves facing one of the grandest sights of earth, for they were "over against the temple," the shadows of whose massive proportions lay across the valley and on the mountain side. No wonder that after gathering about their Master, those disciples ventured to inquire the time set for the destruction of such magnificence as well as for the time of his advent. Remarkable is this reply, for it matched their need, not their want. He gave them not information, but instruction. Better was it for them to be personally prepared than prophetically expert. Their inquiry evidenced danger. Their thinking was not clear. Confusion was imminent, and care must be taken. Judaic false Christs were coming. They did come; fifteen of them, so it is said. But every age has its false Messiahs and its fictitious religiousness. Believers, beware of deceivers.

James Chambers

Enable with perpetual light
The dulness of our blinded sight;
Anoint and cheer our soilèd face
With the abundance of thy grace;
Keep far our foes, give peace at home;
Where thou art guide, no ill can come.
GREGORY THE GREAT *(translated)*.

AUGUST 9.

Is not this the Christ? — JOHN iv. 29.

Go your way, and tell John what things ye have seen and heard. — LUKE vii. 22.

THESE words contain the answer of Jesus to the disciples of John, who came to inquire as to his Messiahship. The Saviour says, "Go tell John what you have seen and heard." And what had these disciples seen and heard in the brief visit to Jesus? They had seen the eyes of the blind opened and the tongue of the dumb loosed; they had seen the lame, at his touch, walk forth with perfect soundness, and the leper, by his word, return to his home and friends perfectly whole; they had seen the dead rising from their graves and going forth in the enjoyment of life. Yes, more, to the poor, the despised, the outcast, a full, free salvation was preached. Go tell John these wondrous things, and he will see in them the fulfilment of the grand old prophecy of Isaiah about the Messiah.

How precious the privilege, that we may take all our care to Jesus! Does Jesus rest his Messiahship upon his works? Then let it be ours to show by our works that we have been with Jesus and learned of him. May our works be such as will open the eyes of those spiritually blind, to see this Jesus as the one altogether lovely, and unstop the deaf ears that they may hear the soul-saving strains of this gospel, and occasion multitudes of dead souls to rise and stand forth to battle for the cause of King Jesus!

J. D. Ewing.

How beauteous were the marks divine,
That in thy meekness used to shine,
That lit thy lonely pathway, trod
In wondrous love, O Son of God!   BISHOP A. C. COXE.

August 10.

Laying up in store for themselves a good foundation against the time to come. — 1 TIM. vi. 19.

And I say unto you, Make to yourselves friends of the mammon of unrighteousness; that, when ye fail, they may receive you into everlasting habitations. — LUKE xvi. 9.

CHRIST here calls money by a hard name. Not that money has any immoral quality in itself, but it gets its stigma from its habitual application by men to selfish and sordid ends. Yet Christ shows us another side, and tells us that this much-abused thing may become a real power in adjusting our relations to the kingdom of God. The selfish lust for money breeds hatred; yet money may be so used as to make friends in heaven.

Christ draws his illustration from a low level. He shows how an unfaithful steward turned his fraud to advantage by making friends of his master's creditors. "Take a lesson from this shrewd worldly policy," says Christ. "Every poor and helpless brother whose load you lighten by your benefactions, is knit to you by grateful love. The poor and sick and burdened shall greet you in heaven, saying, 'I was hungry and ye gave me meat; I was thirsty, and ye gave me drink; I was a stranger and ye took me in.' And the King shall say, 'Inasmuch as ye did it unto one of these my brethren, even these least, ye did it unto me.'"

Marvin Vincent

> But there are joys that cannot die,
>   With God laid up in store;
> Treasure beyond the changing sky,
>   Brighter than golden ore.
>
> PHILIP DODDRIDGE.

August 11.

The Lord knoweth them that are his. — 2 Tim. ii. 19.

I know thy works, and where thou dwellest, even where Satan's seat is: and thou holdest fast my name, and hast not denied my faith, even in those days wherein Antipas was my faithful martyr, who was slain among you, where Satan dwelleth. But I have a few things against thee, because thou hast there them that hold the doctrine of Balaam, who taught Balak to cast a stumblingblock before the children of Israel, to eat things sacrificed unto idols, and to commit fornication. — Rev. ii. 13, 14.

"I KNOW thy works," the Redeemer says to each of the seven angels and to us also. He knows our works and "the thoughts and intents of the heart." He knows that we dwell "where Satan's seat is," in days in which his faithful ones still suffer martyrdom. If by his grace we hold fast his name and do not deny the faith, he is the first to know and to commend it.

"But I have a few things against thee." He is "of purer eyes than to behold evil," and cannot "look on iniquity." The angel and the church are rebuked on account of those "that hold the doctrine of Balaam" and "the doctrine of the Nicolaitanes," for evil teaching leads to evil living. Has he "a few," or many "things" against us? "Who can understand his errors? Cleanse thou me from secret faults!" But few or many, he calls on us to repent.

He knows us, and that we may know him and ourselves, he has given us his Word, "for the word of God is quick and powerful, and sharper than any two-edged sword, piercing even to the dividing asunder of soul and spirit, and of the joints and marrow, and is a discerner of the thoughts and intents of the heart."

G. F. Knotel.

    Yet why, dear Lord, this tender care?
    Why doth thy hand so kindly rear
    A useless cumberer of the ground,
    On which so little fruit is found?

E. Scott.

August 12.

The Lord will perfect that which concerneth me.
PSALM cxxxviii. 8.

And this is the Father's will which hath sent me, that of all that which he hath given me I should lose nothing, but should raise it up again at the last day. And this is the will of him that sent me, that every one which seeth the Son, and believeth on him, may have everlasting life: and I will raise him up at the last day. — JOHN vi. 39, 40.

HOW precious are these texts! They point us to the ineffable joys which the Father has in store for "Christ's own." They twice make known to us "the will of the Father" and so unmistakably that none can doubt that God's thoughts toward us are "thoughts of peace." They proclaim the great salvation to be open and free to all men without exception, and its terms so easy that the serpent-bitten need but "look and live." They banish personal anxiety by demonstrating that they who are the "given to Christ of the Father," are they who "come" to him. In large capitals they set before us the certainty of the final perseverance of the saints. The "wounded spirit," wearied and oft borne back in the conflict, can rally under such an inspiration, and gather fresh strength in the thought, *It is the will of the Father that I should not be lost!*

God does no half-work. Not one of Christ's saints will be found imperfect at the last day. They will all be absolutely fitted for his service. Not one of them will be missing. Nothing that belongs to them will be lost.

A. A. Reinke

> Trust in him, ye saints, forever;
> He is faithful, changing never.
> Neither force nor guile can sever
> Those he loves from him.
>   KELLY.

August 13.

He that toucheth you toucheth the apple of his eye.
ZECH. ii. 8.

Even so, it is not the will of your Father which is in heaven, that one of these little ones should perish. — MATT. xviii. 14.

THE "little ones," whether little children or disciples of childlike character, are very dear to the heavenly Father. Their humility and gentleness may not seem admirable to the world, but in God's sight these qualities are better than the strength, self-confidence, and pride of those accounted great among men.

The good Shepherd, who has reclaimed these "little ones" and brought them to a place of safety, will not cease to care for them. The heavenly Father, who holds them in such estimation that they have guardians among those who ever stand in his presence, will not lightly regard any injury done to them. They who despise or put a stumbling-block before any of these little ones will surely bring upon themselves a terrible punishment; for these are kept by God as the apple of the eye, and he thinks of them continually. Their very helplessness endears them the more to him, and while all human might shall be smitten to the earth, these weak but trustful ones shall be eternally safe in the arms of his love.

Wm Cavan

> Now, these little ones receiving,
> Fold them in thy gracious arm;
> There, we know, thy Word believing,
> Only there, secure from harm.
>
> MUHLENBERG.

August 14.

Lord, shew us the Father. — JOHN xiv. 8.

He that believeth on me, believeth not on me, but on him that sent me. And he that seeth me seeth him that sent me. — JOHN xii. 44, 45.

"JESUS cried;" his voice then rang clearly through the temple's marble courts, as he uttered loudly this mystery of truth. So Jesus cries down through the ages to ourselves. The "cries" of Jesus, loud, loving, entreating, to heedless, self-deafened men!

"To believe, and to see." A few of those to whom he then cried did believe on him, were ready to follow, obey, that blessed voice. So, also, some of those to whom his cry now comes. But the "believing" involves the "seeing" Christ. As the heart yields to the cry of Jesus, in this belief comes, sooner or later, a mental and spiritual "vision" of the adorable One that floods the soul with joyous light.

To believe, and so to see, Christ is to do more, — it is to know the Father too; it is to reach God, the infinite One, and the glory unapproachable. Like Moses, trembling, we too desire to see. Now the truth of Christ's divinity and the mystery of the union of the Persons in the Godhead are here involved; we behold "God in Christ, reconciling the world unto himself." In the rapturous vision of Christ we believe, we see the Father himself; we behold, we reach unto God. O blessed anticipation of heaven's privilege, even here on earth! Think of seeing God! We do, in believing on Christ.

Listen to this "cry" of Jesus; believe Christ, and you shall see his beauty. In him you shall see the Father, and in time the full glories of the home above.

Anson P. Atterbury

    Thou art the way; to thee alone,
      From sin and death we flee.
    And he who would the Father seek,
      Must seek him, Lord, by thee.
                          BISHOP DOANE.

August 15.

What manner of persons ought ye to be? — 2 Peter iii. 11.

Watch therefore: for ye know not what hour your Lord doth come. But know this, that if the goodman of the house had known in what watch the thief would come, he would have watched, and would not have suffered his house to be broken up. Therefore be ye also ready: for in such an hour as ye think not the Son of man cometh. — Matt. xxiv. 42-44.

OUR Lord assured his disciples that he would rise from the dead, ascend to heaven, and when he had prepared a place there, would return and receive them to himself. After his ascension angels came down to repeat the promise. Peter preached it to the wondering Jews. Stephen saw heaven opened and Jesus ready to descend. The Thessalonians waited for the sublime event. Paul proclaimed it the "blessed hope." The Epistles present their exhortations in view of its near approach, — one book is devoted to its details, while the last message the ascended Lord sends down to earth is, "Behold, I am coming quickly," and the recorded prayer of the Church when truly listening is, "Even so come, Lord Jesus."

He is coming, not when men think, nor in the seasons and periods they have fixed, but unexpectedly. Therefore as a Christian discharge your responsibility. See that you really have life, for this sudden advent will break up the great house of Christendom, reveal the emptiness of much profession and the faithlessness of many stewards.

— I. M. Haldeman

Be ye as they that wait
   Always at the Bridegroom's gate;
Even though he tarry late,
   Watch, brethren, watch.

H. Bonar.

August 16.

Who, when he came, and had seen the grace of God, was glad. — Acts xi. 23.

Likewise, I say unto you, there is joy in the presence of the angels of God over one sinner that repenteth.
It was meet that we should make merry, and be glad: for this thy brother was dead, and is alive again; and was lost and is found. — Luke xv. 10, 32.

AMONG the angels, rather than by men. It is a divine inspiration thus to express the love to which our fallen nature wakes at last, and only after the bitter experiences of life. On the one side we see the idea of the celestial messengers, who always do acceptable service in heaven as they, taught by the "ineffable vision," recognize the possibilities of a new manhood in the faint sparks of genuine repentance, and strike anew their harps in praise of the love which saves that which is lost; on the other side, the father of a prodigal son, who has wearied his heart with knowledge of many sins and ingratitude, and felt almost sick unto death with hope deferred, then rushing forth to meet the lost one and take him to his bosom, forgetting the sorrows, blotting out the sins of the past, and lifting the ingrate as near as possible to his old place. Truly, the mind which had learned the heavenly art to join these two thoughts in such harmony and illustrated them in life was the Word of God, — the mind of that which is nearest all that we call God, his only begotten Son.

Charles H. Hall.

Through all the courts the tidings flew,
And spread the joy around;
The angels tuned their harps anew, —
The long-lost son is found.

UNKNOWN.

August 17.

I can do all things through Christ which strengtheneth me. — Phil. iv. 13.

Therefore all things whatsoever ye would that men should do to you, do ye even so to them. — Matt. vii. 12.

THIS command of our Lord was the Golden Rule of his own life. His heart, given to us, won our hearts for him. Love's conquest of self is its victory over others. But how almost impossible to place others on the throne of self! Therefore Jesus joined the hard requirement of duty with sweet words of promise: "If ye, being evil, know how to give good gifts unto your children, how much more shall your Father, which is in heaven, give the Holy Spirit to them that ask him." The promise fulfilled, the duty is easy.

Let us then to-day, communing first with God, go out into the selfish world, hoping and striving to live unselfish lives. If the *how much more* of our Father's heavenly measure shall gauge the power of his Spirit in our hearts, we will indeed be able to "follow the steps" of him who "came not to be ministered unto but to minister." And this measure is to "them that ask."

They may keep the Golden Rule who trust the Golden Promise.

> Grant, then, this one request,
>   Whatever be denied, —
> That love divine may rule my breast,
>   And all my actions guide.
>
> S. STENNETT *(altered).*

August 18.

For to me to live is Christ. — PHIL. i. 21.

He that findeth his life shall lose it: and he that loseth his life for my sake shall find it. — MATT. x. 39.

OUR present life is not an end, but a means to an end. Childhood is but a preparation for manhood and womanhood. If we set up an infantile standard of life, and seek to bring all the years of childhood and youth into subjection to it, we fail to reach the true life. Now, the whole of our earthly existence is but the infancy, the dawn of a life meant to expand and ripen into eternal blessedness. We are here to be educated for eternal life. Whatever of present enjoyment or advantage would interfere with our education for heaven, must be surrendered; and whatever loss of friends or fortune or earthly honor or pleasure may be necessary to maintain our Christian integrity must be accepted. What seems to be gain in the momentary advantages of wrongdoing will prove an eternal loss; and what seems to be loss in adhering to the right will be an everlasting gain.

Isaac Errett

What is my being, but for thee,
  Its sure support? Its noblest end
Thine ever-smiling face to see,
  And serve the cause of such a Friend.
                    PHILIP DODDRIDGE.

August 19.

Resist the Devil, and he will flee from you.
JAMES iv. 7.

Get thee hence, Satan: for it is written, Thou shalt worship the Lord thy God, and him only shalt thou serve. — MATT. iv. 10.

EVERY temptation of Satan is an attempt on his part to usurp what belongs to God. Christ could not worship him, for worship belongs to God alone. To obey Satan's least command is to disobey God. Whatsoever we give to Satan in the way of worship or service we take from God.

Satan is insolently aggressive, and the more dangerous because so. Look at his persistent assault on Christ. Our Lord was angered by his persistency; it is too often successful with us. Instead of growing friendlier with Satan's repetitions of temptation, let us consider each a greater insult than the preceding. The presence of Satan is an abomination to a pure one. He is the sum of evils. His smooth insinuations should excite horror, instead of winning us. We should be afraid to listen to his flattering promises. To effectually rid ourselves of Satan we must peremptorily order him out of our sight. He will blind and inveigle us if we permit him to ply us, — for he can appear as an angel of light. One who temporizes with Satan voluntarily puts himself in his power.

Francis L. Ferguson.

> Hence, Prince of darkness! hence, my foe!
> Another Lord has purchased me:
> My conscience tells of sin, yet know,
> Baptized in Christ, I fear not thee.

J. J. RAMBACH.

August 20.

For all things are for your sakes. — 2 Cor. iv. 15.

And all things, whatsoever ye shall ask in prayer, believing, ye shall receive. — Matt. xxi. 22.

"PRAYER is the cry of faith to the ear of mercy." Our text invites us to pray, encourages us to pray, and promises us the largest and most blessed results, conditioned only upon faith. "Unbelief, like the grub in the tap-root, cuts off the fundamental sources of life." Sincere prayer is altogether reasonable. "Will he who advises you to ask, refuse afterward to give what you ask?" Do not stagger at the broadness of the promise, "all things." He is able; and what is needful, what is best for us, he will not deny. What has not been granted in answer to the prayer of faith! Saint Chrysostom says: "The strength of fire has been subdued; the rage of lions bridled; anarchy hushed; wars extinguished; the elements appeased; demons expelled; the chains of death burst; the gates of heaven opened; diseases assuaged; frauds repelled; cities rescued from destruction; the sun stayed in its course, — in a word, whatever is an enemy to man hath been destroyed," and whatever is a blessing hath been granted. But if we insist upon having "all things" for ourselves let us be careful how and what we ask, keeping in mind that God knows best.

Wm. N. Peacher

> What a friend we have in Jesus,
> All our sins and griefs to bear!
> What a privilege to carry
> Everything to God in prayer!
> Oh, what peace we often forfeit,
> Oh, what needless pain we bear,
> All because we do not carry
> Everything to God in prayer.
>
> Joseph Scriven.

August 21.

Touched with the feeling of our infirmities. — Heb. iv. 15.

I thirst. — John xix. 28.

THESE words fulfilled Scripture, though not spoken simply to fulfil it. They thus became one of the many fingers with which prophecy pointed to Jesus as the one of whom "Moses and the prophets did speak." Every incident of his death was foretold, — the time, the gambling of the soldiers for his coat, the mocking cry of the mob; each act in the mighty tragedy. "He died according to the Scriptures." Thus these words helped to tell the world, even in his death, that he was the Son of God. We rest then with glad confidence on his finished work. "He is *able* to save to the uttermost." *He is God.*

Yet he was a real sufferer. Wounded soldiers make the battle-field pitiful with their cries for "Water!" Jesus felt the thirst. His body was tortured. He knows how to sympathize with us. He wept with Martha and Mary. He ever sympathizes with his people.

We cannot hesitate to trust him, for he is God. We cannot fear to draw nigh to him with confidence, for he is also a loving and tender man.

>   Touched with a sympathy within,
>   He knows our feeble frame.
>   He knows what sore temptations mean,
>   For he has felt the same.
>
>   WATTS.

August 22.

I obtained mercy, because I did it ignorantly.
1 Tim. i. 13.

Father, forgive them; for they know not what they do. — Luke xxiii. 34.

IS this a prayer for my soul? Yes, if I am still among the enemies of the cross, and yet know not what I am doing. It was answered in a few hours for one who railed on him, and for another who was in command of his execution; and in a few days for thousands who were more guilty still. It may be answered for my soul now, but it can be answered in only one way, — by purging my conscience from its ignorance, by pricking me to the heart, and by giving me repentance.

Perhaps the reader is now first enlightened, and made partaker of the Holy Spirit, and tastes the good Word of God, and thus knows for the first time that a sinful life is crucifying the Son of God afresh, and putting him to an open shame. Then this is the solemn hour to be renewed unto repentance and forgiveness.

Wolcott Calkins

> Still our Advocate in heaven,
> Prays the prayer on earth begun:
> "Father, show their sins forgiven;
> Father, glorify thy Son."
>
> C. Wesley.

August 23.

Every man that hath this hope in him purifieth himself.
1 John iii. 3.

Blessed are the pure in heart. — Matt. v. 8.

SWEETEST of beatitudes from the lips of the blessed Jesus! It suggests the parable of the leaven and those kindred words, "Behold, the kingdom of God is within you." Sinners are purchased and then purified, for purity is the condition and the measure of true happiness, of fellowship with God, of fitness for the society, pleasures, and employments of heaven. "That he might purify unto himself a peculiar people," Christ gave himself for us, spake that word through which we are sanctified, shed that precious blood which cleanseth from all sin, and sent the Spirit of holiness, purifying our hearts through faith.

Heart-purity secures purity of life and character, for "out of the heart are the issues of life," and the fountain determines the stream. It secures transforming visions of God, for we "beholding as in a glass the glory of the Lord, are changed into the same image from glory to glory." It is the heavenly character whereby God is seen in his Word and works, and shall be seen in all the splendors of his glory. We know that "we shall be like him, for we shall see him as he is."

"Create in me a clean heart, O God."

J. S. McElroy

See, Lord, the travail of thy soul
   Accomplished in the change of mine,
  And plunge me, every whit made whole,
   In all the depths of love divine.
                             C. Wesley.

August 24.

So shalt thou find favour. — Prov. iii. 4.

If ye keep my commandments, ye shall abide in my love; even as I have kept my Father's commandments, and abide in his love. — John xv. 10.

KEEP my commands, abide in my love, — obedience the condition of favor. Nature everywhere teaches and enforces this same law.

All abiding art, all the triumphs of science and industry, bear witness that success is attained only in strict conformity to Nature's commands. Then even the lightning will become a useful, peaceful partner.

God in Christ, the incarnation of the divine love, wisdom, and power, woos the soul of man, offering forgiveness and seeking to secure in us a voluntary, loving obedience to the unchangeable truth of the universe, — the commands of God. All blessings follow if we " abide in his love."

There is no possible prosperity for the soul of man save in this obedience of faith. The abiding oneness of the Father and the Son, the glory of that loving communion, stands over against the perfected obedience of the Son of God. " My meat is to do the will of him that sent me and to finish his work."

" If ye know these things, happy are ye if ye do them."

Wm. Bayard Craig

    Teach me to do the thing that pleaseth thee;
      Thou art my God, in thee I live and move.
    Oh, let thy loving Spirit lead me forth
      Into the land of righteousness and love!
                                  Monsell.

August 25.

For the transgression of my people was he stricken.
Isaiah liii. 8.

Father, into thy hands I commend my spirit. — Luke xxiii. 46.

THIS last cry of our Lord on the cross betokens perfect poise of spirit, perfect trust in his Father, and perfect confidence in the all-sufficiency of his atoning sacrifice. It is true that he had suffered extreme anguish of soul on account of the hiding of his Father's face. For on the cross he " bare our sins in his own body." There it " pleased the Lord to bruise him." " For he was wounded for our transgressions, he was bruised for our iniquities, and the chastisement of our peace was laid on him." It was then that the Father hid his face from the " Son of his love." It was then that Jesus cried out: " My God, my God, why hast thou forsaken me? " It was then that the sun grew black and the rocks rent, and the veil of the temple was rent in the midst. But now all is calm in the heart of our adorable Redeemer, and he says, " Father, into thy hands I commend [commit] my spirit." The great atoning work was accomplished, so far as it could be on the earth. It is true that as our great High-Priest Christ must appear in the presence of the Father for us, when risen from the dead. But on the cross Jesus cried, " It is finished." Redemption is wrought, and every one that believes may be saved. O blessed and glorious fact! Who can sufficiently adore its divine author?

D. C. Hughes.

> A holy quiet reigns around, —
> A calm which life nor death destroys;
> And nought disturbs that peace profound
> Which his unfettered soul enjoys.
> Barbauld.

August 26.

If so be that we suffer with him, that we may be also glorified together. — ROMANS viii. 17.

Blessed are ye, when men shall revile you, and persecute you, and shall say all manner of evil against you falsely, for my sake. Rejoice, and be exceeding glad: for great is your reward in heaven: for so persecuted they the prophets which were before you. — MATT. v. 11, 12.

GOD'S blessings are so much greater than any possible human afflictions that any man receiving the first is pronounced "blessed," no matter what he may have of the second. Has man ecstasy of agony? God can reverse it all into ecstasy of pleasure. Between two notes in jarring discord he can put a third that shall make all into delicious harmony. Martyrs have moved aloft their blazing fingers like torches, and shouted for the joy of victory, notwithstanding the fire. Bodies have writhed in pain that spectators could hardly endure to see, but the soul has gloried in the rapture of God's visitations. John Huss kneeling beside the fagot-piled stake poured out his soul in prayer, using the words of the Thirty-first Psalm, and closed with its grand pæan, " Blessed be the Lord: for he hath shewed me his marvellous kindness in a strong city. O love the Lord, all ye his saints. Be of good courage, and he shall strengthen your heart, all ye that hope in the Lord."

John says of Christ, " Having loved his own he loved them unto the end." The uttermost of God for good is far beyond the uttermost of man for evil. God *commands* us to rejoice and be exceeding glad. That command is not grievous. It brings one into the goodly fellowship of prophets and martyrs. Is there any other way of attaining to that lofty companionship? Paul even coveted a fellowship of Christ's sufferings.

H. W. Warren

Finding, following, keeping, struggling, Is he sure to bless?
Saints, apostles, prophets, martyrs, answer, Yes.
                                   J. NEALE *(Translation).*

August 27.

𝔏ord, increase our faith. — LUKE xvii. 5.

Verily I say unto you, If ye have faith as a grain of mustard seed, ye shall say unto this mountain, Remove hence to yonder place; and it shall remove; and nothing shall be impossible unto you. Howbeit this kind goeth not out but by prayer and fasting. — MATT. xvii. 20, 21.

CHRIST was away from his disciples for a little. By even that brief absence they lost their power. They could not cast the evil spirit out of the possessed child. When Christ had performed the miracle, they asked why they had failed. He tells them it was because of unbelief. A living faith will work the impossible. A mustard seed being alive can be matched against the inert mass of a mountain. Science tells us that the weakest life is too much for the largest mass of mere matter. The smallest stream will draw down the mountain. Faith in Christ is a living force. It is not hyperbole to say it can move mountains. Besides this, Christ says such an extreme case required special effort. Some victories are easily won: some devils easily cast out. But this was a violent case and of long standing. It needed prayer and fasting, — that is, reliance on God and self-discipline. When our work fails, like the disciples we should seek the reason. That is the first condition of doing better; and the Master tells us we will find the reason either in a lack of faith that takes hold on God, or a lack of self-renunciation. The child's definition of faith covered these two points when she said in a child's simplicity and a saint's knowledge, "Faith is letting go of everything else and taking hold of God."

Chas L Thompson

I am trusting thee for power,
    Thine can never fail;
Words which thou thyself shalt give me
    Must prevail.

F. R. HAVERGAL.

AUGUST 28.

Perfect through sufferings. — HEB. ii. 10.

Get thee behind me, Satan, thou art an offence unto me: for thou savourest not the things that be of God, but those that be of men. — MATT. xvi. 23.

THIS is our Lord's answer to Peter at Cæsarea Philippi. It is the same as his answer to the Devil in the wilderness. The temptations were the same; namely, to gain the blessings of the kingdom without the cross. It is a temptation that comes to us as followers of Jesus. Our answer must be the same. In this world of sin salvation can only be gained by sacrifice. In Jesus' case it was absolutely necessary for him to suffer in order to save men; so sacrifice is necessary for us. We must take up our cross and follow Jesus. What that cross shall be he only can determine. He alone knows our characters; he would perfect them. He alone knows our destiny; he would educate and fit us for it. He alone knows how we can best glorify our Father, and so gives us the opportunity. When, then, his loving heart has prepared, and his hand has brought some cross for us to bear, let us know that all temptation to complain and resist is satanic, and let us bear it with patient cheerfulness, knowing that "*all* things work together for good" to his people.

E. H. Barnett.

> Must Jesus bear the cross alone,
> And all the world go free?
> No, there's a cross for every one,
> And there's a cross for me.
>
> That consecrated cross I'll bear
> Till Christ shall set me free;
> And then go home, my crown to wear,
> For there's a crown for me.
>
> THOMAS SHEPHERD *(altered).*

August 29.

Simon Peter answered and said, Thou art the Christ, the Son of the living God. — Matt. xvi. 16.

This is the work of God, that ye believe on him whom he hath sent. — John vi. 29.

THUS our blessed Lord answered the people's eager question, "What shall we do, that we might work the works of God?" Eternal life, then, cannot be obtained, as the people supposed, by "works," at all; but only by faith. To "believe on him whom he hath sent" is our one primary work, and without it no other work can be acceptable to him. A tireless following of Christ for loaves and fishes is not "the work of God," nor a wondering admiration of his peerless character and life, nor yet, even, a fervent prophesying in his name and a working again of his greatest miracles. We must begin with, "I believe that thou art the Christ, the Son of God, which should come into the world." The sole object of our faith, Jesus must also be all to our faith, — our "wisdom and righteousness and sanctification and redemption."

But "faith, if it hath not works, is dead, being alone." As the body needs the spirit, and trees need foliage and fruit to proclaim life, so the Christian must justify his faith to others by bringing forth the "things that accompany salvation." Indeed, where there is a true saving faith, its "works" will be as spontaneous as the clear streams which flow softly from a living fountain.

Halsey Moore,

My faith looks up to thee,
Thou Lamb of Calvary,
  Saviour divine!
Now hear me while I pray;
Take all my guilt away.
Oh, let me from this day
  Be wholly thine.   Ray Palmer.

August 30.

For none of us liveth to himself.—Romans xiv. 7.

Woe unto the world because of offences! for it must needs be that offences come; but woe to that man by whom the offence cometh! Wherefore if thy hand or thy foot offend thee, cut them off, and cast them from thee: it is better for thee to enter into life halt or maimed, rather than having two hands or two feet to be cast into everlasting fire.
— Matt. xviii. 7, 8.

OUR Lord means by offences *stumbling-blocks*, which cause men to fall into sin, and are therefore a fruitful source of evil in the world. So long as sin and Satan have power over men there will be such stumbling-blocks; and although it is the Evil One who thus seeks to bring dishonor on Christ and his cause, yet those through whom he acts as agents will be held to a strict account for resulting evil.

It is a comforting thought, however, that God can and does often overrule such offences for good. They may serve to strengthen Christian character, and show who can be depended on; and yet no true believer should knowingly or willingly become a tool of Satan to injure Christ's cause. He should be ready promptly to give up any course, practice, employment, or indulgence, however he may value it, which is a stone of stumbling to himself or others, and leads to sin.

Let us, then, never persist in what is plainly misleading to persons of weak faith, and causes them to fall, even though it may not be in itself sinful. Let us abandon everything that is injurious to our spiritual life, exposes us to overpowering temptation, and is a serious drawback to our progress and usefulness as Christians.

> I must the fair example set;
> From those that on my pleasure wait
>   The stumbling-block remove;
> Their duty by my life explain,
> And still in all my works maintain
>   The dignity of love.   C. Wesley.

August 31.

The Lord knoweth the way of the righteous.
PSALM i. 6.

I know thy works, and thy labour, and thy patience, and how thou canst not bear them which are evil: and thou hast tried them which say they are apostles, and are not, and hast found them liars:
Nevertheless I have somewhat against thee, because thou hast left thy first love. Remember therefore from whence thou art fallen, and repent, and do the first works; or else I will come unto thee quickly, and will remove thy candlestick out of his place, except thou repent.
— REV. ii. 2, 4, 5.

THIS declaration of God's omniscience is to impress us with the fact that God looks beyond the professions, resolutions, and desires of his people. Many of these are fair and earnest, but buds and blossoms must bring fruit, or they live and die to no purpose. The Master, as he walks in the midst of his Church, discovers everything. He looks at the internal as well as the external. It is *work* which develops the character. Labor in the Christian life is not pastime; to do the work required of us must be unto *weariness*. The sweat of the face is the result of the labor which brings bread to the hungry; so the sweat of the heart is found in the labor unto weariness of the Christian. Nothing marks the persevering, successful endurance of the Christian like the patience with which he does and suffers for his Lord.

Our Lord's tenderness prompts him first to commend every good act of theirs, and then, as a warning, to condemn what he cannot approve.

Should we wander from thy fold,
And our love to thee grow cold,
With a pitying eye behold.
Lord, forgive and save.

MORRIS.

SEPTEMBER 1.

The friend of the bridegroom . . . rejoiceth greatly because of the bridegroom's voice. — JOHN iii. 29.

Ye are my friends, if ye do whatsoever I command you. — JOHN xv. 14.

EVERY man needs a friend. No one can live alone. He must have companionship, or life would be a dreary solitude. But it must be a true friend; a false friend is worse than none. The flatterer, who tells pleasant falsehoods to deceive, can work more mischief than the worst enemy. The true friend is one who sees things as they are, who perceives the weaknesses of his most intimate companion, but who bears with his infirmities for the sake of all in him that is good.

The divine Friend may be ours if we but return his affection. We can obtain his friendship by giving him our own; and this we are to prove by simple trust and obedience. This giving up of ourselves to him is not an abdication of our personality, an adoption of the Jesuit rule that a man must become a *cadaver* to be vitalized and animated by another intelligence and will than his own. Our Master asks not for the dead body, but for the living soul; and a man is never so full of life, so "vital in every part," with all his faculties strung to their utmost intensity, as when he gives himself up to the control of him whose service is perfect freedom. Once enter into this new life, and we shall find it blessed indeed.

Henry M. Field.

> Hail, Prince of life, forever hail !
> Redeemer, Brother, Friend !
> Though earth and time and life shall fail,
> Thy praise shall never end.
>
> SAMUEL MEDLEY.

September 2.

He that cometh to God must believe. — Heb. xi. 6.

If thou canst believe, all things are possible to him that believeth. — Mark ix. 23.

WHAT inexhaustible possibilities lie in faith! God himself is the unseen author of the visible universe, and it was by faith that the worlds were framed, so that things that are seen were not made of things that do appear.

In the sublime galaxy woven with divine hand all in and through the eleventh chapter of Hebrews, the light that shines from every star is faith.

It was this that carried Noah across the flood. It was this that gave strength to Moses to deliver the people of God from Egypt, to train them in the wilderness, and to transfer them to the Promised Land. It was this that enabled Israel to hold to the hope of the promise until Jesus came. This animated the feeble few of Galilee to carry the gospel to the perishing world. This is the power by which every sainted Christian has triumphed in life and in death and entered home at last. Our blessed Saviour is himself the author and the finisher of faith.

"If *thou* canst believe, all things are possible to him that believeth."

W. W. Page

> Lord, I believe; but oft I know
> My faith is cold and weak.
> My weakness strengthen, and bestow
> The confidence I seek.
>
> J. R. Wreford.

SEPTEMBER 3.

By love serve one another. —GAL. v. 13.

Ye call me Master and Lord: and ye say well; for so I am. If I then, your Lord and Master, have washed your feet, ye also ought to wash one another's feet. For I have given you an example, that ye should do as I have done to you. — JOHN xiii. 13-15.

AN Oriental custom is made to teach an important lesson, as one of the lowliest offices in a servant's work is performed by the world's great Teacher. By a reverse of the ordinary method the Master turns servant and minister, and washes the feet of his disciples and puts upon them the obligation to do for each other as equals the service he had done them as their Lord. Feet-washing as a rite of hospitality is no longer practised, owing to the changed conditions of life and society; but the example of love and humble ministration to our fellow-beings stands for our perpetual imitation.

With such an example we need not deem any service for humanity too lowly. The Master has ennobled it by his divine hand, and our highest dignity in spiritual manhood is attained, when like him, we humble ourselves to do a generous act to some fellow-man. The mission of the Lord's disciples is to carry the means for mental renovation and moral purification to all who need it.

Robt. W. Jones.

Kind deeds of peace and love betray
Where'er the stream has found its way;
But where these spring not rich and fair
The stream has never wandered there.
                                        DRUMMOND.

September 4.

He leadeth me beside the still waters. — Psalm xxiii. 2.

If any man thirst, let him come unto me, and drink. He that believeth on me, as the scripture hath said, out of his belly shall flow rivers of living water. — John vii. 37, 38.

STRONGER symbol of intense unrest it would be difficult to find. The shipwrecked sailor, wave-tossed, under the burning heat of tropical sun, knows its full meaning. Fevered blood, throbbing temples, parched lips, burning throat, swollen tongue, — these combine to produce a climax of agony. Than extreme thirst, there is no worse physical torment. It wrings from the divine One the only expression of bodily anguish as he hangs upon the cross. "I thirst!" This is the *material* culmination. Dives looking up out of his place of torment and seeing Lazarus at rest in Abraham's bosom, begs for a drop of water to cool his thirsting tongue. Thirst, thirst! Fit symbol is it of the fevered unrest of a sin-driven soul. But what if a bubbling fountain has been opened beside the way? Surely thirsty men will halt and drink. What ecstasy as they quaff the crystal liquid and lave their dusty hands and bathe their weary brows! But Christ is such a fountain providentially opened beside life's tortuous way for thirsting souls. He is not some desert mirage, but a "well of living water." They who drink of this water shall cease thirsting. Art thou thirsty? Hark! The mighty Christ tenderly calleth, "Come unto me and drink!"

Henry A. Powell

> Come, then, with all your wants and wounds,
>   Your every burden bring.
> Here love, unchanging love abounds,
>   A deep, celestial spring.   Samuel Medley *(altered).*

September 5.

Heal me, O Lord, and I shall be healed.—JER. xvii. 14.

Wilt thou be made whole?—JOHN v. 6.

OUR text presents unto us another one of those incidents which showeth the mercy and goodness of God, and how anxious Christ as the great Physician was to do good,—the care of the Shepherd for the sheep, the Redeemer for the redeemed.

The great drawback to the world is that it fails to devise methods to fully enhance its glory; we fail to find out in the years we have to spend upon the earth all which a curious mind imagines. If anything has baffled science, it is that scientists have failed to discover and devise methods to enable them to master her fully; if anything has created uneasiness among those of the medical world, it is that which has hindered a successful treatment of patients. But dissimilar to all of these, Christ, the healer divine, walks into the midst of many maladies,—the halt, the blind, and those afflicted for many years,—saying, Wilt thou be made whole? And, behold, him who accepted his overtures of mercy and love is made whole from that hour. The length of time he was sick, and the completeness in the cure, all but increases our faith in him whose very words make one wise unto salvation, and showeth that he is the sinner's friend, and would that all would turn unto God and live.

David W. Frazier

> The great Physician now is near,
> The sympathizing Jesus;
> He speaks, the drooping heart to cheer,
> Oh, hear the voice of Jesus!
>   WILLIAM HUNTER.

SEPTEMBER 6.

If our heart condemn us not then have we confidence toward God. — 1 JOHN iii. 21.

If thou bring thy gift to the altar, and there rememberest that thy brother hath ought against thee; leave there thy gift before the altar and go thy way; first be reconciled to thy brother, and then come and offer thy gift. — MATT. v. 23, 24.

THE enthusiasm of love is the soul of devotion. The rapture of heart to heart communion with God comes only to souls fully "reconciled by the blood of the cross." We can never hope to have God at peace with us if we are not at peace with our brother. The richest gifts and sacrifices will lie like Cain's rotting fruits and wilted flowers upon the altar, unaccepted, if we are conscious of being unreconciled to our brother. Holy affections must conquer all personal antipathies. The injured one can most readily and easily take the first steps toward reconciliation. Jesus was made a sacrifice, and his last words upon the "offering up of himself" were in prayer pleading with the Father for his enemies. When our religion becomes impassioned with Christ's love, like a fire fusing and refining the gold from the dross, we will waive aside weak formalities and travel a long distance to conquer the heart of our brother. When reconciled, our offerings and gifts on the altar will become "a sweet-smelling savor" like Abel's, and we shall hold the inward testimony of the Holy Spirit that we "please God."

Thomas Chalmers Easton

Kindle thou the sacrifice
  That upon my lips is lying;
Clear the shadows from mine eyes,
  That, from every error flying,
No strange fire may in me glow
That thine altar doth not know.
                      FROM THE GERMAN.

SEPTEMBER 7.

From Jesus Christ . . . the faithful witness. — Rev. i. 5.

I Jesus have sent mine angel to testify unto you these things in the churches. I am the root and the offspring of David, the bright and morning star. — Rev. xxii. 16.

THE Patmos revelations are unique. There is nothing like them in the literature of the world. Some are so weird and wild as to seem incredible, — the fancies of an opium-eater rather than sober and stable facts. But the glorified Saviour attests their truth by assuming all responsibility for them, — " I Jesus."

Not only does he certify this apocalypse, he also certifies himself to be eminently trustworthy. " The sure mercies of David " was a covenant phrase in the early times, and verily the author of these mercies, as well as their splendid product, could not deceive his people by playing with their fears or exaggerating their hopes. Therefore, my soul, do not disdain his teachings in the Church and in thyself. Heed his warnings, and exult in his promises. Keep on trusting him; what thou knowest not now thou shalt know hereafter. Earthly life may be lonelier than this island of exile in the Ægean, — the raptures few and the sobs many; but if Jesus shines upon thee all will be well.

We love sweet voices, and God makes them mute;
   We hold no treasure sure to last a day;
We fill our hearts with flowers that have no root;
We build snow huts that summer melts away;
Yet never need our weak lives hopeless roam,
   For One, descended from a brighter land,
Who came to save, will guide his children home,
   And keep secure all trusted to his hand.

SEPTEMBER 8.

He forgetteth not the cry of the humble. — PSALM ix. 12.

Shall not God avenge his own elect, which cry day and night unto him, though he bear long with them? — LUKE xviii. 7.

SUCH is Christ's application of his story of the unjust judge. An officer of the law, set to do justice, is deaf to the appeals of a poor widow, until, wearied by her importunity, he hears and heeds to be rid of the matter. If such be the conduct of an iniquitous magistrate, how certainly shall our compassionate Father, who loves every member of the household of faith, his purpose of discipline being accomplished, open both ear and hand in response to his outcrying children.

Our enemies are many. The world storms upon us. The flesh tempts us. Satan is inquisitive and ubiquitous. Sorrow sits, an unbidden guest, at the hearthstone. Death, with hour-glass and scythe, strides across the threshold. Feeble, affrighted, dazed, where shall we look? What shall we do? Look up! Cry out! Keep looking up! Keep crying out! It is only a question of time. God will surely appear to vindicate our faith and deliver our soul.

Carlos Martyn.

He bows his gracious ear,
  We never plead in vain;
Then let us wait till he appear,
  And pray, and pray again.
                    JOHN NEWTON.

September 9.

What must I do to be saved? — Acts xvi. 30.

Go ye into all the world, and preach the gospel to every creature. He that believeth and is baptized shall be saved; but he that believeth not shall be damned. — Mark xvi. 15, 16.

DUTY, destiny, are the impressive words suggested and held before the mind with growing clearness and power by this, our Lord's last command.

The duty is every Christian's, and is urged by the alternative eternal destiny of every unsaved soul, — a duty whose obligation will not be lessened until every creature in all the world has heard the gospel, and either accepted or rejected the salvation it offers; whose discharge means the telling simply and lovingly to the guilty, of a pitying Saviour; to the penitent, of a pardoning Saviour; to the troubled, of a peace-giving Saviour; to the sorrowing, of a sympathizing Saviour; to the helpless, of an almighty Saviour; to all who will come unto God by him, of a welcoming and sufficient Saviour. And when these receive and trust the good news and believe on Jesus, they shall be saved and not damned.

How startling and wonderful that the eternal destiny of souls already condemned should turn upon the faithfulness to duty of those who are saved! How stimulating and glorious the results and rewards of patient and persevering obedience to our Saviour's parting request, souls saved from death, and they by whom they were turned unto righteousness shining as the stars forever and ever!

Joachim Elmendorf.

Whosoever heareth, shout, shout the sound!
Send the blessed tidings all the world around!
Spread the joyful news wherever man is found,
" Whosoever will, may come."

P. P. Bliss.

SEPTEMBER 10.

The weapons of our warfare are not carnal.
2 COR. x. 4.

Put up thy sword into the sheath; the cup which my Father hath given me, shall I not drink it? — JOHN xviii. 11.

THE servant is to be as his master. That kingdom which is "righteousness and peace and joy in the Holy Ghost" has no need of carnal weapons. How evidently out of place for Peter to draw his sword in defence of one at the mere recognition of whom his enemies had already fallen to the ground! The condition of both safety and power is obedience to God's perfect will. We have reason to fear self-injury far more than injury from our foes. He who was ready to drink the cup could have had for the asking "more than twelve legions of angels."

Let us adoringly remember that the cup which the Saviour was to drink was the full cup of atoning anguish. Yet the fact that it was presented by the Father's hand gave absolute assurance it was to become the cup of blessing! God never lets the final victory go against either himself or his. We miss triumphs for both the kingdom and ourselves because we are not willing to endure suffering. Redeemed by love's agony, we yet shrink from whatever will cost us pain. Saving our life, we lose it!

L. T. Chamberlain.

If thou the cup of pain
  Givest to drink,
Let not the trembling lip
  From the draught shrink;
So by our woes to be
Nearer, O God, to thee,
  Nearer to thee!

W. W. HOW.

September 11.

Unto you it is given . . . to suffer for his sake.
PHIL. i. 29.

These things saith the first and the last, which was dead, and is alive; I know thy works, and tribulation, and poverty (but thou art rich). . . . Fear none of those things which thou shalt suffer: . . . be thou faithful unto death, and I will give thee a crown of life.
— REV. ii. 8, 9, 10.

NOT one of the "seven churches in Asia" received so high a commendation from "the faithful and true witness" as that in Smyrna; yet in outward condition hers was the severest lot. Hers to suffer rather than to serve; to endure rather than to conquer; to have "tribulations" rather than triumphs. Again and again was she swept over by the fires of persecution, yet they did not consume her.

How full of strength and cheer these words to such a church! The assurance of a *reigning Lord, having all power over death and hell*, "the first and the last," "that was dead and is alive again." "No weapon that is formed against her shall prosper." After trial she shall come forth victorious. Her light shines to-day! Are you called, dear child of God, to trial, to disappointment, to sorrow, to see others reaping while you are laid aside? Remember, "they also serve who only stand and wait," that the highest praise fell to Smyrna, and through tribulations patiently endured.

Wm. N. Scott

> Never flinched they from the flame,
>   From the torture never;
> Vain the foeman's sharpest aim,
>   Satan's best endeavor.
> For by faith they saw the land
>   Decked in all its glory,
> Where triumphant now they stand,
>   With the victor's story.
> J. NEALE *(Translation)*.

September 12.

Ye have purified your souls in obeying the truth.
1 Peter i. 22.

Sanctify them through thy truth: thy word is truth. — John xvii. 17.

AS our blessed Lord was himself "set apart and sent into the world" on a special divine mission, it is not strange that he should pray for his apostles that they might be sanctified, — set apart by God the Father to their divine work. They were to possess and proclaim the gospel in its fulness. Neither doctrinal nor preceptive truths must be overlooked; they must be impressed with the authority of their calling and the sublimity of their work.

All sincere believers are called to a divine service. Our Lord's prayer includes them. Every Christian should be a living gospel and the propagator of spiritual truth. The growth of spiritual life and the steady increase of spiritual power depend upon our belief in and appropriation of the Word of God. We are sanctified by the Holy Spirit through belief of and obedience to the truth. Our sanctification must mean both purity of character and enlightened devotion to Christ's work. Our blessed Lord must be our ideal as to the one and our example as to the other. Rightly apprehending the "truth as it is in Jesus," we must cheerfully make it known to others. Let the warm, vital life of godliness be manifest in our conduct. While in thought we mount heavenward, in deed we should go about in angelic labors.

Jas. S. Chadwick.

> I need a cleansing change within,
> My life must once again begin.
> New hope I need, and youth renewed,
> And more than human fortitude;
> New faith, new love, and strength to cast
> Away the fetters of the the past.
> Hartly Coleridge.

September 13.

Your goodness is as a morning cloud. — Hosea vi. 4.

But he that receiveth the seed into stony places, the same is he that heareth the word, and anon with joy receiveth it; yet hath he not root in himself, but dureth for a while: for when tribulation or persecution ariseth because of the word, by and by he is offended. — Matt. xiii. 20, 21.

IN religion, as in agriculture, everything depends upon the thoroughness with which initial processes are conducted. In opening the way for the reception of the gospel, the ploughshare of the Spirit must be permitted to go deep enough not only to stir the thin soil of emotion which lies upon the surface of the "evil heart of unbelief" that is by nature in us all, but to upturn and remove the underlying rock itself. Only thus will the good seed of the kingdom find its way into that deep subsoil where the conditions of permanent vitality and fruitful development can be found. No mere surface-work will do here; nothing but such a radical regeneration as shall "take away the heart of stone out of the flesh," — such as shall make old things to pass away and all things to become new. Emotions are transient; only principles abide. A religion that flourishes in times of revival in the Church, and withers as soon as they are gone, is a miserable cheat. The sooner it is detected and renounced, the better for the soul.

J. D. Witherspoon

  Dear Lord, and shall we ever live
   At this poor dying rate,
   Our love so faint, so cold to thee,
   And thine to us so great?
         Watts.

September 14.

He that hath pity upon the poor lendeth unto the Lord.
Prov. xix. 17.

Verily I say unto you, Inasmuch as ye have done it unto one of the least of these my brethren, ye have done it unto me. — Matt. xxv. 40.

HOW little we know of what we are and have and do! Faith itself does not remove all blindness to the realities of God's kingdom. Burning though be our zeal, and unremitting our work, the veil is still before our eyes, and we cannot conceive of the glory of our calling. Prompted by the love of Christ, we seek to remove misery, but with our Bibles in our hands and hearts, in which these words are so clearly written, forget that all the time it is really the Lord, and not merely suffering men, whom we have cherished and comforted.

How constant, too, the opportunity for such service! "The least of these my brethren;" that is, the very lowest in knowledge, honor, influence, holiness of life. Though full of faults, he is still a brother in whom Christ dwells, and through whom Christ comes.

Homer tells of Ulysses dwelling for a time unknown in his Ithaca, a beggar, abused, insulted, struck by some of his people but kindly treated by others, until the hour when all had been tested came, and the dishonored beggar was found to be the absent lord. The King is here, and this very day he walks our streets and enters our homes. Happy they who even though they do not recognize him, give him the sympathy of their hearts, and freely administer of whatever they have.

Henry E. Jacobs

Oh, may our sympathizing breasts
  The generous pleasure know
Kindly to share in others' joy,
  And weep for others' woe!

Philip Doddridge.

September 15.

Behold, to obey is better than sacrifice. — I Sam. xv. 22.

My meat is to do the will of him that sent me, and to finish his work. — John iv. 34.

HUNGRY, thirsty, and weary, Jesus comes at noon-day to the well of Samaria. He finds rest in labor, drink in holy converse, and food in bringing a lost soul to God.

Not only do physical conditions affect the spiritual life, but in a larger degree than we are wont to imagine, spiritual conditions affect the physical life. Bodily ailments depress the spirit; spiritual exercise invigorates the body. The entire man, body and soul, feels the refreshing and stimulating influence of close companionship with God in will and work. The servant of God forgets his bodily wants in the joy of becoming the channel through which God flows into other lives.

These words are not spoken concerning a purely personal, unrelated experience. Jesus does not find his food, in this instance at least, in contemplation or self-inspection. He does God's will and accomplishes God's work, with a sinful woman as the object in which his activity centres. It is not enough that we know God's will. The blessed truths of revelation will not be food to us except as we assimilate those truths by our activity. The soul has its laws of development and growth. One of the chief of these laws, the law of labor, is given divine emphasis in the words before us.

L. A. Crandall

    Help us through good report and ill
      Our daily cross to bear,
    Like thee to do our Father's will,
      Our brother's grief to share.
                        John H. Gurney.

SEPTEMBER 16.

Therefore shall they eat of the fruit of their own way.
PROV. i. 31.

I am come a light into the world, that whosoever believeth on me should not abide in darkness. And if any man hear my words, and believe not, I judge him not: for I came not to judge the world, but to save the world. — JOHN xii. 46, 47.

DARKNESS is just the word for both the present and the future without Christ. Light is the word to describe what he does for us when we come to him. "He is the true light which lighteth every man that cometh into the world." He lights up life's path with an example of what man should be and do. His is the light which reveals the way of salvation. Till we come to him, we see our sins as scarlet and as crimson; when we have come to him they become white as snow, for "the blood of Jesus Christ his Son cleanseth us from all sin." He lights up heaven, and tells us that there God shall wipe away all tears. He lights up earth by telling us that all power is given him in heaven and on earth, and that he will be with us to the end. Are trials many and severe? Do not forget the light which comes from Gethsemane, the judgment hall, the cross. He not only taught patience and forgiveness, he was patient, he forgave. Remember that he came not to judge, but to save. It is not his wrath, but our unbelief, which condemns us.

A. T. McEwen.

> Jesus, my hope, my rock, my shield,
> Whose precious blood was shed for me!
> Into thy hands my soul I yield;
> I come to thee.
>
> CHARLOTTE ELLIOTT.

September 17.

Let us not love in word, neither in tongue; but in deed and in truth. — 1 John iii. 18.

Give me to drink. — John iv. 7.

IT is Jesus who asks this. It was asked of one who could supply the physical need. It was comparatively a little thing for which he asked, but the woman of Samaria found that he who thus asked could give the water of life, which would quench the thirst of the soul.

Jesus asks still, "Give me to drink," and though we may not be able to quench the physical thirst of the Son of man, we may minister to him by ministering in his name to others, for we have his own word, "Inasmuch as ye did it unto one of the least of these my brethren, ye did it unto me."

The request is one to which every one can accede. Not in the largeness of the gift lies its value, but in the spirit which prompts it. The cup of water only, if given for Christ's sake and for very love to him, he will always regard as for himself.

There are wearied, burdened, bruised, and sorrowing ones of earth to whom we can minister, there are thirsting ones to whom we can bring the "cup of salvation;" and they who thus give Jesus to drink shall from him receive the "gift of God," even the "living water which springeth up into everlasting life."

Lewis Francis.

> May each child of thine be willing,
>   Willing both in hand and heart,
> Every law of love fulfilling,
>   Every comfort to impart!
>
> GODFREY THRING.

September 18.

O send out thy light and thy truth: let them lead me.
PSALM xliii. 3.

This is the condemnation, that light is come into the world, and men loved darkness rather than light, because their deeds were evil. — JOHN iii. 19.

CHRIST, who is at once the Son of God and the Son of man, uttered a truth whose sublimity stands without a parallel, when he said, "I am the light of the world." Light and life, like grace and truth, came by Jesus Christ, the true light which lighteth every man that cometh into the world. "All other lights lead but to bewilder and dazzle but to blind." But in his light we see light revealing at once the exceeding sinfulness of sin and the infinite beauty of holiness, the deepening darkness of the path that leads away from God, and the growing brightness of the way that brings us back to our Father's house. The mischief and the misery of unbelief is that in its love of darkness and its hatred of light, in its rejection of Christ and its retention of sin, the soul is led to refuse that which above all else it needs the most, and to cling to that which multiplies its sorrows and hastens its ruin. With a yearning tenderness like unto that with which a grieved yet loving father laments the folly of a wayward child, the dear Lord addresses the sons and daughters of unbelief, whose unwise choice is the fruitage of their evil deeds, and tells them that impenitence writes its own condemnation, invites its own sentence, and aggravates its own eternal doom.

John J. Brown

> Lord, I believe; thy power I own,
>   Thy word I would obey.
> I wander comfortless and lone,
>   When from thy truth I stray.
>
> J. R. WREFORD.

September 19.

Hearken diligently unto me, and eat ye that which is good. — Isaiah lv. 1.

Verily, verily, I say unto you, Moses gave you not that bread from heaven; but my Father giveth you the true bread from heaven. For the bread of God is he which cometh down from heaven, and giveth life unto the world. — John vi. 32, 33.

THERE is a difference in the gifts from heaven. Some obtain physical blessings and seek no more. "Your fathers did eat manna and are dead." Some seek the hidden manna, and receiving the true "gift of God" never die, for they feed on Christ.

"Moses gave not, no man gives, the bread from heaven." Praise not men because they are God's agents, but give God the glory. Seek not inspiration from man, but drink from the fountain-head. Moses, David, Paul, the noblest men dead or living, are as nothing to the Bread, the Word, which came down from heaven. Go to Christ, follow, lean upon him; let no *man* come between you and your Master.

"The Father giveth you." Does he? He stands offering; have you accepted the food? His hand is stretched out; have you grasped it?

Roderick Terry

Very bread, good Shepherd, tend us;
Jesus, of thy love befriend us;
Thou refresh us, thou defend us,
Thine eternal goodness send us
In the land of life to see.
Thou, who all things canst and knowest,
Who on earth such food bestowest,
Grant us with thy saints, though lowest,
Where the heavenly feast thou showest,
Fellow heirs and guests to be.

H. W. Baker.

September 20.

When Jesus was glorified, then remembered they.
JOHN xii. 16.

But the Comforter, which is the Holy Ghost, whom the Father will send in my name, he shall teach you all things, and bring all things to your remembrance, whatsoever I have said unto you. — JOHN xiv. 26.

HOW imperfect is our apprehension of things heavenly, and how defective our recollection of them! Poor scholars are we in God's school, with our slow learning and quick forgetting, if left to ourselves. Most precious then is our Lord's assurance of the help of the Holy Spirit, so that we shall not fail to attain and retain that knowledge of his teachings which is vital to the welfare and peace of our souls, and which enthrones him in our hearts.

How cheering also the thought of the completeness of the Spirit's teaching, — covering the "all things" of Christ, as twice declared in this one verse. So large is his love for us that he can never be content with anything small in his treatment of us. Thus taught by the Holy Ghost, we shall choose truth rather than error, and ever delight therein. Having clearly and constantly in mind our loving Saviour, we shall learn consolation in sorrow, patience under suffering, courage amid conflict, and fidelity in love and service, even unto death. And so shall this adorable Holy One be unto us indeed "the Comforter."

John C. Bliss.

> Remember that a world unseen
>   Is round thee everywhere;
> That he alone is truly blest
>   Whom God hath in his care;
> Whom his good Spirit, by his might,
> Is leading in a pathway bright.
>
> CRAMFELD.

September 21.

Every one of us shall give account of himself to God.
ROMANS xiv. 12.

And cast ye the unprofitable servant into outer darkness: there shall be weeping and gnashing of teeth. — MATT. xxv. 30.

THE "unprofitable servant" did not meet his fearful doom through accident, sudden temptation, necessity, or lack of knowledge. He admits he *knew* the character of his lord and what would be the natural result of his own negligence. And now our loving Master holds this picture before our eyes that we may escape that servant's doom. This closing sentence is one of the beacon lights kindled by the hand of love, to warn men against the infatuation of sin that pushes them on to ruin. Love divine stands before men to-day who "*know* their Lord's will and do it not," seeking their salvation. It will woo or warn, draw or drive, inspire hope or waken dread, promise peace to the troubled or sting a torpid conscience into life, speak in "the still small voice" or thunder in the storm, and while pointing the weary to the rest in heaven, it will dare to tell the careless of the horrors of hell.

See the Judge, our nature wearing,
  Clothed in majesty divine!
You who long for his appearing,
  Then shall say, "This God is mine!"
    Gracious Saviour,
Own me in that day for thine!

JOHN NEWTON.

September 22.

Before honour is humility. — Prov. xv. 33.

And whosoever shall exalt himself shall be abased; and he that shall humble himself shall be exalted. — Matt. xxiii. 12.

THIS is one of the favorite sayings of our blessed Lord. It teaches that exaltation through humility is the law of spiritual life. The life of Christ is an exemplification of this great principle. Saint Paul writes, "He humbled himself and became obedient unto death, even the death of the cross. Wherefore God hath highly exalted him, and given him a name which is above every name." Humility is the right estimate of ourselves; it is the ascendency of truth in the soul. Consequently, all spiritual life must have its beginnings in humility.

Though the believer may be almost overwhelmed on account of his littleness and unworthiness standing in the searching sight of the eternal Light, yet humility is consistent with the loftiest aspirations and the highest achievements.

The humble find forgiveness and peace through the cross, and discover surpassing sources of life and exaltation in the fatherhood of God, in the brotherhood of Jesus, in the indwelling of the Holy Ghost. Through humility the soul is emptied of self and filled with the divine fulness, and so he that humbleth himself is exalted.

Charles W. Fitts

Thy home is with the humble, Lord!
 The simple are the blest.
Thy lodging is in childlike hearts,
 Thou makest there thy rest.

Dear Comforter! eternal Dove!
 If thou wilt stay with me,
Of lowly thoughts and simple ways
 I'll build a house for thee.
            FABER.

September 23.

***The Lord hath anointed me . . . to proclaim liberty to the captives.* — Isaiah lxi. 1.**

And ought not this woman, being a daughter of Abraham, whom Satan hath bound, lo, these eighteen years, be loosed from this bond on the sabbath day? — Luke xiii. 16.

CHRIST healed this woman on the Sabbath day and in the synagogue. The ruler of the synagogue became indignant, as if Christ had committed some heinous sin. The miracle of Christ and his mercy to this poor woman were nothing to this Pharisee compared to a custom or ordinance. Christ appeals to a custom or common practice among the Jews, of watering their cattle upon the Sabbath day, and applies this act of mercy to the greater need of this woman.

She was "a daughter of Abraham," their sister, — a relation which they should recognize as not belonging to the cattle. Why not be as merciful to her as to a beast? It is so to-day. Cattle can rest on the Sabbath, but servants must work.

She was "bound by Satan;" hence this miracle was more than an act of mercy to the woman. It was piety toward God, as it broke the power of Satan. She had been in this deplorable condition for eighteen years; why delay a single day longer, and add to her misery? Now is the great opportunity.

Christ spent his Sabbaths in the synagogues, and thus gave his testimony to the duty and importance of public worship; and he healed on the Sabbath day, teaching us that acts of mercy and charity belong to the Sabbath and to the true worshipper.

C. T. Marsden

And didst thou pity mortal woe,
   And sight and health restore?
Then pity, Lord, and save my soul
   Which needs thy pity more.
                       Mrs. Amelia Wakeford.

September 24.

As our Lord Jesus Christ hath shewed me.
2 Peter i. 14

Whither I go, thou canst not follow me now; but thou shalt follow me afterwards. — John xiii. 36.

THE Master was ending his mission and passing to the grave. The disciple could not foresee the path through suffering and death to glory, and asking "whither" his Lord was going, desired to follow. The nature and extent of following Christ require tuition and experience, which alone fortify us with grace and strength to follow him closely in the full spirit and conditions of his life. Peter thought he was ready to do this at once; the Lord said, "Not now, but afterwards." Dearly, richly learned he what that meant, when he wrote, "Christ suffered for us, leaving an example that we should follow his steps; that we being dead to sin, should live unto righteousness."

"Not now;" the path of vicarious suffering Christ must tread *alone*. We cannot follow him there.

"Afterwards;" since his bleeding, blessed feet have passed up to the crown heights of God, we may and must follow, not asking "whither," or halting before the presence of suffering, or blanched by fear of enemies, but counting it joy to suffer in his behalf; through good or through evil report, to plant our feet in his own footprints, let them lead us where they will.

Once his disciple, ever "afterwards" follow in life, in death; then "afterwards" in the paths of glory, you shall "follow the Lamb whithersoever he leads."

Horace L. Singleton

> Thy way, not mine, O Lord,
>   However dark it be!
> Lead me by thine own hand;
>   Choose out the path for me.
>   H. Bonar.

September 25.

Behold, the Lord God will come: ... his reward is with him. — Isaiah xl. 10.

Blessed are those servants, whom the lord when he cometh shall find watching: verily I say unto you, that he shall gird himself, and make them to sit down to meat, and will come forth and serve them. — Luke xii. 37.

OUR Lord here emphasizes the importance of an unbroken, progressive life of obedience to the end. He gives notice that such life is the true and decisive test of loyalty to him. He impliedly says to all his servants, Having engaged with me, I assign you to life service. I make no provision for leave of absence, I grant no vacations; but I give assurance of profits to all who serve faithfully, — profits more than equivalent for the service rendered.

Absent for an indefinite period, the Lord puts his servants in charge of his house with instructions to continue the work commenced and guard circumspectly all his interests till he return.

The day of his return he does not reveal, but his servants are assured that he will come; that when he comes their service shall end and their profits be realized. Then to each servant whom he finds "watching" — with house in order, with lamp burning, and with hand on the door ready to open to him — he will say, "Well done, good and faithful servant;" go now to my table and I will serve you; "enter" now "into the joy of thy Lord."

D. R. Miller.

> We long to hear thy voice,
> To see thee face to face;
> To share thy crown and glory then,
> As now we share thy grace.
>
> H. BONAR.

September 26.

Smitten of God, and afflicted. — Isaiah liii. 4.

My God, my God, why hast thou forsaken me? — Matt. xxvii. 46.

STRANGEST as well as saddest words ever uttered. The spotless Son of God passing into the hidings of his Father's face, experiencing that sickening sense of utter desolation, forsaken of God and man; and this that he might know sin's utmost ruin, that man might know love's utmost salvation. Herein is love, not that we loved him, but that he loved us and gave himself for us. He took upon his broad sympathies the burden of a fallen world's sins and sorrows, hiding his Father's face, darkening the heavens, and rolled it off with a bloody sweat and an expiring groan, that guilty man might be saved both the one and the other. He took man's place in the darkness of sin and death that man might take his place in the light of holiness and life. He was abandoned of God that man might be accepted. He went down to hell that man might ascend to heaven. The philosophy is hidden, the fact is revealed. And thank God the fact is all we need to know for our present peace or future welfare. Let us, therefore, gratefully accept the fact that "Him who knew no sin he made to be sin on our behalf, that we might become the righteousness of God in him."

J. A. M. Chapman

> Weary sinner, keep thine eyes
> On the atoning sacrifice.
> There the incarnate Deity
> Numbered with transgressors see;
> There his Father's absence mourns,
> Nailed, and bruised, and crowned with thorns.
>   **Toplady.**

September 27.

He shall have judgment without mercy, that hath shewed no mercy. — JAMES ii. 13.

And his lord was wroth, and delivered him to the tormentors, till he should pay all that was due unto him. So likewise shall my heavenly Father do also unto you, if ye from your hearts forgive not every one his brother their trespasses. — MATT. xviii. 34, 35.

THE merciful man shows mercy, not in the hope of receiving mercy, but because mercy is an element inwrought into the fibres of his moral being. The gospel regards the acts of the life as evidential of the state of the heart. The unmerciful servant was "delivered to the tormentors until he should pay all that was due," not simply on account of a single heartless act, but because that act was the evidence of his possession of an unmerciful disposition. With the infallible Judge it is the state of the heart which secures acquittal or condemnation. Disciples of Christ therefore need to examine their hearts to know of what spirit they are. Further, their lives should clearly show that they have practically learned the lessons taught them in the application of this parable. These are, — that the mercy sinners receive from God should evidence itself in acts of mercy toward their fellow-creatures; that a life lacking in mercy is proof of the falsity of a profession of religion; that they who seek forgiveness from God must be willing to forgive men; and that the prayer of the unmerciful is vanity and their condemnation a certainty. The gospel requires not only that men "do justly," but also that they "love mercy."

B. H. Roberts.

Oh, give us hearts to love like thee!
Like thee, O Lord, to grieve
Far more for others' sins, than all
The wrongs that we receive.   SIR E. DENNY.

September 28.

Followers of God, as dear children. — Eph. v. 1.

And when ye stand praying, forgive, if ye have ought against any: that your Father also which is in heaven may forgive you your trespasses. But if ye do not forgive, neither will your Father which is in heaven forgive your trespasses. — Mark xi. 25, 26.

IT is easy to forgive, when we know ourselves forgiven for Jesus' sake. Whatever our posture in prayer, we must confess that we owe our Lord more than ten thousand talents, and have nothing to pay. Freely forgiven, because of the divine compassion, and the redemption purchased by Christ applied to us by his Holy Spirit, we have neither hand nor heart to take by the throat our fellow-servant, who owes us an hundred pence.

And yet we are not forgiven because we forgive those who trespass against us. We are taught to pray, "Forgive us our debts as we forgive our debtors." But the rule of forgiving and being forgiven is in these words of the Holy Spirit: "Be ye kind one to another, forgiving one another, even as God, for Christ's sake, hath forgiven you" (Eph. iv. 32).

Is there a limit to forgiveness? Yes, even to God's (Mark iii. 29).

And to ours? Yes, again (Matt. xviii. 15-17, 21, 22, and Luke xvii. 3, 4).

Yet we are to love our enemies, who will not let us forgive them (Matt. v. 44, 45).

John D. Wells.

> Think gently of the erring one!
> And let us not forget,
> However darkly stained by sin,
> He is our brother yet.
>
> Fletcher.

September 29.

The only begotten Son ... he hath declared him.
John i. 18.

All things are delivered to me of my Father: and no man knoweth who the Son is, but the Father; and who the Father is, but the Son, and he to whom the Son will reveal him. — Luke x. 22.

WHO is the Father? We know not. He is the focus of all that is high and good.

Who is the Son? We know not; the focus of all that is divine in human history and in the history of each of us.

What is the relation of the Father and the Son? Open, each to each.

What is the knowledge here spoken of, — a thing of definitions? No, of consciousness. It is a fellowship with the Father and with his Son Jesus Christ. Through it the love wherewith the Father loves the Son is in us, and he is in us. It is life eternal. It comes to us through God's commandments, given in love and accepted in simplicity.

And what is the face which God through the Son turns to us? Sympathy with childlike men; willingness to declare his blessed name; promise of an infinitude of experience.

Edward J. Horn

> But what to those who find? ah, this
> Nor tongue nor pen can show;
> The love of Jesus, what it is,
> None but his loved ones know.
> Bernard of Clairvaux *(translated by Edward Caswall).*

September 30.

Lord, evermore give us this bread. — John vi. 34.

I am that bread of life. Your fathers did eat manna in the wilderness, and are dead. — John vi. 48, 49.

A THOUSAND desires may be refused us, but bread we must have. We can do without a thousand things which we regard as necessities, and yet live; but deny us bread and we die. The need is universal and universally confessed, and to supply it the world has become a very bee-hive for industry. But Jesus here reminds us that there is a bread which we need more than this, — namely, the "Bread of life," — which will sustain us when we have done eating the bread of earth. Bread sustains and strengthens the body; but Christ sustains and strengthens the soul. Who but Christ can sustain us when temptations strong beset us? Who but Christ can strengthen us when trials and misfortunes befall us? These are the experiences which make us cry out, "Lord, to whom shall we go? Thou hast the words of eternal life." Besides, bread is good; manna must have been better, for it fell from heaven; but Jesus is the *best bread*. Even those who ate manna died; but he who eats the bread which Jesus gives shall never die. "Lord, evermore give us this bread."

A. H. Crosbie,

> O Bread to pilgrims given,
> O Food that angels eat,
> O Manna sent from heaven,
> For heaven-born natures meet,
> Give us, for thee long pining,
> To eat till richly filled,
> Till, earth's delights resigning,
> Our every wish is stilled.
>
> **Thomas Aquinas** *(translated by Ray Palmer).*

October 1.

I delight to do thy will, O my God. — Psalm xl. 8.

Now is my soul troubled; and what shall I say? Father, save me from this hour: but for this cause came I unto this hour. Father, glorify thy name. — John xii. 27, 28.

THE shadow of the agony in the garden is already falling on the spirit of the Son of man. "Son of man" we must know him to be, no less than Son of God, or there would be no mediation, no at-one-ment, and we should have but half a gospel. "This hour" signifies the consummation of the infinite sacrifice, both at Gethsemane and Calvary. Nowhere is the interior struggle of the cross laid so plainly open. The great Sufferer marks and reveals the successive steps in the secret working of his sacrificial submission. There are two possible prayers. The terrible alternative is distinctly before him; he can ask for rescue, exemption, comfort, an easy lot. How many of us, in a weaker faith, with a feebler vision, do ask these for ourselves, for those we love! That would be the surrender of the Saviour's mission for mankind to self; that is in its degree our constant temptation. No. "For this cause came I unto this hour." Self must be surrendered to God for redemption's sake, for man's sake. Two precious lights, then, shine out of the text, — the glory of self-sacrifice and the intense humanity of our Lord.

"I know," is all the Sufferer saith, —
"Knowledge by suffering entereth,
And life is perfected by death." Mrs. Browning.

October 2.

Let not thine heart be hasty to utter any thing before God. — Eccl. v. 2.

But thou, when thou prayest, enter into thy closet, and when thou hast shut thy door, pray to thy Father which is in secret; and thy Father which seeth in secret shall reward thee openly. But when ye pray, use not vain repetitions, as the heathen do: for they think that they shall be heard for their much speaking. Be not ye therefore like unto them: for your Father knoweth what things ye have need of, before ye ask him. — Matt. vi. 6, 7, 8.

PRAYER enters into the very idea of religion. Genuine prayer is at once most simple and most difficult. To have ease and joy in it is a mark of spiritual soundness and growth; to neglect it is a sure symptom of decline. Prayer has two aspects, worship and petition. In the one it terminates on God, in the other on man. In this passage our Lord treats of it in relation to God. Among the religionists of that day the prevailing motive was the love of man's applause rather than the desire of God's approval. Alms must be done where men can see, fasting paraded before the public gaze, and prayer offered loud and long in the synagogues and at the crossings of the streets, where men "most do congregate." Against this vice in prayer Jesus warns us. Have a place where you may be alone with God, a time when you have an engagement to meet him, and in this privacy, "where none but God can hear," let the soul pour itself out in praise and penitence and petition.

C. R. Hemphill

> O thou by whom we come to God,
> The life, the truth, the way,
> The path of prayer thyself hast trod!
> Lord, teach us how to pray!
>
> J. Montgomery.

October 3.

Love is the fulfilling of the law. — ROMANS xiii. 10.

On these two commandments hang all the law and the prophets. — MATT. xxii. 40.

IN this wonderful statement our Lord declares a great principle, — namely, " that love is the basis of all duty," — the first and great commandment being, " thou shalt love," and the second being like unto it, " thou shalt love." And as in the Sinaitic tables the first commands relate to God and the rest to mutual duties among men, so here the first is " thou shalt love *God*," the second " thou shalt love *men*." All duty to God and man is thus brought into proper relations. Duty has thus twofold development. First, it regards God, who as supreme is entitled to pre-eminent consideration; our relations to him as our Creator, Preserver, Redeemer, involve certain corresponding duties of obedience, gratitude, love. These are our highest obligations; they must be first in our thoughts as controlling all our conduct. Secondly, duty has its development toward men, — we must love our neighbor as ourselves; that is, as we would have him love us, and as by the teaching of the parable of the good Samaritan he makes every man our neighbor who needs our help, he gives a practical rule as well as a precept for our conduct. We thus have practical tests for the interpretation of our religious experiences. " By this shall all men know that ye are my disciples, if ye love " (John xiii. 35).

O. H. Tiffany.

> That blessed law of thine,
> Jesus, to me impart;
> The Spirit's law of life divine,
> Oh, write it on my heart!
>
> C. WESLEY.

October 4.

A door was opened unto me of the Lord. — 2 Cor. ii. 12.

I know thy works: behold, I have set before thee an open door, and no man can shut it: for thou hast a little strength, and hast kept my word, and hast not denied my name. — Rev. iii. 8.

THE church in Philadelphia, the pearl among the seven churches, receives the unmixed praise of him who is holy and true and powerful. He knows her *works* as well as her words. She is orthodox in conduct as well as in creed. She observes both tables of the law, loves God, and lets brotherly love continue. Her deeds evidence her faith.

To such a church the *door* is always open, — the door of gracious opportunity, of blessed usefulness, of ceaseless activity; and no power can *shut* it. He who unlocks it with the key of David will keep it open. The church enjoys this sublime privilege just because she has a *little strength*. Being consciously weak she supplies the condition of power. The law of God's kingdom is that humiliation shall precede exaltation, disintegration fruitfulness, oblivion advancement; and then God employs the weak things of this world with which to confound the mighty. The door stood open because she had been obedient and had kept his word, and had not denied his name. Fidelity to Christ in word and work is the test of loyalty and the condition of blessing.

Cornelius Schenck

Come, labor on!
Away with gloomy doubts and faithless fear!
No arm so weak but may do service here;
By feeblest agents can our Lord fulfil
    His righteous will.

HYMNS FROM THE LAND OF LUTHER.

October 5.

Them also which sleep in Jesus will God bring with him. — 1 Thess. iv. 14.

I am the resurrection, and the life: he that believeth in me, though he were dead, yet shall he live: and whosoever liveth and believeth in me shall never die. Believest thou this? — John xi. 25, 26.

"BY one man sin entered into the world, and death by sin, and so death passed upon all men for that all have sinned." "Jesus Christ hath abolished death, and hath brought life and incorruption to light through the gospel." "He that hath the Son hath life" and can triumphantly say, "O grave, where is thy victory? O death, where is thy sting?" The Psalmist said, "Though I walk through the valley of the shadow of death." A shadow is not substance; that shadow indicates light beyond. Dean Alford wrote the epitaph upon his tomb in Old Canterbury. It reads thus: "The inn of a traveller, on his way to the New Jerusalem." God has said, "If the spirit of him that raised up Jesus from the dead dwell in you, he that raised up Christ from the dead shall also quicken your mortal bodies." His Spirit is the earnest, confirming his word of promise: "That by two immutable things, in which it is impossible for God to lie, we might have strong consolation who have fled for refuge to lay hold upon the hope set before us." And thus we know that "when Christ, who is our life, shall appear, then shall we also appear with him in glory."

L. W. Munhall.

And he, dear Lord, that with thee dies,
And fleshly passions crucifies,
In body, like to thine, shall rise:
  Hallelujah!

W. Cooke *(Translation).*

October 6.

The root of the righteous yieldeth fruit. — Prov. xii. 12.

He that received seed into the good ground is he that heareth the word, and understandeth it; which also beareth fruit, and bringeth forth, some an hundredfold, some sixty, some thirty. — Matt. xiii. 23.

"HEREIN is my Father glorified, that ye bear much fruit," said Jesus. What a possibility, what an inspiration, that we can enhance the glory of "our Father"! Our hearts leap at the thought. How can this be done? By bearing "leaves," — a *profession* of love for him? No. By bearing *some* fruit? No. "That ye bear *much* fruit." In the abundance of the yield is the joy, the glory, of the husbandman. We should therefore aim to be extraordinary, "hundredfold" Christians, satisfied with none but the largest yield. Our lives should be packed with good deeds. Then at harvest-time we can say, "Father, I have glorified thee on the earth." This fruitfulness depends upon the condition of the heart to receive the seed, the way in which we hear the Word. Combining the three versions of this parable, we find that the characteristics of a good hearer are, — he understandeth the Word; he receiveth it; he keepeth it. Apprehension of the Word, faith in the Word, obedience to the Word, — these three are indispensable to fruitfulness. "Take heed, therefore, *how* ye hear." Meditate, believe, obey, "that ye shall neither be barren nor unfruitful in the knowledge of our Lord Jesus Christ."

W. B. Jennings.

> Then let our hearts obey
> The gospel's glorious sound;
> And all its fruits from day to day,
> Be in us and abound.
>
> J. Montgomery.

OCTOBER 7.

The angel of the Lord encampeth round about them that fear him. — PSALM xxxiv. 7.

Take heed that ye despise not one of these little ones; for I say unto you, That in heaven their angels do always behold the face of my Father which is in heaven. — MATT. xviii. 10.

"LITTLE ones," — the children of God; the saved; the heirs of salvation. "In heaven their angels always behold the face," — here an allusion is had to Oriental monarchs, who in their accustomed seclusion received into their presence only the favored courtiers of their realm. The seven princes of the court of Ahasuerus are said in the Book of Esther "to behold the king's face." But the New Testament contains a revelation of the kingdom of God on earth, as set up by our blessed Lord, and accordingly sets forth the agencies by which its affairs are administered and its subjects are protected. Hence, angels are represented as "ministering spirits sent forth" to each individual member of this spiritual kingdom for his guidance, comfort, and aid (Heb. ii. 14).

I think Christ meant to confirm that vague conception of the many of almost every age and clime, that "in heaven," the angelic host have an abiding interest in the welfare of each child of God on earth, and minister to their wants.

While Christ's "little ones," in their earth-life, cannot approach the celestial throne, their angels do; therefore already they have an interest in heaven.

Ezekiel B. Kephart,

> The hosts of God encamp around
> The dwellings of the just;
> Deliverance he affords to all
> Who on his succor trust.
>
> TATE.

October 8.

The oil of joy for mourning. — Isaiah lxi. 3.

Weep not. — Luke vii. 13.

THE words were not spoken out of impatience nor with any tone of rebuke. Jesus knew the depth of her anguish, and in anticipation of what he would do for her he says, "Weep not." It was a promise of comfort, like that given of old: "Refrain thy voice from weeping, and thine eyes from tears, for they shall come again from the land of the enemy." The watcher on the mountain sees the gleam of the coming day, while there is only darkness upon those in the valley; and when in disappointment or affliction or pain, we hearken to the word of the Lord, we will find in it a message of hope and a reason to wait patiently until the end of his work shall appear. It was little the bereaved mother knew of the purpose of Jesus when he uttered his tender appeal; little did Martha of Bethany know of the glory to be revealed because of her sorrow; and how little we know of what Jesus is able to do for us, when we are brought to the point where all human helpers are vain! He is pitiful toward us and able to make all our troubles and sorrows and sins, opportunities of his grace, as our helper and Saviour; and they who trust in him and wait shall be satisfied with his work. Their sorrow shall be turned into joy and their lament into the thankful confession, "Thou hast put off my sackcloth, and girded me with gladness."

> O my soul, what means this sadness?
> Wherefore art thou thus cast down?
> Let thy griefs be turned to gladness,
>   Bid thy restless fears be gone.
>   Look to Jesus,
>   And rejoice in his dear name.
>
> John Fawcett.

October 9.

And became obedient unto death. — PHIL. ii. 8.

O my Father, if it be possible, let this cup pass from me: nevertheless, not as I will, but as thou wilt.
O my Father, if this cup may not pass away from me, except I drink it, thy will be done. — MATT. xxvi. 39, 42.

THESE words, noblest of all words in the gospel of love, reveal to us the secret of Christ's endurance and sublime heroism. When the suffering Son of man in the crisis of his agony amid the shadows of Gethsemane finds God, *he* is his *Father* still. For all the night was growing colder, darker, and more desolate, and his soul was sinking beneath the pressure of an unutterable grief, God was his Father still! "O my Father!" — the infinitely wise, the infinitely holy, the infinitely loving and tender, — the cup which he hath given me shall I not drink it? Surely he will send no needless sorrow, and he will make every agony the birth-pang of an ineffable joy. It must needs be that afflictions come, but it is the will of the Father that they shall work out for us the far more exceeding and eternal weight of glory; and we shall be satisfied when at last we see of the travail of our soul. Oh, then, "sweet will of God," be done!

Friend, hast thou been in the garden with Jesus, and hast thou discerned that the rolling clouds which overshadowed thee with darkness were but the dust of thy Father's feet? If thou hast, then the cup of sorrow has been to thee a cup of blessing; and with the growing conviction of God's fatherhood, strength has poured in upon thy soul, till when Christ has bidden thee rise, thou hast gone forth with solemn gladness in the Master's fellowship, to duty or sacrifice.

J. A. Nelson.

My Jesus, as thou wilt!
  Oh, may thy will be mine!
Into thy hands of love
  I would my all resign;

Through sorrow, or through joy,
  Conduct me as thine own,
And help me still to say,
  My Lord, thy will be done!
    MISS J. BORTHWICK *(Translation).*

October 10.

Declaring what . . . God had wrought among the Gentiles by them. — Acts xv. 12.

As thou hast sent me into the world, even so have I also sent them into the world. — John xvii. 18.

THE Christian is not then an anchorite. By his high calling in Christ Jesus he is not withdrawn from the world, he is sent into the world. And it may startle him a little to hear his Master saying that the errand of the disciple in this world is the same as that of the Master. But the statement could not be stronger; "as," "even so,"—the parallel is as perfect as language can make it.

Jesus Christ never forgot that he was *one sent*. "I came not to do mine own will, but the will of him that sent me." "My meat is to do the will of him that sent me." He says the same thing over and over; and he never forgot the nature of his errand.

He came to learn: from the beginning he "increased in wisdom" as well as in stature. "Though he was a Son, yet learned he obedience by the things which he suffered."

He came to work: "My Father worketh hitherto, and I work."

He came to suffer: "Ought not Christ to have suffered?" he asked the bewildered pair on the road to Emmaus.

He came to save: "The Son of man is come to seek and to save that which was lost;" "I, if I be lifted up, will draw all men unto me."

The servant bears the same commission. "Even so" is he sent to learn, to labor, to suffer, to save.

Washington Gladden

O Lord and Master of us all,
  Whate'er our name or sign,
We own thy sway, we hear thy call,
  We test our lives by thine!   John G. Whittier.

October 11.

By whom also we have access. — Romans v. 2.

Verily, verily, I say unto you, I am the door of the sheep. . . . I am the door: by me if any man enter in, he shall be saved, and shall go in and out, and find pasture. — John x. 7, 9.

A FOLD has but one door; so with the kingdom of heaven. The earthly shepherd *controls* the door; the heavenly Shepherd *is* the door. The earthly shepherd admits whom he pleases; the heavenly Shepherd, — "whosoever cometh unto me, I will in no wise cast out." But he must come while the door is open, for when once the master of the house has risen up and has shut to the door, it is too late. Even a sheep cannot get in when the door is shut. There is no side door, back door, nor little door; there is one door only, and that door is Christ. The door is never ajar; it is either open or shut.

Those that enter the door are safe. They are safe because the door is shut. No use to have a door if you never shut it. When the morning comes, the door is open; no danger now. The sheep are free to go forth and enjoy the green pastures, or lie down beside the still waters. So with the believer. This life is the time of danger. He must come into the fold, and must come through the door. He must *come* in, — no compulsion about it. Once in, the door stands between him and danger. When the morning cometh, all danger is forever past. Henceforth the door "shall not be shut at all by day, for there is no night there." Then the "redeemed shall come forth with songs and everlasting joy," and the "Lamb that is in the midst of the throne shall feed them, and shall lead them to living fountains of waters."

The door stands invitingly open; let us go in.

Joseph H. Reading.

Yes; thou art still the Life, thou art the Way
  The holiest know, — Light, Life, and Way of heaven;
And they who dearest hope, and deepest pray,
  Toil by the light, life, way, which thou hast given.
Theodore Parker.

October 12.

God hath revealed them unto us by his Spirit.
1 Cor. ii. 10.

If any man will do his will, he shall know of the doctrine, whether it be of God, or whether I speak of myself. — John vii. 17.

JESUS here reveals the secret of heavenly wisdom. My doctrine is not mine, but his that sent me. My Father is my teacher. My method of learning is by rendering to him a life of perfect obedience. If you also would learn of him, then follow my example. *Do* his will, prove it by experience, and then you will know of the doctrine, whether it be of God or not.

The principle contained herein is one of widest application. Our best strength and knowledge come from practice. The more we investigate and prove by experience, the more intimate and useful becomes our understanding of them. We know the fragrance of a flower by the sense of smelling. We know the flavor of a fruit by the sense of tasting. We know the faithfulness of earthly friendship by trusting it in some emergency. In like manner, if we enter heartily upon the doing of God's will, we shall find that as we are exercised in it the divinity of its origin will more clearly appear.

Thus the door of heavenly wisdom is opened in the gospel to the humblest as well as the highest. All may attend this school. Not a great mind nor the wisdom of this world is required. The promise is, — the meek will he guide in judgment and teach his way. Let us come then with ready mind and contrite heart, to Jesus, who is meek and lowly, and he will teach us by his Spirit that we may "stand complete in all the will of God."

Bundy S. Backus

Some secret truths, from learned pride concealed,
To maids alone and children are revealed;
What though no credit doubting wits may give,
The fair and innocent shall still believe.

POPE.

October 13.

Then shall I know even as also I am known.
1 Cor. xiii. 12.

What I do thou knowest not now; but thou shalt know hereafter.
— John xiii. 7.

CHRISTIANS should yield implicit obedience and ready submission to the will of Christ. God's ways are not our ways, but they are the best ways. By faith Abraham went out, not knowing whither he went; but God led him to Canaan. Human nature finds it hard to trust. God's providences are intricate. The web seems tangled, the pattern confused; we see as yet only the wrong side, and the stitches seem set at cross purposes. By and by we shall look at it from the right side and shall know that every stitch was ordered by infinite wisdom controlled by boundless love. When we review the experiences of life in the luminous brightness of the great hereafter, we shall see that where the way seemed darkest, even there God was guiding us most tenderly. The reason of every providence will be revealed in heaven. Until then we walk by faith, seeing only one step at a time, but not in darkness, for Christ always gives light for one step. A lantern illumines the whole journey, though it shines only a few feet in advance. A familiar hymn says, —

"It will be all right in the morning."

The Christian adds, "Yes, and it is all right now."

Jesse F. Forbes.

> In vain the ways of Providence
> With anxious gaze I scan;
> To find out God by human sense, —
> It is not given to man.
>
> Thomas MacKellar.

October 14.

Unto God the Lord belong the issues from death.
Psalm lxviii. 20.

Give place: for the maid is not dead, but sleepeth. — Matt. ix. 24.

THREE times during his earth-life Jesus invades death, and calls the loved ones back. First it is the only son of a widow; then the only daughter of bereaved parents; and again the only brother of two sisters. What a comment on the heart of Christ! We are never so bewildered in sorrow that he will not come to us. None but Jesus can speak comfort to a bereaved heart. His tenderness and love and hope are a balm on the wounded spirit. His truth crowns the shadow of death with light. There is no deeper sorrow in a home than when an only daughter lies dead, — so young, so tender, so sweet; and death so cruel! Jesus once in the home of sorrow, all is changed; dead to us, but to him she "sleepeth." There is calm repose, peaceful slumber, sweet rest, certain waking. Where the loving and mighty Christ comes, all sorrow must "give place." Cold philosophy, mournful crying, old death must stand aside. Jesus has conquered death. He gives us again our loved ones in a higher, holier, sweeter, and endless life. His words, " The maid is not dead but sleepeth," in the sorrowing heart commingle ever with the sweet assurance from Bethany, "I am the resurrection and the life." And this is our hope for ourselves, and for those we need so much, and love so well.

> Though we may mourn
>   Those in life the dearest,
> They shall return,
>   Christ, when thou appearest!
> Soon shall thy voice
>   Comfort those now weeping,
> Bidding rejoice
>   All in Jesus sleeping.   Dayman.

October 15.

Lest . . . I myself should be a castaway.
1 Cor. ix. 27.

If a man abide not in me, he is cast forth as a branch, and is withered; and men gather them, and cast them into the fire, and they are burned. — John xv. 6.

How striking is this figure of the vine and its branches! How expressive of that secret but vital union which exists betwixt Christ and his people! — a union as real and essential as that between the vine and its branches.

United to Christ, the believer partakes of the nature, power, and life of Christ. From him we derive our spiritual life and fruitfulness. The Christian graces which adorn and beautify our life and character are the fruits of the Christ-life in us, and by which the " Father is glorified " and men recognize that we are disciples. " Abiding " in Christ, holiness — " the beauty of the Lord our God " — will remain " upon us," and we shall " still bring forth fruit even in old age." But what a fearful doom awaits the unbeliever, the hypocrite, and the apostate!

A branch "apart" from the vine, by an inflexible law of nature, " withers," is fit only to be " cast forth," " gathered," " cast into the fire," and " burned." Such in the very nature of things must be the inevitable result of the soul's separation from Christ, who is the source and fountain of all spiritual life. *In* him is life eternal. *Apart* from him is death everlasting. Beloved reader, seek union with Christ, abide in Christ.

E. Humphries,

Abide in thee, in that deep love of thine,
My Jesus, Lord, thou Lamb of God divine;
Down, closely down, as living branch with tree,
I would abide, my Lord, my Christ, in thee.
J. D. Smith.

October 16.

𝕷𝖔𝖔𝖐 . . . also on the things of others. — Phil. ii. 4.

Which now of these three, thinkest thou, was neighbour unto him that fell among the thieves? . . . Go, and do thou likewise. — Luke x. 36, 37.

THOUGH apart from his original design, yet our Lord gives us an apt illustration in this narrative of the helpless and wretched condition of all men in their natural state, and also of his own gracious interposition in their behalf. We have all of us been badly handled by the great adversary of God and man. We have not only been robbed and stripped and wounded and left more than half dead, but we have been left altogether "dead in trespasses and sins."

Our blessed Lord, he in whom dwelt all the fulness of the Godhead, not by chance, but "according to his eternal purpose," has been pleased to pass this way; and looking upon us in our undone state, and knowing that we were entirely "without strength," he had compassion upon us and graciously interposed between us and eternal death. " He gave himself to redeem us from all our iniquity," bound up our broken hearts, poured his healing balm into our bleeding wounds, and promised "never to leave nor forsake us," until he had brought us to the house of many mansions.

In view of what Christ has done for us when we were yet enemies and rebels against him, we should be constrained to "go and do likewise," even to our bitterest enemy, for Christ's sake. So far from confining our compassions and our contributions, we should ever bear in mind that Christian benevolence takes in an indefinitely wide sphere.

Jno. Gaslin

Thy neighbor? It is he whom thou
Hast power to aid and bless.   William Cutter.

October 17.

When he is tried, he shall receive the crown of life.
JAMES i. 12.

Every branch in me that beareth not fruit he taketh away: and every branch that beareth fruit, he purgeth it, that it may bring forth more fruit. — JOHN xv. 2.

THE fruits of the Spirit are the only evidence of a man's being a true Christian. Where there is no fruit there is no vital union to Christ. A person may be a Christian in name and have a nominal union to Christ, but there will be no fruit. Fruit must be seen in holiness of life and character. He that is destitute of these is "dead while he liveth."

There are different degrees spoken of, — "fruit," "more fruit," and "much fruit." If the Christian only bear "fruit," Christ is pleased: but he desires "more fruit" and "much fruit," and hence he often uses the pruning-knife of trial and affliction that he may make his children more holy. God never intends to do us harm by trial or to make us suffer for the sake of suffering, but "for our profit, that we may be partakers of his holiness." Am I united to Christ as the branch to the vine by a living faith? Then let me endure with patience any pruning, that I may not only bear "more fruit" but "much fruit;" for "herein is my Father glorified, that ye bear much fruit."

Samuel N. Hoadley.

Then let me never more repine
  Beneath the chastening stroke,
And be the willing spirit mine
  To wear the Saviour's yoke.
THOMAS MACKELLAR.

October 18.

I seek not your's, but you. — 2 Cor. xii. 14.

Follow me, and I will make you fishers of men. — Matt. iv. 19.

WHENEVER Christ says, "Follow me," he has in view the highest good of men. The call in this verse is more than a call to personal discipleship. It meant in the case of Andrew and Simon their work for others as well as their own personal surrender to him. To follow him would inspire them with a new love for men; to follow him would make them know something of the divine yearning to save men. Theirs would be an intense desire to "catch men" for the kingdom of God. One of the rewards of following Christ is the enlargement or exaltation of our aim in life. We need not minutely or elaborately define the figure which our Lord here uses. The simple truth is that the following of him is the condition of our highest usefulness. Discipleship makes a man a positive blessing to the world; it fills his soul with a grand evangelistic purpose. The final commission interprets the first call to Simon and Andrew. They were made disciples in order that they might go into the world to "make disciples."

If we would be "fishers of men" we must "follow him" in his methods; and thus both to obtain and to become a blessing men must heed the same gracious call, still made by the same Lord, — "Follow me."

 A glorious band the chosen few,
  On whom the Spirit came.
 Twelve valiant spirits, their hope they knew,
  And mocked the cross and flame.
 They climbed the dizzy steep to heaven
  Through peril, toil, and pain:
 O God! to us may grace be given
  To follow in their train!   HEBER.

October 19.

Not that we loved God, but that he loved us.
1 John iv. 10.

Ye have not chosen me, but I have chosen you. — John xv. 16.

CUSTOM, which is higher than law, makes it impossible for a true woman to choose her husband. She must be chosen by him. If a king should say to his peasant-bride, "You did not choose me, but I chose you," he would pay a high tribute to her worth and modesty. He would also delicately suggest the fervor and depth of his own affection.

The disciples could not have chosen Jesus. They were sinners : he was holy. They were weak; he was almighty. They were ignorant; he was omniscient. They were mortal; he was eternal. They were human; he was divine. His choice was a tribute to their worth; true love can never choose the unworthy. His choice was the evidence of infinite love. True love delights in lavishing liberal gifts upon its object; he gave himself. His choice was their exaltation, but his own humiliation; it was their salvation, but his own crucifixion. To die for love's sake is the climax of sacrifice. He who dares to die for the friends he has chosen, can fitly say to them, "Love one another as I have loved you."

Jay Benson Hamilton.

'T is done, the great transaction's done;
I am my Lord's, and he is mine.
He drew me, and I followed on,
Charmed to confess the voice divine.
PHILIP DODDRIDGE.

October 20.

Whosoever believeth that Jesus is the Christ is born of God. — 1 John v. 1.

Dost thou believe on the Son of God? — John ix. 35.

ALL men believe. Faith is an instinct of human nature, a necessity in human life. Therefore the question is not, "Dost thou believe?" but "Dost thou believe on the Son of God?"—"Dost thou acknowledge him as thy Lord, and trust him as thy Saviour?"

Momentous question, indeed, as addressed to any human soul!—for everything of value turns upon its answer. None but this Son of God can solve for any man the mystery of his being, or make sure to him his highest destiny. Only to the soul that trusts him can he become "wisdom from God, and righteousness and sanctification and redemption."

There are those in whose loving faith he is enthroned; who know his power to save and sanctify; who rejoice in the certainty, the comfort, the beauty, of their Christian faith; to whom, both for service and suffering, it is a regenerating force, a steadfast hope, a heavenly inspiration; in whom it is the source of such purity of character and peace of spirit as are even now the beginning of heaven within them.

Can I say to Jesus Christ to-day, "Lord, I believe"? Is my worship of him a proof of my faith?

Herman C. Riggs.

> Jesus, I hang upon thy word;
> I steadfastly believe
> Thou wilt return and claim me, Lord,
> And to thyself receive.
>
> C. Wesley.

October 21.

Against thee, thee only, have I sinned. — PSALM li. 4.

And the publican, standing afar off, would not lift up so much as his eyes unto heaven, but smote upon his breast, saying, God be merciful to me a sinner. — LUKE xviii. 13.

THIS publican, despised and hated of men, now spiritually convicted, knows, and therefore condemns and hates himself. Utterly humbled, he dares only to step over the threshold of the temple, because there dwells God, against whom he has sinned. He does not presume to look up to heaven, because God is there. In agony he smites upon his now broken heart, out of which so much sin has come. His sense of utmost need no longer lets him be silent. Deeply penitent he cries, not for his fancied rights, not for some earned reward, but for mercy, unmerited forgiveness. Earnestly he cries to God, that God against whom he has sinned. He feels that no other can reach his desperate case. Twin-born with his penitence is faith, appropriating belief in God's ability and willingness to save even him.

"To me, *the* sinner." He no more mistakes his condition than its cause, sin. Not "to me" as a publican, as one unfortunate, an unwilling victim of others, but "to me, *the sinner*." This prayer of humble faith earnestly offered by a self-condemning, penitent, believing sinner, always has been, always will be heard. "He went down to his house, justified."

A. Huntington Clapp.

> Behold, we fall before thy face;
> Our only refuge is thy grace.
> No outward forms can make us clean;
> The leprosy lies deep within.
>   WATTS.

October 22.

In the wilderness shall waters break out.
ISAIAH xxxv. 6.

I am Alpha and Omega, the beginning and the end. I will give unto him that is athirst of the fountain of the water of life freely.— REV. xxi. 6.

WE have here a statement, " I will give," etc.; a fact, "it is done." The speaker is (verse 5) "he that sat upon the throne," the Omnipotent; here he is "Alpha and Omega, the beginning and the end," the eternal.

This is therefore a fundamental, spiritual law on the authority of the Omnipotent and with the witness of the Eternal. Material laws exist in and with matter as essentials. This is an essential law of the spirit universe. Nature, with forces always omnipotent in their realm, abhors and fills a vacuum. Omnipotence and eternity make a spiritual vacuum forever impossible. The soul thirsts; it is satisfied. It cries out for God; God is its possession; the want is the realization.

The measure is, "freely;" the quantity, what Omnipotence can give; the continuance, while eternity endures.

When the sinner, like the prodigal, "comes to himself," he has fact, not promise only. Jesus says, "Come, for all things are *ready.*" In Jesus Christ "the Almighty," "the same yesterday, to-day, and forever," the soul, thirsting, is forever satisfied; and whosoever drinks has in him "a well of water springing up into everlasting life."

Geo. D. Hulst.

Here see the bread of life; see waters flowing
  Forth from the throne of God, pure from above.
Come to the feast of love; come ever knowing
  Earth has no sorrow but heaven can remove.

October 23.

He shall deliver the needy when he crieth.
PSALM lxxii. 12.

Verily I say unto thee, To day shalt thou be with me in paradise.
— LUKE xxiii. 43.

THUS began the fulfilment of the Saviour's prophecy, " I, if I be lifted up from the earth, will draw all men unto me." Christ crucified was the object upon which the malefactor's faith rested. It is an affecting thought that the penitent thief was probably at that hour the only human being who unwaveringly believed in the power and coming of Jesus. Never had his claims and promises seemed so preposterous; never had his cause looked so dark. But though all men had forsaken him, this dying sinner anticipated the glorious advent of the dying Saviour and made his petition, " Lord, remember me."

One might almost think that he would want to forget himself and drop from the remembrance of the just and the pure. But faith in Christ enables the sinner to forgive himself and to say of the man that he was, " It is no longer I." The new man within him does not think of hiding from the face of him that sitteth on the throne, but asks as his greatest boon to be held in the memory of a pitiful Lord.

How kingly is the Saviour's response! How far it exceeds the breadth of the petition! The mercy of Christ can reach to the vilest sinner. It can save him in his greatest extremity. It can save him completely. From the place of his penitence it is not even a day's journey to the Paradise of God.

George Alexander.

> The dying thief rejoiced to see
> That fountain in his day;
> And there may I, though vile as he,
> Wash all my sins away.
> COWPER.

October 24.

Jesus Christ who is the faithful witness. — Rev. i. 5.

Thou hast said: nevertheless I say unto you, Hereafter shall ye see the Son of man sitting on the right hand of power, and coming in the clouds of heaven. — Matt. xxvi. 64.

CHRIST spoke the truth with respect to his Messiahship and his divine sonship. The apostle Paul calls this "witnessing a good confession." He came into the world to bear witness to this truth. In his life also he was the Truth. His life manifests the eternal realities of the spiritual universe, and so he is essentially the king of men. As Christ's earthly life manifested God, so will every true, loving disciple of Christ manifest the same life, and so be a witness for Christ. As a new incarnation, Christ's life is to become the life of the world.

Besides his rule and kingship among men, he will be seen hereafter on the right hand of power, exalted in the heavens, as the judge of all men. He is now judged by a human tribunal; hereafter *he* will sit in judgment. In these perils and indignities of his trial and condemnation, Christ's consciousness of his own essential glory kept him true to his divine purpose.

After this divine pattern, every true, faithful life will be a perpetual witness to the truth, — serene and patient in the presence of perils; counting the sufferings of the present not worthy to be compared with the glory that will be revealed in us.

A. R. Bentoro

We shall see him in our nature
  Seated on his lofty throne;
Loved, adored, by every creature,
  Owned as God, and God alone!
There the hosts of shining spirits
  Strike their harps and loudly sing
To the praise of Jesus' merits,
  To the glory of their King.   M. Pyper.

October 25.

Whosoever shall call upon the name of the Lord shall be saved. — Romans x. 13.

Verily I say unto you, That the publicans and the harlots go into the kingdom of God before you. — Matt. xxi. 31.

IN this parable our Lord points out two classes of men, — manifest sinners and hypocrites. In the first class we have the general reply of the unsaved, "I will not." In the second class we have the declaration of hypocrites, who promise much and do but little. Better not promise at all than to promise and not fulfil. All who openly profess the religion of Christ, say by that act, "I go." I accept of Christ and his religion for all there is in it and all there is of it, — soul, body, and spirit, — all for Christ. But alas, how few comparatively do this! They say, "I go," but go not. Publicans and harlots, the worst of sinners, who have all along said, "I will not," will go into the kingdom of God before such hypocritical professors. A mere profession of Christ's religion will not suffice; there must be an inward conformity to the divine will, and a consecration of the whole being to God. "Thou shalt love the Lord thy God with all thy heart, and with all thy soul, and with all thy mind." It requires all this to be a true follower of Christ. All this is implied in the words, "I go, sir." Our Lord throws a ray of light upon the pathway of the unsaved. Although they have often said, "I will not," yet if they turn to God with an honest, sincere heart and say, "I go," they will find the door into the kingdom of God wide open. "Whosoever will" may enter in.

J. Weaver

Long from thee my footsteps straying,
 Thorny proved the way I trod;
Weary come I now, and praying,
 Take me to thy love, my God!   Ray Palmer.

October 26.

The greatest of these is charity. — 1 Cor. xiii. 13.

If ye love me, keep my commandments. — John xiv. 15.

GREAT is faith and great is hope, but greater than these is love. Faith is mighty even to the moving of mountains; it sails the wildest seas; it can open blind eyes, can do many a miracle; it justifies the soul and anticipates heaven. Great is faith; but love is greater. Faith tires betimes; love is unwearied. Faith is not always welcome; love is at home everywhere and travels all the world without a passport. Faith is now and again a day late. Love stayed last at the cross and came first to the sepulchre. Faith and hope long for heaven. Love *is* heaven; for God is love, and when we love we are in heaven.

Would you get out of a man the best that is in him, the appeal must be to love. One may learn geometry, yet may not know nor have even so much as heard of Euclid. But we cannot rightly accept "these sayings of mine" without taking to our hearts him who said them. We cannot separate Christ's precept from Christ's person. "Never man spake like this man." As he continues to speak, follow him up and presently you will cry, "My Lord and my God! Thou alone hast the words of eternal life; to whom else can we go?" "Lord, thou knowest that I love thee." "If ye love me, keep my commandments," — do my will; "Be doers of the word and not hearers only." Let your deeds be your eulogists. More eloquent than words, more effective than self-assertion, is the doing of the Master's will, prompted out of a heart full of love for the Master and deeply imbued with his truth.

John R. Paxton

Speak to me by name, O Master!
  Let me know it is to me;
Speak, that I may follow faster
  With a step more firm and free,
Where the Shepherd leads the flock
  In the shadow of the rock.   F. R. Havergal.

October 27.

He brought me to the banqueting-house, and his banner over me was love. — Song of Solomon ii. 4.

With desire I have desired to eat this passover with you before I suffer. — Luke xxii. 15.

WHAT a wealth of love these words reveal! How they discover also the reality and intimacy of our Lord's union with his chosen ones! His love, in this pathetic renewal of tender regard, seems literally to close them in in its marvellous fulness. Truly in this last passover they and he are one. The intensity of our Lord's desire is seen in the scrupulous care he had taken to secure its quiet and uninterrupted enjoyment. Why was this desire to eat with them so great? Partly because in the heaviness of his sorrow now he yearned for the solace of the disciples' sympathy and communion of love, just as he did later amid the agonies of Gethsemane. He loved his own, and rejoiced in their love for him. Partly, also, because he was glad to give these loyal ones an unmistakable exhibition of his relation to them as their Saviour. He had sadly felt their slowness to understand his mission in its spiritual meaning. Now he so uses the passover memorial, whose significance they know, though it will cease with his own death, that they cannot fail to see the true meaning of his work; and the symbolism is so clear that they can never forget him. Thus he makes the feast the fellowship of intelligent love with his sufferings for sinners.

Let us come to his table with like desire for him, and not grieve him by any heartless formality or chilling indifference. Let us make it the communion of reciprocal yearning.

William McCauslee

This is the hour of banquet and of song;
This is the heavenly table spread for me.
Here let me feast, and feasting still prolong
The brief, bright hour of fellowship with thee.
                                                                H. Bonar.

October 28.

The unity of the spirit. — Eph. iv. 3.

Neither pray I for these alone, but for them also which shall believe on me through their word; that they all may be one; as thou, Father, art in me, and I in thee, that they also may be one in us: that the world may believe that thou hast sent me. — John xvii. 20, 21.

THE eye of the Saviour runs forward through time to the end of the world. It embraces all the Christians of all the ages in a single glance. What a foresight!

He prays for their unity. It is to be like the oneness of the Father and the Son. Christians should be united in love, in purpose, and in endeavor. God in redemption is the centre of Christian unity, "one in us." "God was in Christ reconciling the world unto himself." Christians come to unity as they become more and more absorbed in entreating men, "Be ye reconciled to God." Christian missions are the path to Christian union. Differences otherwise magnified vanish before pagans in foreign lands or in the presence of degraded classes within Christendom. It must be so if the world is to believe that God in infinite love sent his Son for its salvation.

It is within my power to fulfil in a measure the prayer of my dying Saviour. I can abolish all spirit of party or sect in myself. I can make myself one with all Christians of whatever name or nation. Let me not fail to offer to Christ that desire of his heart.

P. F. Leavens.

    Bind thy people, Lord, in union,
      With the sevenfold cord of love;
    Breathe a spirit of communion
      With the glorious hosts above.
    Let thy work be seen progressing;
      Bow each heart and bend each knee,
    Till the world, thy truth possessing,
      Celebrates its jubilee.   Aveling.

October 29.

The letter killeth, but the spirit giveth life. — 2 Cor. iii. 6.

It is the spirit that quickeneth; the flesh profiteth nothing: the words that I speak unto you, they are spirit, and they are life. — John vi. 63.

THIS passage suggests such important distinctions as letter and spirit, form and power, ordinance and grace conveyed. As the soul to the body of Adam, the spirit is to the letter, the power to the form, and the grace to the ordinance. Without an appropriating faith in Jesus, the bread of God, no good could come of a literal eating of his flesh or drinking of his blood. Adam's body was but fashioned clay until the Creator breathed upon it. The breathing made the moving, living soul, invested with rule among the creatures. Empty formalism receives rebuke in these words. The Church may not usurp the prerogatives of her founder and substitute connection with herself for union with her living Head. The spiritual discernment of Christ in his sacraments makes them means of replenishing to the soul. Apart from the washing of regeneration, baptism may *signify*, but it will not *convey* cleansing to the heart. Void of gracious sustenance the supper becomes, where the Lord's body is not discerned. In the knowledge of God and his Son Jesus Christ standeth our eternal life; but the condition of that saving knowledge is supplied in the Spirit's twofold work of *revelation* and *illumination*. The lack of the latter leaves the wondrous things in the law unseen, and the Bible forever a sealed book. "For we are the circumcision which worship God in the Spirit, and rejoice in Christ Jesus, and have no confidence in the flesh" (Phil. iii. 3).

> God through himself we then shall know,
>   If thou within us shine,
> And sound, with all thy saints below,
>   The depths of love divine.   C. Wesley.

October 30.

All the ends of the earth shall see the salvation of our God. — Isaiah lii. 10.

All power is given unto me in heaven and in earth. Go ye therefore, and teach all nations, baptizing them in the name of the Father, and of the Son, and of the Holy Ghost: teaching them to observe all things whatsoever I have commanded you: and, lo, I am with you alway, even unto the end of the world. — Matt. xxviii. 18-20.

THESE words become his lips who spake them, and his alone. They are the climax to which all that went before led up. They give to the gospel story its deepest meaning. They crown it with its highest glory. They declare Jesus in power and purpose Saviour of mankind. They constitute his imperative, perpetual commission to his disciples.

How comprehensive their content! — "all power," sufficient for all undertakings, oppositions, difficulties, delays, and triumphs; "all nations," — not one to be left undiscipled; the entire race, redeemed by his blood, to be discipled and made one in him; "all the days," — each day and all day, till time shall end.

How vital their connection, — the foundation fact his universal *power*; on this fact, the *precept*, "Go!" to this precept joined, the *promise*, "Lo, I am with you!" Power, precept, promise, all so joined that they cannot be dissevered. No power? then no obedience. No obedience? then no presence. No presence? then no power.

Lord, by thy power make thy people willing, and by thy presence give them power to obey thy precept, that so thy glory may soon fill the earth!

Henry N. Cobb

Baptize the nations; far and nigh
    The triumphs of the cross record;
The name of Jesus glorify,
    Till every kindred call him Lord. J. Montgomery.

October 31.

Behold, he prayeth! — Acts ix. 11.

I thank thee, O Father, Lord of heaven and earth, because thou hast hid these things from the wise and prudent, and hast revealed them unto babes. Even so, Father: for so it seemed good in thy sight. — Matt. xi. 25, 26.

WHAT a graceful yet sublime veil of mystery envelops like a glistering robe the person of the praying Saviour! These communings of the incarnate Son with the eternal Father must in some aspects remain inexplicable to finite minds. They constitute a part of that central mystery of the Trinity which it is not given to man to comprehend. God hides even while he reveals.

And yet how precious are the records of the praying as well as the teaching, the acting, the suffering Christ. Four times in his intercessions we hear from his lips that tender word, *Father!* In this instance it stands in what strange contrast with the judicial utterance just preceding! Here also the prayer changes into an outburst of thanksgiving such as never before or since ascended to the throne where in august sovereignty the Father is seated.

Oh, the sad estate of those from whose eyes the things of God, the precious verities of grace, are hidden! wise and prudent in earthly things, they fail to see heavenly things, and their loss is utter and everlasting. Oh, the blessedness of those who in the simplicity of childhood hear and believe what Christ has spoken! Though babes in the earthly sense, they are the true children of the Father and heirs through Christ of all the promises.

Edward D. Morris.

Glorified apostles raise,
Night and day, continual praise.
Hast thou not a mission too
For thy children here to do?
With the prophets' goodly line
We in mystic bond combine, —
For thou hast to babes revealed
Things that to the wise were sealed.
Millard (*Translation*).

November 1.

God . . . now commandeth all men every where to repent.
ACTS xvii. 30.

Go out into the highways and hedges, and compel them to come in, that my house may be filled. — LUKE xiv. 23.

THE disciple must go to those who need him; they will not come to him. Earth's highways and byways are alike filled with the neglected and perishing, and the disciple, like his Master, has a special mission to them. "As the Father hath sent me into the world, even so send I you." Like our blessed Saviour, we too must seek and save the lost. We are ever prone to turn to those who have not gone astray, but such was not the spirit of the Master. God has in these latter days brought all the ends of the earth together, and now the earnest worker can go to almost any part of the globe without difficulty, and bring in the wanderer and the outcast to the royal feast of heaven. With hands of holy violence and yet with the voice of love and the touch of gentleness we should go after the most needy and neglected ones of earth in the assured confidence that God's blessing will follow us, and that our labors shall not be in vain. In the great banqueting house of heaven may it be ours to see some among the happy guests who shall have been gathered in by our faithful obedience to this command!

J. M. Thoburn

Whoever will — O gracious word ! —
 May of this stream partake;
Come, thirsty souls, and bless the Lord,
 And drink for Jesus' sake!

SAMUEL MEDLEY *(altered)*.

November 2.

I believe that Jesus Christ is the Son of God.
Acts viii. 37.

Blessed art thou, Simon Bar-jona: for flesh and blood hath not revealed it unto thee, but my Father which is in heaven. And I say also unto thee, That thou art Peter, and upon this rock I will build my church; and the gates of hell shall not prevail against it. — Matt. xvi. 17, 18.

IN these words Christ inaugurates his church and unfolds its constitution and destiny. His church is to be henceforth the organized and visible form of God's kingdom in the world. Men enter it through a faith and confession wrought in them by the Holy Spirit. Simon Bar-Jona is "blessed," and made "Peter" (a rock) by this spiritually inwrought faith and confession.

When he through the Holy Spirit received and confessed Jesus as the Christ, the Son of the living God, he laid the first stone in that building in which as living stones are builded all who, taught by the Spirit, possess the same faith and make the same confession. When therefore Christ says "On this rock I will build my church" he says his church shall be built on this *petrine* quality, be built on, and out of Peters, — on and out of characters and lives such as are produced by acceptance and confession of Christ under the teaching of the Holy Ghost, of which Peter is a type. Thus builded, it will endure unshaken every assault and conquer every foe. "The gates of Hades," or all the powers of evil, of darkness, and of death, shall not prevail against it.

John B. Drury.

Crowns and thrones may perish,
 Kingdoms rise and wane,
But the church of Jesus
 Constant will remain.

Gates of hell can never
 'Gainst that church prevail;
We have Christ's own promise,
 And that cannot fail.
  Baring-Gould.

November 3.

There was given him . . . a kingdom, that all . . . should serve him: . . . and his kingdom . . . shall not be destroyed. — DANIEL vii. 14.

My kingdom is not of this world : if my kingdom were of this world, then would my servants fight, that I should not be delivered to the Jews: but now is my kingdom not from hence. — JOHN xviii. 36.

JESUS was charged with the assumption of an earthly kingship by the Jews. On this false accusation he was delivered unto Pilate. Pilate said unto him, "Art thou the King of the Jews?" Jesus made no denial, but explained in the words of this passage the true nature of his kingdom, — a hidden spiritual kingdom. He said, "If my kingdom were of this world, then would my servants fight, that I should not be delivered to the Jews, but now is my kingdom not from hence." He aspired to no earthly regal power and glory. All he asks is to be enthroned in the hearts and lives of men, — to rule their wills, affections, passions, motives, and acts. These are his subjects, and with these under his guidance and control, he rules the world. With these at his command every individual soul becomes a glorious habitation, and every life pure and beautiful to behold.

Dear reader, have you this divine kingdom set up in your heart? If not, then please do *now* open the door that "the King of glory may come in."

Wm. J. Shuey

> Hasten, Lord, the glorious time
>   When, beneath Messiah's sway,
> Every nation, every clime,
>   Shall the gospel call obey!
> Then shall wars and tumults cease;
>   Then be banished grief and pain;
> Righteousness and joy and peace,
>   Undisturbed, shall ever reign.   HARRIET AUBER.

November 4.

What time I am afraid I will trust in thee. — PSALM lvi. 3.

It is I; be not afraid. — JOHN vi. 20.

HOW human for the disciples with minds somewhat tinged with the superstitions of their age to be afraid of such a marvellous manifestation! True, Christ was all the while surprising them with some new phase of his divinity and love. Nevertheless, they were fearful, requiring frequently some gentle rebuke, — "Fear not," "Why are ye fearful?"

Our blessed Lord was more apt and ready to deliver the disciples from the perils of their fears than they were to recognize the form so clear and visible in the dark, as their Lord walking upon the boisterous and turbulent waters.

Fear and doubt cramp the action and chill the life of our faith, clouding our sight of Jesus. Thus was it that he was so prompt to assure them that what they beheld was not a vision of fright and evil, but that it was their best friend. "It is I; be not afraid."

Fear is a treacherous foe of faith. It alarms and weakens its subject, making it a more possible prey for the enemy without. Jesus would have us to be Christian heroes, never surrender to our fears. Certainly he knows how hard we toil to make a headway against the resistless forces of life. His ever active sympathy and tender love bring him to our rescue in the hour of danger.

If we would realize the more that Jesus is always with us in our trials, not only may we hear his still and inspiring voice, but also obtain the needed help that makes our burdens light. In the midst of the tempests of life, Jesus comes to fellowship with us.

Wm H. Thomas

Thou who in darkness walking didst appear
Upon the waves and thy disciples cheer,
When all is dark may we behold thee nigh,
And hear thy voice, "Fear not, for it is I"!
C. WORDSWORTH.

November 5.

Haste thee, escape thither. — GEN. xix. 22.

Enter ye in at the strait gate. — MATT. vii. 13.

THIS thought should be an incentive to earnest action in this probationary life, that it may issue in a joyful eternity. The man at the railway-gate sees pleasure beckoning him within as he journeys to his family, and pain mocking him without, if like the foolish virgins he hears the saddest of words, "too late." The gate is a definite, plain entrance, and is shown in mercy by him who said, "I am the door." It implies action, for he who would enter must move and not debate. He must not be overladen, for the young man loved by Christ could not get his large burden of worldly goods through the strait passage. The narrow defile introduces to the beautiful valley, and the celestial city shines before the Christian traveller. The strait gate of repentance leads to the wide gate of Paradise. As Saint Chrysostom teaches, though the gate is strait, the heavenly city is wide. It contains "a great multitude, which no man could number" (Rev. vii. 9). Let us with Saint Ignatius not desire "even to breathe apart from" Christ in self-denial and devotion and holy sacrament, that the "gate of death" may bring us to the gate of resurrection, to eternal life, and we "may enter in through the gates into the city" (Rev. xxii. 14).

S. F. Hotchkin

I see not the way before,
But I go at thy command,
Entering gladly duty's door,
Led by thy directing hand.

THOMAS MACKELLAR.

NOVEMBER 6.

Let every man take heed how he buildeth. — 1 COR. iii. 10.

And every one that heareth these sayings of mine, and doeth them not, shall be likened unto a foolish man, which built his house upon the sand: and the rain descended, and the floods came, and the winds blew, and beat upon that house; and it fell: and great was the fall of it. — MATT. vii. 26, 27.

AN inverted pyramid is an impossibility. A ship must have ballast. A balloon must have a car. In air, on water, on land, a good foundation is the most important thing.

In religion there is but one foundation. "Other foundation can no man lay than that is laid, which is Jesus Christ." All others are sand. The silica may sparkle in them, but they are sand. Without Christ, God's mercy is sand; the cement of grace is lacking. Without Christ, man's excellence is sand; the cement of faith is lacking.

Every man's foundation will be tested, thoroughly tested. "The rain *descended*." It will be tested by God and by the Devil. "The floods came" from the deep. It will be tested by men and circumstances. "The winds blew" from all quarters, and these all *beat* upon the house. Whoso has built on sand *must* fall. Is it harsh to call such an one foolish?

Yes, great will be the fall! Not a leaning tower of Pisa has fallen, but *a man!* Fallen! — not prone upon the earth, but down, down, down into outer darkness. Fallen! A building, every stone and timber and fresco of which was instinct with life, is in ruins, yet *still lives*.

These verses close the Sermon on the Mount. God grant they may not portray the close of your life!

J. B. Caldwell

> My gracious Lord, I own thy right
> To every service I can pay;
> And call it my supreme delight
> To hear thy dictates and obey.
>
> PHILIP DODDRIDGE.

NOVEMBER 7.

This is life eternal, that they might know thee the only true God, and Jesus Christ, whom thou hast sent. — JOHN xvii. 3.

If ye had known me, ye should have known my Father also: and from henceforth ye know him, and have seen him. — JOHN xiv. 7.

BY the examination of the context of this passage it is apparent that these disciples knew many things concerning Christ; that is, they knew him so far as *faith* enabled them to know him to be the Son of God, the true Messiah, and the Saviour of the world. But this is a tacit reproof because they did not know him more fully and perfectly as one with the Father, similar in meaning to John viii. 19, where in answer to the question, "Where is thy Father?" Jesus answered, "Ye neither know me nor my Father: if ye had known me, ye should have known my Father also."

Wheelock H. Parmly

The Father is in God the Son,
And with the Father he is one;
In both the Spirit doth abide,
And with them both is glorified.

O Father, thou most holy One!
O Son of God, eternal Son!
O Holy Ghost, thou Love divine,
To join them both is ever thine!

Eternal Father, thee we praise!
To thee, O Son, our hymns we raise!
O Holy Ghost, we thee adore,
One mighty God forevermore!

H. W. BAKER.

NOVEMBER 8.

Whatsoever he saith unto you, do it. — JOHN ii. 5.

Whosoever therefore shall break one of these least commandments, and shall teach men so, he shall be called the least in the kingdom of heaven: but whosoever shall do and teach them, the same shall be called great in the kingdom of heaven. — MATT. v. 19.

WHATEVER we do is a lesson. The breaking or teaching of a commandment is always a teaching of the same. The most trifling and concealed transgression declares itself in an evil influence upon others. The most insignificant and modest act of obedience instructs all and is an impulse to goodness.

Least and greatest in the kingdom! How shall we avoid falling so low, and how succeed in rising so high? Give heed to the little things. To be unfaithful in the least sinks us in spiritual degradation; to be faithful in the least lifts us to crowned eminence before God.

Oh, these conclusive little things! We step over them in our daily path and drop them on either side, — too trivial for notice. Yet they determine character and influence, acceptance and rank before God.

Each command gives opportunity to gain or lose position. Where shall be our place, — low down or high up? That depends upon the day's, yea, the moment's, obedience. What shall be the reach of our influence, — narrow or wide? That depends upon immediate and constant example. Even a little faithfulness wins a large acknowledgment.

Edwin A. Bulkley

    Give me to know thy will, O God!
        And may I see to-day
    A light from heaven upon my road
        To clearly point the way!
    That I may know just what to do
        And what to leave undone,
    And be unto thy service true
        From dawn to setting sun.
                      THOMAS MACKELLAR.

November 9.

Overcome evil with good. — ROMANS xii. 21.

Love your enemies, bless them that curse you, do good to them that hate you, and pray for them which despitefully use you, and persecute you; that ye may be the children of your Father which is in heaven: for he maketh his sun to rise on the evil and on the good, and sendeth rain on the just and on the unjust. — MATT. v. 44, 45.

JEWISH rabbi and heathen sage had taught alike the maxims of love for friends and hatred for enemies. But here is a new departure in the field of ethics, — an announcement that must have strangely startled the hearers of Jesus. How should they, indeed, love an enemy, reward bitterness and hate with blessing, or make intercession for the defamer and persecutor? But Jesus followed quickly with a reason for his tenet, a consideration the highest that could be conceived of. They who do these things shall be called the children of God. There is no higher character ascribed to God than that in which he appears as offering forgiveness to offenders. They, then, who cherish this perfect spirit of forgiveness are in the highest and best sense like God, and accounted worthy to be named his children. To acquire this spirit, to attain this divine likeness and this exalted recognition, should demand our best ambition and noblest strife. Blessed Saviour, thou Prince among teachers, may we sit humbly at thy feet until thou dost teach us perfectly this lesson, and dost put into our hearts the spirit which enabled thee to pray, " Father, forgive them, for they know not what they do!"

D. Berger

> Thy foes might hate, despise, revile,
>   Thy friends unfaithful prove;
> Unwearied in forgiveness still,
>   Thy heart could only love.
>   SIR E. DENNY.

November 10.

Partakers of Christ, if we hold the beginning of our confidence stedfast unto the end. — Heb. iii. 14.

But he that shall endure unto the end, the same shall be saved. — Matt. xxiv. 13.

A WARNING note the Master sounds as he "sits upon the Mount of Olives." The love of the majority shall cool, therefore "endure." To begin is not to finish; profession is not possession, neither is confession conquest. Admiration for the character of Christ is far different from submitting to the will of Christ. "He endured the cross." "And from that time many of his disciples went back and walked no more with him." The multitudes who shouted, "Hosanna," cried also, "Crucify." The disciple who said, "Though I should die with thee, yet will I not deny thee," likewise declared, "I do not know the man;" and it was "one of the twelve who betrayed him." "Blessed is the man that endureth temptation," trial, tribulation, who has patience to submit to the command of his Lord, and who has perseverance to press forward in the face of difficulty and in spite of all opposition. "They starve well," was the comment of an old commander on his patient troops. "They charge well," was the encomium which a veteran general gave to his leal-hearted warriors. To starve, to charge, to be patient, to persevere, "to hold fast that which thou hast, that no man take thy crown," and "to press toward the mark for the prize of the high calling of God in Christ Jesus," — this is to endure; "and he that endureth to the end, the same shall be saved."

A. M. Halsey.

Ne'er think the victory won,
Nor lay thine armor down;
Thine arduous work will not be done
Till thou obtain the crown.

HEATH.

November 11.

If any man's work abide ... he shall receive a reward.
1 Cor. iii. 14.

Behold, I come quickly; and my reward is with me, to give every man according as his work shall be. — Rev. xxii. 12.

THE disciples came to Jesus and asked, "What shall be the sign of thy coming, and of the end of the world?" He replied, Many deceivers and many false prophets shall arise, iniquity shall abound, and the love of many wax cold before the end comes. And this gospel of the kingdom shall be preached in the whole world for a testimony unto all the nations; and then shall the end come. This will be the prelude to the judgment. Then shall appear the sign of the Son of man in heaven. No one will be able to anticipate the time of these events, and the appearing of the Lord will be with the suddenness and vividness of lightning; and he will have "wages" with him to give to each as his labor merits. It will be a day of vengeance to the wicked, but a day of reward to the righteous. Note the contrast: "Depart from me, ye cursed," and "Enter into the joy of thy Lord." The coming of the Lord Jesus will be the occasion of the greatest joy to his saints. They will behold him coming to be glorified in his saints; they will greet him with unending praises. What manner of persons ought *we* to be in all holy living, looking for the coming of the day of God? Shall we not wait with holy longing, ready at any moment when we shall hear his voice anew — "Yea, I come quickly" — to cry out, "Amen; come, Lord Jesus"?

P. J. Pockman

> Haste the day of thy returning
>   With thy ransomed church to reign;
> Then shall end our days of mourning,
>   We shall sing with rapture then,
>   Thou art worthy!
>   Come, Lord Jesus, come; Amen!

J. G. Deck.

NOVEMBER 12.

Give me this water, that I thirst not.—JOHN iv. 15.

I am the bread of life: he that cometh to me shall never hunger; and he that believeth on me shall never thirst.—JOHN vi. 35.

THIS is one of the "I ams" of Christ, and one which is very precious to the believer. Christ is the source and support of spiritual life. As bread is necessary to the body, so is Christ essential to the soul. As the grain has to be crushed in order to become bread, so Christ's body had to be broken and his blood shed on the cross, that he might become the bread of life.

Unless bread is eaten it is useless. In like manner Jesus Christ must be partaken of by faith. He who uses this bread of life shall never hunger and never thirst. He shall never again hunger for this world, as formerly. He has found the grand elixir of life, so that even though he passes through the valley of Baca, he can make in it a well. He shall not hunger and thirst always, but can look forward to a glorious time when he shall join the throng "who shall hunger no more, neither thirst any more . . . for the Lamb, which is in the midst of the throne, shall feed them and shall lead them to living fountains of waters."

H. W. Kidd.

Thou, Saviour, art the living bread;
Thou wilt my every want supply.
By thee sustained and cheered and led,
I'll press through dangers to the sky.
RAY PALMER.

November 13.

With the mouth confession is made unto salvation.
ROMANS x. 10.

Whosoever therefore shall confess me before men, him will I also confess before my Father which is in heaven. But whosoever shall deny me before men, him will I also deny before my Father which is in heaven.—MATT. x. 32, 33.

TO confess Christ before men is to make a public acknowledgment of him as the Saviour of the race, but especially to express one's acceptance of him as his personal Saviour, to espouse actively his cause, to ally one's self with the disciples of Christ. He that announces his trust in Jesus for forgiveness, who is truly baptized into the name of Christ, and partakes of the Lord's Supper, who unites with the Church and labors for the upbuilding of Christ's kingdom, in all these ways confesses Christ. So also a life of obedience, humility, piety, godly zeal, which is Christ-like, is a witness for Christ and a testimony to his transforming power. Such an one will Christ not only formally acknowledge before the Father, but give him a glorious share in his heavenly honor.

To deny Christ is to do the opposite of the above. To do this it is not necessary publicly and formally to declare one's renunciation of Christ as an infidel might do, but simply neglect to confess him in the ways above indicated. If we in any such way disown Christ, we are none of his, and it cannot but be that he must disown us.

Let us, then, accept and confess Christ as our Lord and Saviour.

J. P. Landis,

> I'm not ashamed to own my Lord,
>   Or to defend his cause;
> Maintain the honor of his Word,
>   The glory of his cross.
>
>   WATTS.

November 14.

Who hath despised the day of small things?
ZECH. iv. 10.

Gather up the fragments that remain, that nothing be lost. — JOHN vi. 12.

THIS utterance of our Lord is one of the many side-lights to be found in the gospel narratives. It ushers us into the realm of purely temporal things and is nothing more than a commonplace order such as any one might find in the mouth of an average housewife. This homely injunction not to waste even the remains of a dinner is severely practical, and forms a sharp contrast to the sublime spiritual truths which our Saviour had so recently given his disciples on the mountain-top. A great descent, we exclaim, and yet what a testimony to the completeness of Christ's character! Unlike the majority of men, our Lord was many-sided. He was not so lost in contemplation as to be unmindful of the wants of the body. He who discoursed so eloquently upon the glories of God's kingdom was not above practising the little economies of life and inculcating the importance of frugality. Both by precept and example Christ taught that wastefulness is sin. Saving may be one of the minor virtues perhaps, still, let us remember that the command to "gather up the fragments" came from him who was able to feed five thousand. The liberal Christian is usually the man who has learned this lesson of economy. It is not given us to multiply loaves of bread; but where is the man who cannot save something and become instrumental in sending the bread of life to those who have it not?

John L. Scudder

Scorn not the slightest word or deed,
  Nor deem it void of power;
There's fruit in each wind-wafted seed
  That waits its natal hour.

ANONYMOUS.

November 15.

I dwell . . . with him also that is of a contrite and humble spirit. — Isaiah lvii. 15.

Blessed are the poor in spirit: for their's is the kingdom of heaven.
Matt. v. 3.

THIS is our Lord's protest against the self-satisfied but self-deceived righteousness of the scribes and Pharisees, and against the ethical legalism and self-wrought virtue on which so many estimable people base their hope of heaven. Christ came not to press upon men a salvation not needed. He does not offer "unsearchable riches" to those "who are rich and increased with goods and have need of nothing," but to the poor in spirit, those who are utterly destitute of spiritual resources and have come to know it, and with profound self-abasement are ready to acknowledge it. They have come to themselves as did the starving prodigal; and in this deeply felt consciousness of guilty bankruptcy, their real blessedness has its beginning. A little divine light begins to shine into their hitherto darkened hearts, and they see how poor they are. Oh, how our blessed Lord loves to fill an emptied heart! while one that is already full of satisfactory riches and resources has no place for him. This beatitude necessarily begins the series. It is the first of the rising steps which lead to the portal by which we must enter the kingdom of heaven. "God resisteth the proud but giveth grace unto the humble."

A. W. Cowles

    The heaven where I would stand complete
        My lowly love shall see;
    And stronger grow the yearning sweet,
        My holy One, for thee.
                        T. H. Gill.

November 16.

I shall be satisfied, when I awake, with thy likeness.
PSALM xvii. 15.

Be ye therefore perfect, even as your Father which is in heaven is perfect. — MATT. v. 48.

THE child of God must not be content with the pharisaic interpretation of the law. Nor must he share the publican's conception of his duty of kindness toward his fellows. God commendeth his love toward us in that while we were yet sinners Christ died for us. God is love, and love is the fulfilling of the law. Be like God; let the child reproduce the Father's virtues. The Father's house is to be his lasting home. His eternal associations are to be with the holy, ever blessed Trinity. The intimate relations of heaven demand entire sinlessness in all who abide there. It would surprise us if God demanded less than perfection in those who are to be fellow-heirs with Christ. Holiness is your duty and your destiny. It is a distant goal, but it will be reached. "I shall be satisfied," said the Psalmist, "when I awake, with thy likeness." Let life's day be filled with service toward God and toward man. Then let the night of death come. Your awaking shall be blessed; you will see the King in his beauty.

J. W. Dulles.

Holy Lamb, who thee receive,
Who in thee begin to live,
Day and night they cry to thee,
" As thou art, so let us be!"
ANNA S. DOBER.

NOVEMBER 17.

Whatsoever doth make manifest is light. — EPH. v. 13.

For every one that doeth evil hateth the light, neither cometh to the light, lest his deeds should be reproved. But he that doeth truth cometh to the light, that his deeds may be made manifest, that they are wrought in God. — JOHN iii. 20, 21.

THIS passage of Scripture occurs at the close of Christ's conversation with Nicodemus. It contains the two fundamental doctrines of the whole Bible, — sin and salvation. The unregenerate man hates the light, shuns the light, fears the light. He would have you believe that he can be a Christian in his own way, that a public profession is not necessary, that the Lord's Supper is not of sufficient importance to require his compliance with the dying injunction of the Redeemer. His whole course is in direct opposition to the revealed will of God. "The carnal mind is enmity against God; for it is not subject to the law of God, neither indeed can be" (Romans viii. 7). The regenerate man is the opposite of this. He loves the light because God is light, and he delights to honor God by a cheerful and willing obedience to the divine commands. Whatever good he may do he gives God the credit for it. "In me dwelleth no good thing," but "I can do all things through Christ." Reader, this is a test by which you can easily find out where you stand; is it in the twentieth or twenty-first verse of this wonderful chapter?

George H. Smyth.

> Behold the servant of the Lord!
>   I wait thy guiding hand to feel;
> To hear and keep thy every word,
>   To prove and do thy perfect will;
> Joyful from my own works to cease,
> Glad to fulfil all righteousness.
>   C. WESLEY.

NOVEMBER 18.

If we ask any thing according to his will, he heareth us.
1 JOHN v. 14.

If ye abide in me, and my words abide in you, ye shall ask what ye will, and it shall be done unto you. — JOHN xv. 7.

HERE we have the conditions of *prevailing prayer*. First, *The abiding in Christ*.
O blessed union, — oneness with the Saviour; fulness of love and fellowship with him; a relationship never to be broken, not even death itself can sever it; one continued life in union with divine life, and the same nature unfolded. As is the "vine," so is the "branch" with one life-giving power. As is the "body," so is each "member" sustained by one and the same element of existence. Thus our body, united to Christ's body, is united to Christ's will, "joined unto the Lord in one spirit;" and the body being the "temple," we are made partakers of his nature. He is "glorified" in us, and we are "fashioned" like unto him.

Second, *The abiding word*. In this heavenly relationship Christ's words are received into believing hearts, without exception, and become our words, and shape our lives. So that in the abiding with him, and his words abiding in us, our will is brought into humble submission to his will, and the union will be such a sweet and harmonious one, his Spirit inditing the petition, that every request will come to him acceptably, and the answer will surely be given.

J Lester Wells

My prayer hath power with God; the grace
  Unspeakable I now receive;
Through faith I see thee face to face;
  I see thee face to face and live!
In vain I have not wept and strove;
  Thy nature and thy name is love.

C. WESLEY.

November 19.

The Lord knoweth how to deliver the godly out of temptation. — 2 Peter ii. 9.

Because thou hast kept the word of my patience, I also will keep thee from the hour of temptation, which shall come upon all the world, to try them that dwell upon the earth. — Rev. iii. 10.

FAITHFUL adherence to the Word of God, — which is the expression of the divine patience, forbearance, and love toward mankind, — exposes the believer to great temptations. The world, the flesh, and the Devil use their most seductive arts to compass his fall; but here is the assurance of sufficient grace. He who says, " I also will keep thee from this hour," prayed for Peter the very instant he knew that Satan desired to sift him as wheat; and in like manner the prayer of our great High-Priest and Intercessor precedes the temptations of every saint.

How comforting to know that our sorrows and complaints, which the world treats with such indifference, enter the heart of our Father in heaven, and bring us unfailing relief!

The church in Philadelphia was the only one in Asia that escaped unscathed from the bitter persecutions of Trajan; and this is an earnest and an assurance of our Lord's protecting presence to every soul who keeps "the word of his patience."

W. S. Bowman,

O Lamb of God, who cam'st to take
The sin of man away,
Fast hold me for thy mercy's sake,
And I shall never stray!

Thomas MacKellar.

NOVEMBER 20.

Love covereth all sins. — Prov. x. 12.

Take heed to yourselves: If thy brother trespass against thee, rebuke him; and if he repent, forgive him. And if he trespass against thee seven times in a day, and seven times in a day turn again to thee, saying, I repent; thou shalt forgive him. — Luke xvii. 3, 4.
I say not unto thee, Until seven times: but, Until seventy times seven. — Matt. xviii. 22.

THIS parable teaches the lesson of unbounded forgiveness. The Jews, it is said, forgave the third offence, but not the fourth. Peter doubles the number, and thinks, perhaps, he has reached the limit of Christian forgiveness. But Christ says, "I say not unto thee, until seven times, but until seventy times seven."

By this he does not mean "seventy-seven times," nor four hundred and ninety times. He uses a definite number for an unlimited multitude. Boundless forgiveness is the divine law. But this boundless pardon has its condition. *"If he repent*, forgive him." " I forgave thee all that debt, *because thou desiredst me.*"

To the penitent only is forgiveness boundless. Forgiveness is a test of character; it is an index of the new birth. The unrenewed heart does not thus forgive. "Take heed to yourselves," an unforgiving spirit is proof of ungodliness: "O thou wicked servant, etc." It is a forerunner of doom: "His lord was very wroth, etc.;" "so likewise shall my heavenly Father do also unto you, if ye from your hearts forgive not every one his brother their trespasses."

W. H. Bixby

Oh, may I learn the art,
With meekness to reprove;
To hate the sin with all my heart,
But still the sinner love.
C. Wesley.

November 21.

Ye shall not tempt the Lord your God. — Deut. vi. 16.

Thou shalt not tempt the Lord thy God. — Matt. iv. 7.

"LET these sayings [of Christ] sink down into your ears," for here is the secret of holiness and happiness. We must come up to the standard of God's holy will and not attempt to drag him down to that of our sinful desires.

Christ's example is rich with suggestions for our own successful resistance of temptation. Before the temptation, John the Baptist attests he saw "the Spirit descending and remaining" on Christ. The heart on which the Holy Spirit descends and remains is a citadel that Satan can never capture. The weapon Christ employed to repel the Tempter was "the sword of the Spirit, which is the word of God." A mind stored with Bible truths and a life which exemplifies them can best repel Satan. Christ also availed himself of "the shield of faith." Implicit faith in God acts as water on flames; it "quenches all the fiery darts of the wicked." Be not afraid of the Devil, but only of sinning against God. Satan is a coward; "resist the Devil, and he will flee from you." One of the Christian's sweetest experiences comes after successfully resisting temptation. At the end of the struggle, "Behold, angels came and ministered unto him."

John Chester.

> Think not thy Saviour does not see
> When Satan casts a dart;
> No arrow ever wounded thee
> That did not pierce his heart.
>
> THOMAS MACKELLAR.

November 22.

Shall I hide from Abraham that thing which I do?
GEN. xviii 17.

Henceforth I call you not servants; for the servant knoweth not what his lord doeth: but I have called you friends; for all things that I have heard of my Father I have made known unto you. — JOHN xv. 15.

THESE inspiring and comforting words of Jesus were addressed to the eleven on the night before he suffered. The revelations made to them at the passover table, in the early evening, concerning his betrayal and death, had blasted all their earthly hopes and expectations. They saw themselves poor, outcast, and alone in the world; and "sorrow had filled their hearts." Could they have grasped the blessed import of these wonderful words, what light would have fallen on their darkness! "Henceforth" the relation of the disciple to his Lord is no more that of a servant (the conception of rabbinical discipleship) not knowing what his Lord does, but the endearing, confidential relation of friend, loved even as the Father hath loved his only begotten Son, and admitted to the secrets of his Lord through the abiding Comforter, and made co-worker together with him, constrained by his unspeakable love. Yea, more; having received "the adoption" he is made "joint-heir" with him, "if he abides in his love," "if so be that he suffers with him," "that they may be glorified together."

J. Fred Sutton

Not a brief glance I beg, a passing word,
But as thou dwell'st with thy disciples, Lord,
Familiar, condescending, patient, free,
Come not to sojourn, but abide with me.
              LYTE.

November 23.

Neither shall the flame kindle upon thee. — Isaiah xliii. 2.

He that overcometh shall not be hurt of the second death. — Rev. ii. 11.

THIS is what the Head of the Church says by the Spirit to encourage our fidelity and perseverance to the last. This solves beforehand the problem of our future. The conflict is to be won by devotion and service to the Master, in opposition to that heartless apathy which surrenders everything to the force of circumstances, to the spirit of the age, and the eddying course and drifting fashions of the world. This is an appeal to faith, — to that far-reaching sense of the soul which apprehends "the glory that shall be revealed in us," "*ready to be revealed* in the last time," the unseen but eternal inheritance undefiled. Have we an "ear" for this revelation? The Spirit speaks this promise to the churches; but does he find faith among us? Do our souls respond to the voice from heaven, — the still small voice of God? Faith in these things ever waxing, shall be more than a match for the blatant gabble, the glitter and glare, the noise and show of the world. The promise allures us to the future for our rest, our satisfaction, and exceeding great reward. We have the *promise* of exemption from the "second death," and its fulfilment confers "immortal life" through Jesus Christ. O Christian, let the full power of the immortal future come upon you!

Matthew. Henry Pogson.

> But to those who have confessèd,
>   Loved, and served the Lord below,
> He will say, "Come near, ye blessed,
>   See the kingdom I bestow;
>   You forever
>   Shall my love and glory know."
>
> — John Newton.

NOVEMBER 24.

Let him be your fear. — ISAIAH viii. 13.

And fear not them which kill the body, but are not able to kill the soul: but rather fear him which is able to destroy both soul and body in hell. — MATT. x. 28.

THERE is a place for fear and hope in the life of faith. God deals with men by holding forth as motives the rewards and punishments of the future. He warns through fear and woos through hope. Fear catches the note of alarm, and the wise soul shuns the evil. Nor does it stop with mere warning; it goes on with help to the end. The fear meant in this verse is awe without terror. It is filial fear that loves while it venerates, and trusts while it adores.

There is a right fear and a wrong fear. The wrong fear is the fear of man, — for the worst he can do is bound up with time, and can but hurt the body. It is always evil and bringeth a snare. It did much for King Saul's ruin; it led David to most unseemly conduct; it brought Peter to great sin and grief in his shameful fall. There is also a wrong fear of God, which is ignorant and hard and cruel as the grave. The right fear is that which knows God's power to destroy both soul and body in hell, and then turns from sin to the way of righteousness, seeking divine truth and a nobler life. And so the wise soul turns to Christ, himself the way, the truth, and the life.

Perfect love casteth out all wrong fear; but the right fear of God abides. It is the beginning of wisdom, a fountain of life. "The fear of the Lord is clean, enduring forever."

A. O. Davies

Fear hath no dwelling there;
Come to the mingling of repose and love,
Breathed by the silent spirit of the dove,
Through the celestial air!
FELICIA D. HEMANS.

November 25.

The God of our fathers hath glorified his Son Jesus.
Acts iii. 13.

This sickness is not unto death, but for the glory of God, that the Son of God might be glorified thereby. — John xi. 4.

"LORD, behold, he whom thou lovest is sick." This is the touching, suggestive message which comes from two troubled hearts at Bethany to Jesus in his Perean retreat. "This sickness is not unto death." This is the short strange answer which the messenger is bidden to take back. Perhaps before the words were spoken, certainly before they could reach the sisters, their brother was dead. Did the Master mean to mock their grief, or was he too for the once mistaken? Ah, there is a ray of resurrection-light gleaming in that dark message, if they would only see it! A saint's sickness is never unto death. He may seem to die, but it is death in seeming only. The heavenly Father will have no dead children. What seemed to be the death of Lazarus was only the occasion for kindling in the hearts of his friends the flame of a heavenly hope. His grave was only a door through which the glory of the divine love and power shone anew upon the paths of men. Earthly affliction is but a means of manifesting and magnifying the love of God in Jesus Christ our Lord. Sickness in the Master's friends is not unto death, but unto discipline, and the discovery of his glory to us, and through us to others.

J. M. Frible

    Without murmur, uncomplaining,
        In his hand
    Lay whatever things thou canst not
        Understand;
    Though the world thy folly spurneth,
    From thy faith in pity turneth,
    Peace thy inmost soul shall fill,
        Lying still.

H. A. P. *(Translation).*

November 26.

Though he wist it not, yet is he guilty. — Lev. v. 17.

But he that knew not, and did commit things worthy of stripes, shall be beaten with few stripes. For unto whomsoever much is given, of him shall be much required: and to whom men have committed much, of him they will ask the more. — Luke xii. 48.

THINGS "worthy of stripes," wrong things, committed in ignorance, are not so blameworthy as things committed against conscience. In the former case, they are committed without purpose of wrong; in the latter case, they are actuated by evil intent. Ignorance of duty and contempt of duty may be followed by precisely the same form of wrong-doing, but not involving the same degree of guilt, as a *few* stripes and *many* stripes are adapted to this diversity of guilt. But stripes, few or many, are the merited and certain penalty of all sin. And "unto whomsoever much is given, of him shall be much required," because his obligation is proportioned to his privilege and opportunity, — to the stewardship which demands his faithfulness. So man deals with his fellow-man. It is common-sense justice, and Jesus Christ indorses the principle in the above words which fell from his lips of infinite wisdom. What then must be the degree of guilt of those to whom the unspeakable riches of Christ are freely offered, and who refuse to accept them, but cleave to the beggarly elements of sin instead? "How shall we escape, if we neglect so great salvation?"

Wm. J. Findley.

Freely from me ye have received,
Freely in love to others give;
Then shall your doctrines be believed,
And by your labors, sinners live.
Unknown.

November 27.

The meek shall inherit the earth. — Psalm xxxvii. 11.

Blessed are the meek: for they shall inherit the earth. — Matt. v. 5.

WHAT is it to be meek? He who pronounced this beatitude said, "I am meek." To be meek, then, is to wear the yoke he wore, — to submit to the will of the Father as he did. A mild manner, a sweet expression, a retiring disposition, are but the superficialities of meekness. Essentially, it is of the heart, not of the face. The Master was meek in self-assertion, as in self-devotion and self-denial. The same spirit spoke in the "nevertheless" of the court of Caiaphas as in the "nevertheless" of the garden of Gethsemane. Meekness is conformity to the will of God in perception, motive, choice, and act. What, then, is the blessedness of the meek? Is it that of the Dives who had not "where to bestow his goods"? Is the reward of submission to the will of God such an "inheritance of the earth" as can be measured by the acre, or counted in coin? The questions answer themselves. Such was not the reward of the Master's meekness. To "inherit the land" is a proverbial phrase. Every Jew understood it. After the conflict for Canaan, then its undisputed possession; so the people of God were "given rest as he promised them," and their fathers before them. The blessedness of the meek is restful self-possession in view of the soul's heritage in God. "The Lord is the portion of mine inheritance; yea, I have a goodly heritage." This is the song of the meek.

John Hunstone.

Lord, when I all things would possess,
 I crave but to be thine;
Oh, lowly is the loftiness
 Of these desires divine!

T. H. Gill.

NOVEMBER 28.

The word of the Lord endureth for ever. — 1 PETER i. 25.

Heaven and earth shall pass away, but my words shall not pass away. — MATT. xxiv. 35.

HOW amazing the prescience here evinced! Immutable as are Nature's laws, vast as is the seeming magnitude and age, long as is the obvious duration of the physical universe, Jesus yet calmly declared that it shall finally perish; and modern science confirms the remarkable declaration. Equally amazing is the confidence with which this man deliberately affirms the imperishability of his own words. Without having committed to writing a single line, he yet declares that his words shall outlive the very universe, are literally immortal. Certain it is that these words were never more vital or influential than to-day, — abiding utterly unwasted the white light of even this wonderful nineteenth century.

Who is this man that thus spake, that is responsible for this most astounding statement? What philosophical historian has ever accounted for him, or ever will?

All men, manifestly, have a direct and personal interest in these "wonderful words of life," — particularly in those relating to human destiny and the terms of salvation. Let the unbeliever ponder them and tremble! Let the believer read them and rejoice!

R. H. Howard

> The mountains melt away
>   When once the Judge appears,
> And sun and moon decay,
>   That measure mortal years;
> But still the same in radiant lines
> The promise shines through all the flame.
>
> PHILIP DODDRIDGE.

November 29.

All that will live godly in Christ Jesus shall suffer persecution. — 2 Tim. iii. 12.

Blessed are they which are persecuted for righteousness' sake: for their's is the kingdom of heaven. — Matt. v. 10.

THIS is the last of the Beatitudes; and while it confirms and seals the sevenfold blessedness of the righteous, it points out what the Christian has to expect from the world's enmity in his endeavor to obtain these precious jewels. Strange that the world should return hatred for love, persecution for peace-making, malignancy for mercy! Yet so it is. Nor does the blessed Master conceal this truth, even as his disciples enter his service. Frankly, unreservedly, he unfolds to them what salary they may expect in his service here on earth. Listen to him: "Men shall revile you and persecute you and expel you from their society, and say all manner of evil against you falsely, *for my sake*." That is the key to this persecution. The surest evidence and the most distinctive mark of genuine discipleship is thus announced by the Holy Ghost, "All that will live godly in Christ Jesus shall suffer persecution." What then? "Rejoice, and be exceeding glad: for great is your reward in heaven." If the world curses you, God calls you "blessed." If the world will not tolerate you beneath the heavens, God will take you up into heaven. If the world's salary be death, God's reward is eternal life.

A. Q. Wedekind.

Brethren, while we sojourn here,
Fight we must, but should not fear.
Foes we have, but we've a Friend,
One that loves us to the end.
Forward, then, with courage go;
Long we shall not dwell below.
Soon the joyful news will come,
"Child, your Father calls; come home!"
                                        Joseph Swain.

NOVEMBER 30.

The dead shall be raised incorruptible. — 1 COR. xv. 52.

Marvel not at this: for the hour is coming, in the which all that are in the graves shall hear his voice, and shall come forth; they that have done good, unto the resurrection of life; and they that have done evil, unto the resurrection of damnation. — JOHN v. 28, 29.

IMMORTALITY, then, is not conditional. It is inherent in human nature. It does not depend upon good behavior; it cannot be forfeited by sin. Even the most desperate of criminals cannot escape from it, much less the most ignorant of agnostics. Until all have stood before the judgment seat of Christ, until some have gone away into eternal punishment and other some into eternal life, until every man reaps that which he has sown, and having been judged according to the deeds done in the body, has received his reward, the Word of God affords no possible hope of escape from the truth of inherent and inalienable immortality, and after that none could wish for one. "It is appointed unto men once to die, and after that the judgment." If death is universal, so must judgment be; and if judgment be universal, it must be because the identity of each individual is retained beyond the grave, for judgment would be impossible or absurd without identity in the person judged.

Here, then, is a joyous hope for the believing, as well as a faithful warning — an affectionate, tender, truthful, and therefore faithful warning — for the unbelieving.

Geo. S. Payson

> Then shall nature stand aghast,
> Death himself be overcast;
> Then, at her Creator's call,
> Near and distant, great and small,
> Shall the whole creation rise,
> Waiting for the great assize.
> STANLEY *(Translation)*.

December 1.

For this cause he is the mediator of the new testament. — HEB. ix. 15.

It is finished. — JOHN xix. 30.

WITH these words Christ closes his work of sacrifice. He had offered himself as "a lamb without spot and without blemish:" and thenceforth, wrote one to whom that one offering was the spell that at once broke his hard heart and transformed his life, "this man, after he had offered one sacrifice for sins forever, sat down at the right hand of God." And yet his work had not wholly ended. We turn from the scene on Calvary, and a little later hear him saying to his disciples, "Go ye," build, preach, and suffer, "and lo, I am with you alway, even to the end of the world." The work of sacrifice is ended only that the work of founding, inspiring and transforming shall begin. "Ye shall be witnesses unto me," he says; and then we read, "And they went forth and preached everywhere, *the Lord working with them.*"

So he means it to be with us. Ah! how often, when the burden is heavy and the way lonely, we would fain say of all that makes life a labor and a pain, "It is finished." And so we shall; but not, surely, to pass on into an inglorious ease. As with the best lives and the noblest powers competency rises side by side with the task, so it will be with us and with our work. One day the cross-bearing will be done, and we shall be privileged to say, "It is finished."

Henry C. Potter

"It is finished!" Oh, what pleasure
Do these precious words afford!
Heavenly blessings without measure
Flow to us from Christ the Lord.
JONATHAN EVANS.

December 2.

𝔚𝔥𝔶 persecutest thou me? — Acts ix. 4.

Inasmuch as ye did it not to one of the least of these, ye did it not to me. — Matt. xxv. 45.

THESE words assign the reason for the dread sentence pronounced upon the lost. The righteous and wicked have been finally separated. The great company on the right hand of the Judge have heard the welcome, "Come, ye blessed," and now the irrevocable doom descends upon "them on the left hand." Here Christ as the King and Judge identifies himself with his people. The lost are not condemned for sins of which they have been found guilty, but for opportunities of serving the Master which they have selfishly neglected. The hungry, the sick, the naked, the stranger, and prisoner had not been ministered unto. Inasmuch as they had neglected to serve the least of these his brethren, they had neglected to serve Christ himself. It is the love of Christ which constrains his people to gentle deeds of loving ministration. Behind all doing lie thought and feeling. As we think of Christ and feel toward him so will our actions ever be. Neglecting to help and comfort his afflicted disciples implies lack of love to Christ and Christ's. Therefore doom falls upon the lost because they preferred an unloving, self-indulgent, utterly selfish life, to the loving self-denial which finds its truest happiness in imitating him "who came not to be ministered unto, but to minister."

David Walker

And we believe thy word,
   Though dim our faith may be;
Whate'er for thine we do, O Lord,
   We do it unto thee.

W. W. How.

December 3.

The righteousness of God. — Romans x. 3.

For I say unto you, That except your righteousness shall exceed the righteousness of the scribes and Pharisees, ye shall in no case enter into the kingdom of heaven. — Matt. v. 20.

IN the preceding verses Jesus has been declaring the majesty of the law; then having made this startling announcement, he proceeds to illustrate the many ways in which both its spirit and letter were violated by the traditional "doers" and "teachers." He demands a distinguishing righteousness in his followers which shall sharply differentiate them from these traditionalists. They are to show a righteousness which shall exceed anything conceived by these old religionists, which shall have grained into its very life a love for truth and a respect for the interests of others. This spotlessness is demanded as the legitimate and convincing fruit of faith, the supreme test of the new kingdom. This demand is uncompromising. But here, as elsewhere, Jesus is insisting on the sacredness of the *spirit* of the law. The righteousness of the Pharisees consisted of an unwearying observance of the letter; but white and clean without, their hearts were far from God. The Christian disciple is to come by faith into such fellowship with Christ that obedience is the result of harmony. He has passed out from the schoolhouse. His renewed nature acts from an intelligent acquiescence in the *spirit* of the requirement. His righteousness exceeds that of all scribes and Pharisees because it *is* righteousness and not mere commandment-keeping.

Watson L. Phillips

> Our God is love; and all his saints
> His image bear below.
> The heart with love to God inspired
> With love to man will glow.
>
> Thomas Cotterill *(altered).*

DECEMBER 4.

His Father's name written in their foreheads.
REV. xiv. 1.

Him that overcometh will I make a pillar in the temple of my God, and he shall go no more out: and I will write upon him the name of my God, and the name of the city of my God, which is new Jerusalem, which cometh down out of heaven from my God: and I will write upon him my new name. — REV. iii. 12.

WHO would not rejoice in the grace qualifying him, the honor attaching to him, and the usefulness that would justify him in being a pillar in the temple of God, in a temple wide as the sanctified universe, and so all-inclusive of what is essentially divine as to admit of no humanly builded temple within itself?

He shall be this pillar, and upon *him* shall be inscribed the threefold name " of my God, the City of my God, and my new Name, " — the first a general piety, the second loyalty to the kingdom, the third affectionate devotion to the personal Redeemer: the first Faith, the second Hope, the third Love. Upon him that overcometh shall this threefold, perfect name be written, identifying him as the Lord's possession and servant, and guaranteeing continuous watch, guidance, and preservation of him; all which in turn shall give him further emboldenment, stimulation, and enterprise.

All this to "him that overcometh," not in his own strength, but through faith in the indwelling Spirit and the outworking providence of Christ.

[signature]

  Thy nature, gracious Lord, impart;
   Come quickly from above;
  Write thy new name upon my heart, —
   Thy new best name of Love.
           C. WESLEY.

December 5.

We have the petitions that we desired of him.
1 JOHN v. 15.

Go thy way; and as thou hast believed, so be it done unto thee.
MATT. viii. 13.

IN quick transition the human and the divine in Christ pass before us. The great wonder-worker himself marvels at the miracle of faith. How artlessly human!

Unembarrassed at the strange proposition, prompt as an echo comes the response, "Go thy way." What sublime divinity!

It was not the hasty dismissal of impotence or indifference or impatience, but the certain answer of a mighty, all-sufficient helpfulness to the cry of a simple, obedient faith. Christ acted like "one having authority." The same sublime almightiness that "arched the heavens" is here. "Go; be it done." And this same almightiness seems obedient to a Gentile's faith; what more unpromising? What could be mightier? Absolutely limitless in its own nature, it so accounted of God's ability; and so it put all the powers at its control in perfect accord with the divine purpose. What a mighty combination was that! What indeed are obstacles when God and man are *one?*

J. W. Weilus.

Oh, make but trial of his love!
Experience will decide
How blest are they, and only they,
Who in his truth confide!
TATE.

December 6.

Some to everlasting life, and some to shame and everlasting contempt. — Daniel xii. 2.

And these shall go away into everlasting punishment: but the righteous into life eternal. — Matt. xxv. 46.

THESE words were prompted by eternal love. Let us not turn away from them as we should if some mere man had spoken them. He who loved us and gave himself for us would not do such a cruel thing as to leave us in any doubt about the future state. Sinners are not going to be left to perish if it is possible to bring them to repentance and forgiveness. God does not take pleasure in the infliction of punishment, but rather desires that they may turn and live.

The awfulness of sin is a fact which cannot be avoided, and its consequences reach out endlessly. There is no possible escape from this issue. Therefore let us take the blessed warning at the lips of him who at the same time held out his arms, saying, "Come unto me . . . and I will give you rest." And oh, how precious the promise to every one who thus flies to Jesus! Not one single blow shall reach him forever and forever! Eternal life with all its possibilities of hope, and joy, and friendship with Jesus, whose life bought ours! Friend, don't wait a single day. Choose this day Christ and eternal life.

Lyman D. Calkins

O thou who canst not slumber,
  Whose light grows never pale,
Teach us aright to number
  Our years before they fail!
On us thy mercy lighten,
  On us thy goodness rest;
And let thy Spirit brighten
  The hearts thyself hast blessed!
BICKERSTETH.

December 7.

Is not this the Christ? — JOHN iv. 29.

Because I said unto thee, I saw thee under the fig tree, believest thou? thou shalt see greater things than these . . . Hereafter ye shall see heaven open, and the angels of God ascending and descending upon the Son of man. — JOHN i. 50, 51.

ONE little word of Christ revealed to Nathaniel that he was no more hidden from him than from the Father. The self-disclosure which Nathaniel made to God when hidden from all other eyes under the fig-tree, is wholly known to Jesus. This was the first revelation to Nathaniel of that wisdom of which Christ promises him further knowledge, and on it he based his faith and his confession. He had personal evidence of the divinity of Christ.

Is it not clear that the Being who shows man to himself is the true God? This view Christ had given Nathaniel and said, " As clearly will I disclose heaven to thee. Messengers shall come from its open portals and by me make known to you the secrets of the skies. They shall return also to heaven, and bear the revelation of men to write in the book of God's remembrance." So this one first proof by which Nathaniel knew his Lord shall be augmented with other evidence, abundant, continuous, and complete.

Be thou my guide into all truth divine;
  Give me increasing knowledge of my God.
Show me the glories that in Jesus shine,
  And make my heart the place of his abode.

C. FORSYTH.

December 8.

Let every one of us please his neighbour for his good to edification. — ROMANS xv. 2.

It is more blessed to give than to receive. — ACTS xx. 35.

THOUGH not recorded in the gospels, these are his own words, doubtless like many another saying of Jesus preserved by oral tradition and treasured in the memory of his disciples. The words are just like him. He was himself God's unspeakable gift; his life was one constant giving.

This maxim contradicts the common creed. Men measure gladness by the abundance of good received. The true blessedness is to impart. It matters not what is given, or how accepted, if the giving be but sincere. It is the altar which sanctifieth the gift. It may be a cup of water, a word of common comfort, a helping hand; it may be a kindly judgment, unspoken sympathy; it may be the sacrifice of ease, health, life, — blessedness attends the gift. What a fulness has this blessedness! It is a well of water within the soul; it is the very joy of the Lord.

Here is medicine for the sad heart. Here are riches for the poorest. Silver and gold if I have it; if not, such as I have give I. Every day brings its opportunities. What a day would that be in the life of any man, whose opportunities for this blessing were proved to the full!

W. W. Atterbury

Help us, O Lord, thy yoke to wear,
Delighting in thy perfect will;
Each other's burdens learn to bear,
And thus thy law of love fulfil.
THOMAS COTTERILL.

December 9.

He shall feed his flock like a shepherd. — Isaiah xl. 11.

I am the good shepherd, and know my sheep, and am known of mine. — John x. 14.

DEFENCELESS by nature, timid and subject to alarm, the sheep, of all animals, is the most utterly dependent upon human protection. Great, therefore, is the importance of a shepherd of undoubted qualifications and fidelity. How truly is a man like a sheep! How impotent against sin, how unsuspicious of its approach, how easily deceived as to its nature! Nor is he without a shepherd's care; for he can sing with the Psalmist, "The Lord is my shepherd." That shepherd is Jesus, nor is there need for another. Does the Christian need food? The good Shepherd says for his comfort, "I am the door; by me if any man enter in, he shall be saved, and shall go in and out and find pasture." Following him you can sing, "He maketh me to lie down in green pastures." Is the Christian sore beset so that he cries out, "My soul is among lions," while terror chills his heart? Then can he find comfort in the words of his Shepherd, "I lay down my life for the sheep." His soul's alarm is stilled, and he can say, "He restoreth my soul." Does Satan lay claim to the child of God, and fill him with apprehension? He is reassured by the words of Jesus, "He calleth his own sheep by name; ... I know my sheep, and am known of mine." Hearing that voice speak my name, I find myself relieved from fear, and following the Shepherd of my soul, am led in "the paths of righteousness."

Chas. R. Barnes.

   Jesus my Shepherd is;
     'T was he that loved my soul;
     'T was he that washed me in his blood;
       'T was he that made me whole.
   'T was he that sought the lost,
     That found the wandering sheep;
   'T was he that brought me to the fold;
     'T is he that still doth keep.   H. Bonar.

December 10.

Received me... as Christ Jesus. — GAL. iv. 14.

He that receiveth whomsoever I send receiveth me; and he that receiveth me receiveth him that sent me. — JOHN xiii. 20.

THE passage teaches two exalting truths. First, the perfect identification of Christ with his disciple. "He that receiveth whomsoever I send"—that is, you, my disciples—"receiveth *me*." More vividly still he announces this truth to Saul persecuting the children of God: "Why persecutest thou *me?*" Christ virtually says in the passage we are studying, "I am in you. To receive you is to receive *me*. To reject you is to reject me. A blow at your honor is a stab at my heart. The arm uplifted against a disciple is a threat against the Son of God." Are you a disciple? Think that invisible spiritual nerves, whose seat is the divine soul, reach forth and cover you with their sensitive tissue?

The second truth is like unto this. So Jesus, the Son, is identified with the Father. "He that receiveth *me* receiveth him that sent me." Jesus alone reveals the Father. Only through him incarnate can we conceive of God as a spirit. "I and my Father are one." "He that hath seen me hath seen the Father."

If, then, Christ is in the Father, and the Father in him, and if the disciple is in Christ, and Christ in him, truly are *we* the sons of God!

J. Clement French.

From Christ they all their gifts derive,
And fed by Christ, their graces live;
While, guarded by his mighty hand,
'Midst all the rage of hell they stand.
       PHILIP DODDRIDGE.

December 11.

He shall save the humble. — Job xxii. 29.

Except ye be converted, and become as little children, ye shall not enter into the kingdom of heaven. Whosoever therefore shall humble himself as this little child, the same is greatest in the kingdom of heaven. — Matt. xviii. 3, 4.

TO be converted is to be turned about, implying a real renewal of the heart and a radical reformation of the life. It is to "be born again," "born of the Spirit," "born not of blood, nor of the will of the flesh, nor of the will of man, but of God." No man is fully alive till he is converted. Our loftiest faculties are tuneless till divine inspiration breathes through them. The new life is the supreme need of human nature. The soul is dead till it receives the light, life, and love of God.

The new birth gives the childlike spirit. We "become as little children;" fear gives way to filial assurance, wilfulness to loving obedience, servitude and formalism to spiritual freedom; grief yields to gladness, and pride is cast out by humility. Heavenly crowns cannot be won by great talents; they cannot be bought by great wealth; and great pretensions and great performances are equally powerless to obtain them. They are freely bestowed upon those who have the childlike spirit. God's kingdom is God's family; all of his children, his "little children," are royal. Those who feel that they are nothing without God are the greatest in the kingdom of God.

J. E. C. Sawyer.

> I would not have the restless will
>   That hurries to and fro,
> Seeking for some great thing to do,
>   Or secret thing to know;
> I would be treated as a child,
>   And guided where I go.
>
> Anna L. Waring.

December 12.

Taught of God to love one another. — 1 Thess. iv. 9.

This is my commandment, That ye love one another, as I have loved you. — John xv. 12.

THE words are last words of the Christ. They are repeated for the emphasis. The truth is, the first clause is a sort of summary of all he had to say, just as the last clause is a summary of all he did and was.

Christ's work began and was wrought in love. His victory was won through love. His greatness lay in his love. God is love, and God in Christ was only manifested love, — love working at all costs. Man's greatness was to be like Christ's. Christ contradicts the human instinct about being great. Men were to rise above other men, become truly great within themselves, and do truly great things in the world, not by rivalries and hate, but by helpfulness and love. God would measure men by that. Men who had felt Christ would measure themselves by that. And the world should be redeemed, the evil in it overcome, wrongs righted, men be saved, Christ's kingdom come, — all by the power of love. It all would cost men suffering. It cost Christ suffering; but there was no other way. There is no other hope of redemption for the world, save in this love — Christ's and men's — Christ's working through men.

Edward Caldwell Moore

> Hence may all our actions flow, —
> Love the proof that Christ we know;
> Mutual love the token be,
> Lord, that we belong to thee.
> Love, thine image, love impart;
> Stamp it now on every heart.
> Only love to us be given;
> Lord, we ask no other heaven!
>
> C. Wesley.

December 13.

Deceitful above all things, and desperately wicked.
JER. xvii. 9.

Not that which goeth into the mouth defileth a man; but that which cometh out of the mouth, this defileth a man. For out of the heart proceed evil thoughts, murders, adulteries, fornications, thefts, false witness, blasphemies. — MATT. xv. 11, 19.

WE are taught by these words that right living is a weightier matter than to wash the hands oft, eat clean meats, and make a fair show in the flesh.

In such practices the Pharisees excelled, but with no better results than self-righteousness and pride. Their experience should convince us that moral progress is not attainable by that road.

According to Jesus, the source of sin is corrupt human nature. Universal consciousness attests the same. The things which defile a man come from within, as when unholy passions master the bodily parts and set them to deeds of shame.

And reformatory forces to be successful must operate within. King David shows how to start, when he prays, "Create in me a clean heart, O God, and renew a right spirit within me." As we learn to "delight in the law of God after the inward man," the strength to yield our members servants of righteousness unto holiness will be forthcoming. Gracious strength! — which Saint Paul felt the touch of when he exclaimed, "I thank God, through Jesus Christ!"

R. H. Fulton.

  I need thee, precious Jesus!
   For I am full of sin;
  My soul is dark and guilty,
   My heart is dead within.
  I need the cleansing fountain,
   Where I can always flee, —
  The blood of Christ most precious,
   The sinner's perfect plea.

F. WHITFIELD.

December 14.

This man shall be blessed in his deed.—JAMES i. 25.

If ye know these things, happy are ye if ye do them.—JOHN xiii. 17.

CHRIST, as teacher and Lord, in washing the disciples' feet, gave an effective example of humility and service. How selfish ambition and self-righteous ease are rebuked! Our divine Redeemer, emptying himself in self-denying offices for lost sinners, here emphasizes the thought that with him for model and leader, knowledge and service must co-exist, and will insure supreme happiness.

Divinely enlightened to know experimentally the riches of being justified freely through the redemption that is in him, so that Christ is formed in our hearts an example, a hope, and a royal priest, our living faith will shine by useful ministries. No Christian service can be mean service.

Christ-like works will make us Christ-like, as doers of his word. Jesus' ministry in our new birth, and since in washing away our daily stains, fills us with glowing love. We must exulting tell abroad such good news, and touch weary burden-bearers with our sympathetic and uplifting brotherhood. Such knowledge and service kindle on earth beacon-fires that live beyond heaven's verge. We, not forgetful hearers, but humble doers of Christ-like deeds, through sovereign grace are forever happy in our Lord.

L. C. Vass,

> Now to our eyes display
> The truth thy words reveal;
> Cause us to run the heavenly way,
> Delighting in thy will.
>
> BENJAMIN BEDDOME.

December 15.

Filled with the fruits of righteousness which are by Jesus Christ. — Phil. i. 11.

I am the vine, ye are the branches: he that abideth in me, and I in him, the same bringeth forth much fruit: for without me ye can do nothing. — John xv. 5.

THIS parable teaches the *essential oneness* of Christ and his people. The inevitable result of that union is *fruit-bearing.* It needs especially to be noted that Christ is himself the whole vine — root, stock, and branches, — just as in 1 Cor. xii. 12, the whole body of believers is called "Christ."

The meaning is that in this vine, which is Christ, the branches represent believers, who are "in him" and the life of each branch is the life of the whole vine. The believer is not to ask himself, "Am I a branch of the vine?" but rather, "Have I the life of the vine in me?" Nor is it a question of my trying to produce fruit, which always ends in failure, but of my "abiding in Christ, the vine." "The branch cannot bear fruit of itself," — "without me ye can do nothing." The branch simply brings forth what the vine produces.

The fruitage is not so much outward services, which often are merely the energy of the flesh, but rather those affections and graces called "the fruit of the Spirit." And the blessed result will continually be "fruit," "more fruit," "much fruit."

"And now, little children, abide in him, that when he shall appear, we may have confidence, and not be ashamed before him, at his coming."

Albert Erdman

Not in my self, O Lord, not mine the good;
I cannot do the holy thing I would.
My strength, my hope, my life, are all in thee.
Thou hast abundance for thyself and me;
Not in myself I strive.

December 16.

The dead in Christ shall rise first. — 1 Thess. iv. 16.

Our friend Lazarus sleepeth; but I go, that I may awake him out of sleep. — John xi. 11.

JESUS called Lazarus his friend, — blessed title, glorious privilege, friend of Jesus! Am I his friend? He gives us the test, — " Ye are my friends if ye do whatsoever I command you." His command is, trust me, love me, serve me. Do I obey this? Then I am Jesus' friend, and what is more, he is my friend. This friendship is a treasure neither time nor chance, men nor devils, life nor death can take away. Let us not imagine Christ is not our friend because we suffer. He allowed Lazarus to die, yet we are told Jesus loved Martha and her sister and Lazarus. Jesus' friends now upon earth may all die, may all sleep; but he has not forgotten them, one day he will say to the angels: " My friends sleep, but I go to awake them." Then the Lord himself shall descend with a shout, with the voice of the archangel and with the trump of God. And the dead in Christ shall rise first; then we which are alive and remain shall be caught up together with them in the clouds to meet the Lord in the air, and so shall we ever be with the Lord.

E. H. Harding.

Asleep in Jesus! Oh, for me
May such a blissful refuge be!
Securely shall my ashes lie,
And wait the summons from on high.
                        Mrs. Margaret Mackay.

December 17.

Where I record my name I will come unto thee ... and bless thee. — Ex. xx. 24.

If two of you shall agree on earth as touching any thing that they shall ask, it shall be done for them of my Father which is in heaven. For where two or three are gathered together in my name, there am I in the midst of them. — Matt. xviii. 19, 20.

CHRISTIANS are brethren. With a community of interests, they have common needs and wants. Here is our Lord's special promise to them when they meet together to ask for what they in common desire. There are promises to private prayer, to family prayer, to public prayer; this promise is to the *symphony* of prayer. Giving the smallest number that could form a union, Christ gives the largest encouragement to united prayer. Very sweet is the assurance of his presence then: that is enough. He is the Shechinah in this Holy of Holies. It is he who binds the saints together when they say "our." When he is one of a praying company, what wonder that "it shall be done for them"? As Westcott says, "Their prayer is only some form of his teaching transformed into a supplication, and so it will necessarily be heard." They ask *in his name;* that pleads his authority and his wisdom. Christ has omnipotence and omniscience; we have neither. It were not to be desired, if this large promise offered the first and not the second. Let us therefore have faith, and "keep not silence till he establish Jerusalem."

John Reid

Oh, joy, that we, who pray for all, by all
Commended are to God in daily prayer!
Yea, now, as in time past, and yet again
Through time to come, that church which shall not fall
From night to morn breathes forth upon the air
Meek intercession for the sons of men.   Sir Aubrey de Vere.

December 18.

He spake, and it was done. — Psalm xxxiii. 9.

I will; be thou clean. — Matt. viii. 3.

HERE is conscious power. The petition of the leper had been in faith in the power, but in question as to the willingness to exercise it in his particular case. The answer reveals both power and willingness. "I will;" there is simple majesty in the words. It is as if the Lord said, "I have the power, and I will exercise it. Thy faith hath not been reposed upon me in vain."

But, further, it is power for cleansing, — "Be thou clean." How much that cleanness meant! No longer an outcast shunned of men, but clean, — the defilement, the loathsomeness removed by that omnipotent word! The poor leper was reinstated in the privileges of his birthright.

The two essential things in soul-cleansing are thus brought into view, — faith on the human side, power on the divine side. "Lord, if thou wilt, thou canst make me clean," — this is the soul's cry in weakness, but in trust. The Lord's answer, full of divine power, is sure to follow, "I will; be thou clean." Oh, the blessedness to all eternity of a clean soul!

O. A. Kingsbury.

> Up to the place of thine abode
> I lift my waiting eye;
> To thee, O holy Lamb of God,
> Whose blood for me so freely flowed,
> I raise my ardent cry.
>
> Thomas Hastings.

December 19.

Our hands have handled of the Word of life.
1 John i. 1.

Reach hither thy finger, and behold my hands; and reach hither thy hand, and thrust it into my side: and be not faithless, but believing. — John xx. 27.

ON the evening after his resurrection Christ appeared to his disciples. Thomas was absent. When the disciples informed him of the visit of their risen Lord, he refused to accept their testimony. Nothing but an ocular demonstration would satisfy him. He specified with great particularity of detail the only evidence that would remove his incredulity. He continued in this state of unbelief for a week. He did not abandon his faith in the Christ he had known; he simply claimed that so astounding an event as the resurrection of the Lord should be made as plain to him as it had been to the others with whom he was on an official equality. He acted perhaps unconsciously, as if to have "seen the Lord" was essential to the office and work of an apostle. His devotion to Christ, his courage, his willingness to suffer death (John xi. 16), show him to be of strong character. He still clung to the disciples, although their statements were incredible to him. At the end of a week, he went with them to the place of meeting. He expected something or he would not have gone. He waited for the manifestation. According to his faith it was done unto him. Christ graciously appeared and spoke in the words of the text. Let us be cautious in our judgment. Every one must see Christ for himself if he would show him to others.

Robert Lowry.

God with us! oh, wondrous grace!
Let us see him face to face,
That we may Immanuel sing,
As we ought, our Lord and King.

Sarah Slinn.

December 20.

Thou canst do every thing. — JOB xlii. 2.

With men this is impossible; but with God all things are possible.
MATT. xix. 26.

WE mortals are continually "troubled about many things." Our responsibilities, perplexities, and crosses are so many and so overwhelming that failure and loss seem inevitable, as we cry concerning life's problem, "With men this is impossible." Yet back of the single, apparently meaningless stitches we are weaving into life's pattern, there is a plan, simple, wise, divine. Near the weary worker stands one ready to transmute the plain, coarse metal of human love and toil into the shining gold of divine acceptance. By the bedside of the sufferer wasting under the power of disease is one whose touch will soon release the imprisoned spirit and soothe the aching flesh, and afterwards reunite body and spirit in glorified manhood forever. Beside the dark open grave, into which our hopes and affections often seem to be hurrying, stands the Conqueror of death and the grave, ready to brighten our pathway down into the valley, and to open for us on the other side a glorious path up the heavenly heights.

There is, there can be, no distress so great, no emergency so sudden, no enemies so strong, as to defeat or mar the plans of our strong One. While we listen to these words of Jesus, "With God all things are possible," we may also hear him saying, "All things are possible to him that believeth."

John C. Van Deventer.

> Lord, we pray, and know thou hearest,
> For thy promises are true!
> Grant the heart-wish that is dearest;
> He who knows can also do!
>
> SYMINGTON.

December 21.

Jesus Christ the same yesterday, and to day, and for ever. — Heb. xiii. 8.

I am Alpha and Omega, the beginning and the end, the first and the last. — Rev. xxii. 13.

HOW sweet this announcement of his name must have been to the aged and persecuted disciple in his lonely banishment! Our Lord makes special revelations of himself to his afflicted servants. This name tells of his unchanging faithfulness and grace. The tones of the voice are readily recognized by the disciple whom Jesus loved, and awaken memories of the blessed fellowship of his early life. The first courteous greeting, "Whom seek ye?" the kindly invitation, "Come and see;" the first day spent in his company, — these and many other events come back with great clearness and force.

This name also indicates that his doctrines have not changed. Our Lord is the Alpha and Omega of divine revelation. He is the metropolis of the Scriptures, and all the doctrines, as the king's highways, lead directly to the city of our God. The doctrines are simply *facts* about Christ in his covenant relations to his people. Election is his love choosing us from eternity; justification, his obedience and death providing righteousness for us; adoption, his grace putting us into the family of our Father; and the perseverance of the saints, the fact that "having loved his own which were in the world, he loved them unto the end." O believer, he is all thy salvation! Blessed are they that trust in him!

Rich. S. Campbell

'Tis Jesus, the first and the last,
  Whose Spirit shall guide us safe home;
We'll praise him for all that is past,
  And trust him for all that's to come.
JOSEPH HART.

December 22.

That no man put a stumblingblock . . . in his brother's way. — Romans xiv. 13.

Whoso shall receive one such little child in my name receiveth me. But whoso shall offend one of these little ones which believe in me, it were better for him that a millstone were hanged about his neck, and that he were drowned in the depth of the sea. — Matt. xviii. 5, 6.

"IN my name." In these words you have once more that solemn truth, so often taught in the Bible, that with God, *motive is of infinite moment.*

As in the day when Samuel looked on Eliab, comely and tall, and confidently declared, "Surely the Lord's anointed is before him!" and the Lord answered and said, "The Lord seeth not as man seeth: for man looketh on the outward appearance, but the Lord looketh on the heart," even so to-day the heart and its motives will before everything else be remarked by God. The widow's two mites, the cup of cold water, the receiving of one such little child *in his name*, is a kindness done to himself.

My soul, seek for thyself *the right motive*, and thine shall be the rich reward!

"But whoso shall cause one of these little ones to stumble and fall" shall surely and sorely be punished! Awful thought!—my care is not only for my own soul, but also for the souls of others. "No man liveth unto himself." I am not only fearfully and wonderfully *made*, but also fearfully *placed*. My acts, my words, my very looks affect others for weal or woe! See that thy walk be circumspect, so shalt thou be free from the blood of all men!

D. Parker Morgay.

> No act falls fruitless; none can tell
> How vast its power may be,
> Nor what results infolded dwell
> Within it silently.
>
> Anonymous.

December 23.

With joy shall ye draw water out of the wells of salvation. — Isaiah xii. 3.

If thou knewest the gift of God, and who it is that saith to thee, Give me to drink; thou wouldest have asked of him, and he would have given thee living water. — John iv. 10.

IF the puzzled woman had but known that the mysterious stranger then talking with her was no mere Jew, but the divine Creator of all the floods of waters, and the divine Friend and Redeemer of the soul that is at the same time sin-smitten and athirst for heavenly blessings, she would have become a suppliant herself and would have sued for that "gift of God" which Christ, the gracious and omnipotent Jehovah, had it in his power to bestow upon her. Nor would he have denied her request, but would have conferred upon her that true inward "fountain of living water" so faintly symbolized by the freshly bubbling fountain-heads and leaping streams of this earth, Eternal Life.

He who, as some think, pointed to the rising sun when he exclaimed, "I am the light of the world," stood amidst the pillared galleries of Herod's temple when the golden flagon was brought from the pool of Siloam on the last day of the feast and poured on the altar, and cried, "If any man thirst, let him come unto me and drink."

A. C. Alexander.

> We taste thee, O thou living Bread,
> And long to feast upon thee still;
> We drink of thee, the Fountain-head,
> And thirst our souls from thee to fill.
>
> **Bernard of Clairvaux** *(translated by Ray Palmer).*

December 24.

The just shall live by his faith. — Hab. ii. 4.

He that believeth on him is not condemned: but he that believeth not is condemned already, because he hath not believed in the name of the only begotten Son of God. — John iii. 18.

THE issues of the final judgment are anticipated and virtually determined in this world. Character is the key to destiny. Faith and salvation, unbelief and condemnation, are severally united in the eternal fitness of things.

The believer is not judged. He is passed from death unto life. He has accepted the proffered remedy as the bitten Israelites did when they looked on the serpent of brass.

Judgment is for those who believe not. Sin has wages; those who choose to abide in it and who reject the Saviour pronounce sentence on themselves. Primarily, it is not Christ who condemns them; they have been judged already. The quality and measure of their guilt are shown in this cumulative indictment: they believe not on Jesus, the Son of God, the only begotten, who is most high in the glory of God the Father, and besides whom there is no other deliverer.

"How shall we escape, if we neglect so great salvation?" But if we accept it, if we humbly urge our title to that blessed estate for which there is no judgment, we can vindicate our hope only by walking in the light and making our deeds manifest that they are wrought in God.

J. Ralston Smith.

Believe in him who died for thee,
And sure as he hath died,
Thy debt is paid, thy soul is free,
And thou art justified.
C. Wesley.

December 25.

The gift of God is eternal life through Jesus Christ our Lord. — Romans vi. 23.

God so loved the world, that he gave his only begotten Son, that whosoever believeth in him should not perish, but have everlasting life. — John iii. 16.

THE grandest doctrine of the Word of God to my mind is the doctrine of the atoning sacrifice of Christ. I will contend for every letter of truth, but if I must give up something, I will hold tenaciously to this: "Without shedding of blood there is no remission of sin;" "the blood of Jesus Christ his Son cleanseth us from all sin."

As to this doctrine of sacrifice, — to put it plainly, this truth of substitution, — Christ Jesus was made sin for us, though he knew no sin, that we might be made the righteousness of God in him. When God the Holy Ghost led you to receive this fact, did it not satisfy the intense craving of your spirit? Did you ever know what perfect rest about sin was till you saw it laid upon Christ, carried away by Christ up to the tree, borne by him upon the tree, and there made an end of by the shedding of his precious blood?

Would anything short of that, do you think, content you now? I am sure it would not. There is a thirst in the human heart that nothing can ever satisfy, but "God so loved the world, that he gave his only begotten Son, that whosoever believeth on him should not perish, but have everlasting life."

C. H. Spurgeon

Oh, may we keep and ponder in our mind,
God's wondrous love in saving lost mankind!
Trace we the Babe who hath retrieved our loss
From his poor manger to his bitter cross,
Treading his steps, assisted by his grace,
Till man's first heavenly state again takes place.
                                                    BYROM.

December 26.

I count all things but loss for the excellency of the knowledge of Christ Jesus. — Phil. iii. 8.

Again, the kingdom of heaven is like unto a merchant man, seeking goodly pearls: who, when he had found one pearl of great price, went and sold all that he had, and bought it. — Matt. xiii. 45, 46.

THIS is a parable for believers; the man was "seeking goodly pearls." But there are some converted people who are not represented by this eager merchantman. They are satisfied with the salvation which grace gives to penitent faith. These have found *a* pearl in the possession of a hope: but they have not found *the* pearl of great price, — they do not know Jesus as a personal friend. The knowledge that I am saved is the lowest round on the ladder of Christian attainment; there is a richer knowledge than this. It is the knowledge of Christ, who is *the* truth.

This knowledge has two conditions. One is intense eagerness, "I *press* toward the mark." Christ does not reveal the riches of his grace to him who is not longing and praying for clearer light. The other condition is sacrifice, — "He sold all that he had and bought it." When we have caught a glimpse of his preciousness, we count all things but loss to "know him and the power of his resurrection." They are the true "higher life" disciples who can say, "I live, yet not I, but Christ liveth in me."

Abbott E. Kittredge

  I bless the Christ of God,
   I rest in love divine,
  And with unfaltering lip and heart
   I call this Saviour mine.
          H. Bonar.

December 27.

Happy are these thy servants . . . that hear thy wisdom.
 1 Kings x. 8.

The queen of the south shall rise up in the judgment with the men of this generation, and condemn them: for she came from the utmost parts of the earth to hear the wisdom of Solomon; and, behold, a greater than Solomon is here. — Luke xi. 31.

CHRIST'S are never careless words; we do right to take out all they contain.

"The queen of the south." Then that romantic story of 1 Kings x., and again of 2 Chron. ix. is true. This queen of Sheba did live when Solomon lived. In her remote land she did hear how great and wise he was, and with camel-loads of spices, gold, and jewels, did journey to ask him hard questions, and acknowledge him greater and grander than her thought. How Christ's touch livens up such old pictures!

"A greater than Solomon." Not in rank, gold, power, but in divine nature and perfect character. He says it who alone has right to say it.

"Rise up in the judgment." Then there will be a judgment, and destinies be weighed, and spiritual comparisons settled. She will be there. Christ's generation of a thousand years later will be there. *We* shall be there.

"Shall condemn them." With little light, she came far to get more. Those to whom Christ spake faced brighter light, but saw it with shut eyes. We have more and better than all they; God grant we may so see by it that the rule which convicted them condemn not us!

Henry M. Dexter.

Father, in us thy Son reveal;
Teach us to know and do thy will;
Thy saving power and love display,
And guide us to the realms of day!
 JOHN FAWCETT.

December 28.

Praying always with all prayer, . . . and watching thereunto. — Eph. vi. 18.

Watch and pray, that ye enter not into temptation: the spirit indeed is willing, but the flesh is weak. — Matt. xxvi. 41.

THE disciples were under trial in Gethsemane. They had entered the garden, doubtless, with deep concern for the Master, but the simplest temptation speedily overcame them. Bidden to watch with their Lord, *they slept.* Any other form of danger might have been more easily predicted. Had they been cautioned they would have answered in Jesus' own words, "What! can we not watch with thee one hour?" But now they have no excuse to offer till divine love reveals the source of weakness and its remedy. What ample emphasis for the admonition to the habit of watchfulness with prayer!

Drowsiness is the easy path to disloyalty. The disciple must watch himself if he would be fitted to watch with Christ. He may have been waiting to become involved in some large undertaking, and yet find himself asleep before some very humble duty. David prayed to be upheld with a willing spirit; but the most willing spirit has a heavy drag upon it in the weakness of the flesh. Our petitions too depend upon our watchfulness. The wary eye, that is keenest to discern its special dangers, is always the eye most readily, intelligently, and prevailingly turned "to the hills whence cometh strength."

> O gracious God, in whom I live,
> My feeble efforts aid!
> Help me to watch and pray and strive,
> Though trembling and afraid!
>
> Anne Steele.

December 29.

The promise is unto you, and to your children.
ACTS ii. 39.

Suffer little children, and forbid them not, to come unto me: for of such is the kingdom of heaven. — MATT. xix. 14.

THE children were brought for the symbolic touch of Jesus' hands, for the gracious power of Jesus' prayer; and even the disciples rebuked them, perhaps because they deemed the children an untimely intrusion, too young for consideration. Not so. "But Jesus said"—the immortal words which ideally lift the children of every age into his arms. Those who know Jesus better than these disciples did, those who have themselves become as little children in their trust, love, hopefulness, and that wonder which may be touched into worship, both recognize their children's need of being brought, and instinctively desire to bring them unto him. They are burdened with the fact that the child's nature is liable to the touch of Satan and of sin, whose touch is death, and they long for the laying on of those hands that bless because they are accompanied by the prayer which is prophetic of salvation. Christian parent, let not your ambition for the child's worldly welfare, your sinful failure to know Jesus in the fulness of his grace, hinder your child from coming, or yourself from bringing him to Jesus. Your children may die. Hear then the words, "Suffer little children and forbid them not, to come unto me: for of such is the kingdom of heaven."

W. C. Stitt

"Let them approach," he cries,
"Nor scorn their humble claim;
The heirs of heaven are such as these,
For such as these I came."

ONDERDONK.

December 30.

That they be rich in good works. — 1 Tim. vi. 18.

Lay not up for yourselves treasures upon earth, where moth and rust doth corrupt, and where thieves break through and steal: but lay up for yourselves treasures in heaven, where neither moth nor rust doth corrupt, and where thieves do not break through nor steal: for where your treasure is, there will your heart be also. — Matt. vi. 19–21.

HUMANITY'S road to enduring wealth is here indicated by the One who, though he was rich, became poor that we through his poverty might be rich. The same lesson opens his mouth in the parables of the rich fool, the unjust steward, and the rich worldling. This passage is the moral with which he points the choice of the young ruler.

The kernel of this statement lies in the significance of the word *heart*. "For where your treasure is, there will your heart be also." The rich fool's earth-sphered heart stamped him as "one who layeth up treasure for himself and is not rich toward God." The unjust steward's worldly prudence should make us wise enough to bring the mammon of unrighteousness under the *heart* control of an heir to the "everlasting habitations." The rich worldling's *heart* dissection takes place when Abraham says, "Son, remember that thou in thy lifetime receivedst thy *good* things." The young ruler's *heart* sorrow is revealed as the loving Saviour declares, "How hardly shall they that have riches enter into the kingdom of God!"

"Never treat money affairs with levity," says one of earth's noted writers; "money is character." Let us weigh the treasures of earth in the balance of the Sermon on the Mount.

Their works of piety and love,
  Performed through Christ, their Lord,
Forever registered above,
  Shall meet a sure reward.

HARRIET AUBER.

December 31.

Even so, come, Lord Jesus. — Rev. xxii. 20.

Behold, I come quickly. — Rev. iii. 11.

"QUICKLY." The little church at Jerusalem fixed her eye upon that "blessed hope," the visible appearing of her Lord. It was a reality present to her heart, projected full on the vision of her faith. Ever since, she has journeyed on as one journeys toward a high mountain, the way being long, rough, and sometimes weary. At times the end seemed farther off than at the beginning, but at last the stretch is well-nigh complete, and she lifts up her head and rejoices in the Lord.

The sun of the gospel is to-day penetrating to the heart of old continents in the East. Its light has come to the very western edge of this most western land, having encircled the whole earth.

In arts men are now working with the subtlest forces, like electricity. In science they are studying the origin of life. Everywhere the human mind is busying itself with the last analysis of things. All things are pushing themselves to extremes. Good men seem to be growing better and bad men growing worse. Missions, charities, love, longings for unity and a godly fear, anarchy, greed, blasphemy, hate! The tares and the wheat manifestly "grow together." As the Lord said: "The vision is yet for an appointed time, but at the end it shall speak, and not lie. Though it tarry, wait for it; because it will surely come, it will not tarry."

W. M. Ahles.

> Five! and the tapers now
>   In rosy morning dimly burn!
> Stand, and be girded thou;
>   Thy Lord will yet return.
> Hark! 't is the matin-call;
>   Oh, when our Lord shall come again,
> At prime or even-fall,
>   Blest are the wakeful men!
>
> ARTHUR CLEVELAND COXE.

INDEX OF AUTHORS,

WITH PLACE OF SETTLEMENT, ETC.

January.

1. Rev. W. M. TAYLOR, D.D. .... Broadway Tabernacle Congregational Church, New York.
2. Rev. T. W. CHAMBERS, D.D. ... Collegiate Reformed Dutch Church, New York.
3. Rev. T. DE WITT TALMAGE, D.D. Brooklyn Tabernacle Presbyterian Church, Brooklyn, N. Y.
4. Rev. A. H. BRADFORD, D.D. ... Congregational Church, Montclair, N. J.
5. Rev. HOWARD CROSBY, D.D. ... Fourth Avenue Presbyterian Church, New York.
6. Rev. H. M. KING, D.D. ...... Emanuel Baptist Church, Albany, N. Y.
7. Rev. WILLIAM AIKMAN, D.D. .. Presbyterian Church, Atlantic City, N. J.
8. Rev. H. S. BURRAGE, D.D. .... Baptist Church, Portland, Me.
9. Rev. WENDELL PRIME, D.D. ... Editor New York "Observer."
10. Rev. W. F. BAINBRIDGE, D.D. .. Baptist Minister; Superintendent City Missions, Brooklyn, N. Y.
11. Rev. GEORGE MACLOSKIE, D.D. . Professor of Biology and Botany, Princeton College, N. J.
12. Rev. R. T. JEFFREY, D.D...... Caledonia Road United Presbyterian Church, Glasgow, Scotland.
13. Rev. B. B. WARFIELD, D.D. ... Professor Didactic and Polemic Theology, Princeton Seminary, N. J.
14. Rev. E. WALPOLE WARREN .... Holy Trinity Protestant - Episcopal Church, New York.
15. Rev. M. McG. DANA, D. D. .... Kirk Street Congregational Church, Lowell, Mass.

INDEX OF AUTHORS.

16. Rev. HENRY VAN DYKE, D.D. . . Brick Presbyterian Church, New York.

17. Rev. C. F. THWING, D.D. . . . . . Plymouth Congregational Church, Minneapolis, Minn., Associate Editor of the "Advance," Chicago.

18. Rev. W. T. SABINE, D.D. . . . . . First Reformed Episcopal Church, New York.

19. Rev. M. H. HUTTON, D.D. . . . . Second Reformed Church, New Brunswick, N. J.

20. Rev. GEORGE S. MOTT, D.D. . . . Presbyterian Church, Flemington, N. J.

21. Rev. Z. GRENELL, D.D. . . . . . . First Baptist Church, Detroit, Mich.

22. Rev. A. B. MACKAY . . . . Crescent Street Presbyterian Church, Montreal, Canada.

23. Rev. J. S. BRIGHT, D.D. . . . . . Congregational Minister, Dorking, England.

24. Rev. HUBERT W. BROWN . . . . . Presbyterian Missionary, City of Mexico, Mexico.

25. Rev. C. F. HOFFMAN, D.D. . . . . Protestant - Episcopal Church of All Angels, New York.

26. Rev. A. H. MOMENT, D.D. . . . . Westminster Presbyterian Church, Brooklyn, N. Y.

27. Rev. JOHN E. TODD, D.D. . . . . . Congregational Church of the Redeemer, New Haven, Conn.

28. Rev. W. F. CRAFTS . . . . First Union Presbyterian Church, New York.

29. Rev. MARK STAPLE . . . . Methodist-Episcopal Church, formerly in the Methodist (now Methodist Protestant) Church, and at one time President of the New York Conference.

30. Rev. S. W. BOARDMAN, D D. . . . Presbyterian Church, Stanhope, N. J.

31. Rt. Rev. C. C. PENICK, D.D. . . . Protestant - Episcopal Missionary Bishop, residing at Louisville, Ky.

February.

1. Rev. Canon C. D. BELL, D.D. . . . St. Mary's Church, Cheltenham, England.

2. Rev. JOHN H. SHEDD, D.D. . . . . Presbyterian Missionary, Oroomiah, Persia.

INDEX OF AUTHORS. 369

3. Rev. ARTHUR BROOKS, D.D. . . . Protestant - Episcopal Church of the Incarnation, New York.
4. Rev. GILES H. MANDEVILLE, D.D. Secretary Board of Education, Reformed Church in America.
5. Rev. T. T. EATON, D.D. . . . . . Walnut Street Baptist Church, Louisville, Ky.
6. Rev. GEORGE DOUGLAS, D.D. . . . President Methodist College, Montreal, Canada.
7. Rev. S. H. KELLOGG, D.D. . . . . St. James Square Presbyterian Church, Toronto, Canada.
8. Rev. H. A. STIMSON, D.D. . . . . Pilgrim Congregational Church, St. Louis, Mo.
9. Rev. BURDETT HART, D.D. . . . . First Fairhaven Congregational Church, New Haven, Conn.
10. Rev. THOMAS A. HOYT, D.D. . . . Chambers Presbyterian Church, Philadelphia, Pa.
11. Rev. D. D. DEMAREST, D.D. . . . Professor of Pastoral Theology and Sacred Rhetoric, Reformed Church Seminary, New Brunswick, N. J.

12. Rev. F. BOTTOME, D.D. . . . . . Asbury Methodist-Episcopal Church, New York.
13. Rev. J. E. TWITCHELL, D.D. . . . Dwight Place Congregational Church, New Haven, Conn.
14. Rev. GEORGE P. HAYS, D.D. . . . Second Presbyterian Church, Kansas City, Mo.
15. Rev. ALEXANDER McKENZIE, D.D. Shepard Memorial Congregational Church, Cambridge, Mass.
16. Rev. R. R. BOOTH, D.D. . . . . . Rutgers Presbyterian Church, New York.
17. Rev. W. W. CLARK . . . . Reformed Church in America, now laboring as an evangelist.
18. Rev. PETER STRYKER, D.D. . . . Andrew Presbyterian Church, Minneapolis, Minn.
19. Rev. A. J. ROWLAND, D.D. . . . . Franklin Square Baptist Church, Baltimore, Md.
20. Rev. E. N. POTTER, D.D. . . . . . President Hobart College, Geneva, N. Y.
21. Rev. G. C. BALDWIN, D.D. . . . . Formerly Pastor First Baptist Church, Troy, N. Y.
22. Rev. T. B. M'LEOD, D.D. . . . . . Clinton Ave. Congregational Church, Brooklyn, N. Y.
23. Rev. JOHN HOWLAND. . . . . . . Congregational Missionary at Guadalajara, Mexico.
24. Rev. ADOLPH SAPHIR . . . . . . Presbyterian Minister, London, Eng.

25. Rev. DANIEL BLISS, D.D. . . . . . President Syrian Protestant College, Beirut, Syria.
26. Rev. S. H. VIRGIN, D.D. . . . . . . Pilgrim Congregational Church, New York.
27. Rev. JOSIAH TYLER. . . . . Congregational Missionary Umsunduzi, Verulam, South Africa.
28. Rev. H. M. SANDERS . . . . Baptist Minister, recently Pastor of Forty - Second Street Baptist Church, New York.
29. Rev. R. M. OFFORD . . . . Minister in the Reformed Church in America, and one of the editors of the New York "Observer."

March.

1. Rt. Rev. T. M. CLARK, D.D. . . . Protestant-Episcopal Bishop of Rhode Island.
2. Rev. H. M. LADD, D.D. . . . . . . Euclid Avenue Congregational Church, Cleveland, O.
3. Rev. E. P. INGERSOLL, D.D.. . . . Congregational Church of the Puritans, Brooklyn, N. Y.
4. Rev. T. L. CUYLER, D.D. . . . . . Lafayette Ave. Presbyterian Church, Brooklyn, N. Y.
5. Rev. JOHN NEWTON, D.D. . . . . . Presbyterian Missionary, Lahore, India.
6. Rev. D. R. FRAZER, D.D. . . . . . First Presbyterian Church, Newark, N. J.
7. Rev. MYRON ADAMS, D.D. . . . . Plymouth Congregational Church, Rochester, N Y.
8. Rev. ROBERT F. SAMPLE, D.D. . . Twenty-Third Street Presbyterian Church, New York.
9. Rev. WAYLAND HOYT, D.D. . . . Memorial Baptist Church, Philadelphia, Pa.
10. Rev. C. F. DEEMS, D.D. . . . . . . Church of the Strangers, New York.
11. Rev. N. W. CONKLING, D.D. . . Minister in the Presbyterian Church, New York.
12. Rev. J. L. AMERMAN, D.D. . . . . Missionary of the Reformed Church in America, Professor in Theological School, Tokio, Japan.
13. Rev. W. R. HUNTINGTON, D.D. . Grace Protestant-Episcopal Church, New York.
14. Rev. DAVID GREGG, D.D. . . . . . Park Street Congregational Church, Boston, Mass.

INDEX OF AUTHORS. 371

15. Rev. E. TRUMBULL LEE . . . . . . First Presbyterian Church, Pueblo, Col.
16. Rev. J. B. REMENSNYDER, D.D. . . St. James Lutheran Church, New York.
17. Rev. W. G. BLAIKIE, D.D. . . . . Professor Free Church College, Edinburgh, Scotland
18. Rev. I. E. DWINELL, D.D. . . . . Professor of Homiletics and Pastoral Theology, Pacific Theological Seminary, Oakland, Cal.
19. Rev. A. T. PIERSON, D.D. . . . . . Bethany Presbyterian Church, Philadelphia, Pa.
20. Rev. RUDOLF KOENIG . . . . Free Church of Scotland, Budapest, Hungary.
21. Rev. G. R. LEAVITT, D.D. . . . . Plymouth Congregational Church, Cleveland, O
22. Rev. J. E. COOKMAN, D.D. . . . . Twenty-Fourth Street Methodist-Episcopal Church, New York.
23. Rev. C. H. PARKHURST, D.D. . . . Madison Square Presbyterian Church, New York
24. Rev. STEPHEN YERKES, D.D. . . . Professor of Biblical Literature, Exegetical Theology, &c., Danville Theological Seminary, Danville, Ky.
25. Rev. ROBERT WATTS, D.D. . . . . Professor Belfast College, Belfast, Ireland.
26. Rev. H. M. MACCRACKEN, D.D. . . Presbyterian Church, and Vice Chancellor of the University of New York.
27. Rev. H. M. PARSONS, D.D. . . . . Knox Presbyterian Church, Toronto, Canada.
28. Rev. CORNELIUS BRETT . . . . . . Reformed Church, Bergen, N. J.
29. Rev. GEORGE BURROWES . . . . . Professor Greek and Hebrew Exegesis, San Francisco Theological Seminary, San Francisco, Cal.
30. Rev. W. P. BREED, D.D. . . . . . Emeritus, West Spruce Street Presbyterian Church, Philadelphia, and President of the Board of Publication and Sabbath-School Work.
31. Rev. GOYN TALMAGE, D.D. . . . . Reformed Church in America, now honorably retired.

April.

1. Rev. BYRON SUNDERLAND, D.D. . First Presbyterian Church, Washington, D. C.
2. Rev. JOHN H. DENISON, D.D. . . . Williams College Church, Williamstown, Mass.
3. Rev. EDWARD L. STODDARD, Ph. D. St. John's Protestant - Episcopal Church, Jersey City Heights, N. J.
4. Rev. J. G. VOSE, D.D. . . . . Beneficent Congregational Church, Providence, R. I.
5. Rev. WILLIAM HARVEY . . . . . . United Presbyterian Missionary, Cairo, Egypt.
6. Rev. ELIAS RIGGS, D.D. . . . . . . Presbyterian Missionary at Constantinople, Turkey.
7. Rev. J. M. ALLIS . . . . Presbyterian Missionary, Santiago, Chili, S. A.
8. Rev. DAVID COLE, D.D. . . . . . . Reformed Church, Yonkers, N. Y.
9. Rev. R. R. MEREDITH, D.D. . . . Tompkins Avenue Congregational Church, Brooklyn, N. Y.
10. Rev. ALEXANDER MILLER . . . . . St. Andrew's Presbyterian Church, Sydney, New South Wales.
11. Rev. W. H. CLARK . . . . Second Reformed Church, Philadelphia, Pa.
12. Rev. ALEXANDER GRANT . . . . . . Baptist Book Rooms, Toronto, Canada.
13. Rev. G. D. BOARDMAN, D.D. . . . First Baptist Church, Philadelphia, Pa.
14. Rev. W. V. KELLEY . . . . Bedford Avenue Methodist-Episcopal Church, Brooklyn, N. Y.
15. Rev. J. M. WORRALL, D.D. . . . . Thirteenth Street Presbyterian Church, New York.
16. Rev. G. S. BISHOP . . . . Reformed Church, Orange, N. J.
17. Rev. J. A. HODGE, D.D . . . . . . Presbyterian Church, Hartford, Conn.
18. Rev. F. B. MEYER . . . . Regents Park Baptist Church, London, England.
19. Rev. L. F. STEARNS, D.D. . . . . . Professor Systematic Theology, Bangor Theological Seminary, Bangor, Me.
20. Rev. O. J. HARDIN . . . . Presbyterian Missionary, lately at Tripoli, Syria.

INDEX OF AUTHORS. 373

21. Rev. A. P. HAPPER, D.D. . . . . . President of the Presbyterian College, Canton, China.
22. Rev. K. M. FENWICK . . . . Zion Congregational Church, and formerly Professor Congregational College, Montreal, Canada.
23. Rev. S. B. ROSSITER, D.D. . . . . North Presbyterian Church, New York.
24. Rev. ROBERT SHINDLER . . . . . . Baptist Minister, Addlestone, Surrey, England.
25. Rev. JOEL SWARTZ, D.D. . . . . . Lutheran Church, Gettysburg, Pa.
26. Rev. C. C. TIFFANY, D.D. . . . . . Zion Protestant-Episcopal Church, New York.
27. Rt. Rev. S. D. FERGUSON, D.D. . . . American Protestant-Episcopal Missionary Bishop, of Cape Palmas, Liberia, West Africa.
28. Rev. J. E. RANKIN, D.D. . . . . . Congregational Church, Orange Valley, N. J.
29. Rev. H. H. JESSUP, D.D. . . . . . Presbyterian Missionary, Beirut, Syria.
30. Rev. F. N. ZABRISKIE, D.D. . . . Reformed Church in America, at one time Associate Editor of the "Christian Intelligencer," resides at Princeton, New Jersey.

May.

1. Rev. T. S. HASTINGS, D.D. . . . . President, and Professor of Sacred Rhetoric, Union Theological Seminary, New York.
2. Rev. E. A. REED . . . . Second Congregational Church, Holyoke, Mass.
3. Rev. W. N. CHAMBERS . . . . Congregational Missionary at Erzroom, Persia.
4. Rev. J. J. BULLOCK, D.D. . . . . . Southern Presbyterian Minister, Washington, D. C.
5. Rev. A. J. GORDON, D.D. . . . . . Clarendon Avenue Baptist Church, Boston, Mass.
6. Rev. J. H. BARROWS, D.D. . . . . First Church, Chicago, Ill.
7. Rev. THOMAS DAVIES, D.D. . . . . The College Haverfordwest, Wales.
8. Rev. G. D. ARMSTRONG, D.D. . . . First Presbyterian Church, Norfolk, Va.

Index of Authors.

9. Rev. C. A. Stoddard, D.D. . . . Editor New York "Observer."
10. Rev. J. V. N. Talmage, D.D. . . Missionary of the Reformed Church, America, at Amory, China.
11. Rev. J. M. King, D.D. . . . . Park Avenue Methodist-Episcopal Church, New York.
12. Rev. Adolph Spaeth, D.D. . . . . Lutheran Pastor Philadelphia, Pa., and Associate Editor "Lutheran Church Review."
13. Rev. P. D. Van Cleef, D.D. . . . Wayne Street Reformed Church, Jersey City, N. J., and Stated Clerk of General Synod.
14. Rev. Smith Baker, D.D. . . . . . First Congregational Church, Lowell, Mass.
15. Rev. J. F. Riggs . . . . Reformed Church, Bergen Point, N. J.
16. Rev. C. C. Clever . . . . German Reformed Church, Baltimore, Md.
17. Rev. D. C. Marquis . . . . Professor New Testament Literature and Exegesis, McCormick Theological Seminary, Chicago.
18. Rev. Jacob Fry, D.D. . . . . Lutheran Pastor, Reading, Pa.
19. Rev. F. J. Newton . . . . Presbyterian Missionary, Ferozepur, India.
20. Rev. J. G. Lansing, D.D. . . . . . Professor of Old Testament Languages and Exegesis, in the Reformed Church.
21. Rev. E. B. Coe, D.D. . . . . Reformed Collegiate Church, New York.
22. Rev. W. M. Paxton, D.D. . . . . Professor of Ecclesiastical, Homiletical, and Pastoral Theology, Princeton Seminary, New Jersey.
23. Rev. S. M. Hamilton, D.D. . . . Scotch Presbyterian Church, New York.
24. Rev. Merrett Hulburd, D.D. . Trinity Methodist-Episcopal Church, New York.
25. Rev. G. R. Brackett, D.D. . . . Second Presbyterian Church, Charleston, S. C.
26. Rev. W. J. R. Taylor, D.D. . . . Clinton Avenue Reformed Church, Newark, N. J.
27. Rev. E. O. Guerrant, D.D. . . . Presbyterian Church, Troy, Ky.
28. Rev. G. A. Tewksbury, D.D. . . . Pilgrim Congregational Church, Cambridgeport, Mass.
29. Rev. A. J. Brown, D.D. . . . . . . Lutheran Pastor, Blountville, Tenn.

INDEX OF AUTHORS. 375

30. Rev. W. W. NEWTON, D.D. .... Protestant-Episcopal Church, Pittsfield, Mass.
31. Rev. W. E. LOCKE .... Congregational Missionary, Philipopolis, Bulgaria.

June.

1. Rt. Rev. E. G. INGHAM ...... Bishop of Sierra Leone, Africa (Established Church of England).
2. Rev. A. H. PLUMB, D.D. ...... Walnut Ave. Congregational Church, Boston, Mass.
3. Rev. E. P. TERHUNE, D.D. .... Williamsburgh Reformed Church, Brooklyn, N. Y.
4. Rev. J. B. STRATTON, D.D. .... Presbyterian Church, Natchez, Miss.
5. Rev. S. M. HOPKINS, D.D. .... Professor of Ecclesiastical History and Church Polity, Theological Seminary, Auburn, N. Y.
6. Rev. J. H. ECOB, D.D. ...... Second Presbyterian Church, Albany, N. Y.
7. Rev. HARVEY GLASS, D.D. .... Presbyterian Minister, Danville, Ky.
8. Rev. H. M. BAIRD, D.D. ...... Professor of the Greek Language and Literature, University of New York.
9. Rev. J. T. SMITH, D.D. ...... Central Presbyterian Church, Baltimore, Md.
10. Rev. J. H. A. BOMBERGER, D.D. . Professor Ursinus College and Seminary of German Reformed Church, Collegeville, Pa.
11. Rev. A. W. PITZER, D.D. ..... Central Presbyterian Church, Washington, D. C.
12. Rev. W. J. HARSHA .... First Presbyterian Church, Omaha, Neb.
13. Rev. G. N. BOARDMAN, D.D. ... Professor Systematic Theology, Chicago, Ill.
14. Rev. J. W. NEIL, D.D. .... Presbyterian Church, San Antonio, Texas.
15. Rev. J. M. P. OTTS, D.D. ..... Presbyterian Church, Talladega, Ala.
16. Rev. B. C. HENRY .... Presbyterian Missionary, Canton, China.
17. Rev. MICHAEL BURNHAM, D.D. . . First Congregational Church, Springfield, Mass.

18. Rev. Frederick Merrick . . . . . Methodist-Episcopal Church, Delaware, O.
19. Rev. J. M. Ludlow, D.D. . . . . . . Presbyterian Church, East Orange, N. J.
20. Rev. J. W. Lupton, D.D. . . . . . Presbyterian Church, Clarksville, Tenn.
21. Rev. G. C. Noyes, D.D. . . . . . . Presbyterian Church, Evanston, Ill.
22. Rev. F. D. Power, D.D. . . . . . . Church of the Disciples, Washington, D. C.
23. Rev. S. M. Woodbridge, D.D. . . Professor of Ecc'esiastical History and Government in the Reformed Church Seminary, New Brunswick, N. J.
24. Rev. S. J. Niccolls, D.D. . . . . . Second Presbyterian Church, St. Louis, Mo.
25. Rev. W. N. McVickar, D.D. . . . Holy Trinity Protestant-Episcopal Church, Philadelphia, Pa.
26. Rev. L. S. Handley, D.D. . . . . . First Presbyterian Church, Birmingham, Ala.
27. Rev. B. K. Pierce, D.D. . . . . . . Methodist-Episcopal Church, Newton, Mass., formerly Editor " Zion's Herald," Boston, Mass.
28. Rev. C. Cuthbert Hall . . . . . First Presbyterian Church, Brooklyn, N. Y.
29. Rev. Josiah Strong, D.D. . . . . Secretary Evangelical Alliance, New York.
30. Rev. R. P. Kerr, D.D. . . . . First Presbyterian Church, Richmond, Va.

July.

1. Rev. John Hall, D.D. . . . . . . Fifth Avenue Presbyterian Church, and Chancellor of the University of New York.
2. Rev. T. H. Capp . . . . Church of Disciples, St. John, New Brunswick.
3. Rev. R. M. Sommerville . . . . Second Reformed Presbyterian Church, New York.
4. Rev. Robert Moffett . . . . . . Church of Disciples, Cleveland, O.
5. Rev. H. M. Booth, D.D. . . . . . Presbyterian Church, Englewood, N. J.
6. Rev. David Trumbull, D.D. . . . Editor, Valparaiso, Chili.

INDEX OF AUTHORS. 377

7. Rev. F. W. E. PESCHAU, D.D. . . Lutheran Church, Wilmington, N. C.

8. Rev. M. B. RIDDLE, D.D. . . . . . Professor New Testament Literature and Exegesis, Western Theological Seminary, Allegheny, Pa.

9. Rev. T. N. HASSELQUIST, D.D. . . . Lutheran Church, Rock Island, Ill.

10. Rev. J. R. WILSON, D.D. . . . . . Professor South-Western University, Stated Clerk Southern Presbyterian General Assembly, Clarksville, Tenn.

11. Rt. Rev. W. R. NICHOLSON, D.D. Bishop of the Reformed Episcopal Church, Philadelphia, Pa.

12. Rev. S. D. ALEXANDER, D.D. . . . Phillips Presbyterian Church, New York, and Stated Clerk Presbytery of New York.

13. Rev. R. S. MACARTHUR, D.D. . . Calvary Baptist Church, New York.

14. Rev. HENRY BLODGET, D.D. . . . Congregational Missionary, Pekin, China.

15. Rev. W. V. V. MABON, D.D. . . . Professor of Systematic Theology Reformed Church Seminary, New Brunswick, N. J.

16. Rev. D. E. KLOPP . . . . Trinity German Reformed Church, Philadelphia, Pa.

17. Rev. J. H. M KNOX, D.D. . . . . President Lafayette College, Easton, Pa.

18. Rev. B. B. TYLER, D.D. . . . . . . Church of the Disciples, New York.

19. Rev. M. D. HOGE, D.D. . . . . . . Second Presbyterian Church, Richmond, Va.

20. Rev. J. S. KIEFFER, D.D. . . . . . German Reformed Church, Hagarstown, Md.

21. Rev. B. BAUSMAN, D.D. . . . . . . German Reformed Church, Reading, Pa.

22. Rev. ANDREW A. BONAR, D.D. . . Free Church, Glasgow, Scotland.

23. Rev W. F. V. BARTLETT, D.D. . First Presbyterian Church, Lexington, Ky.

24. Rev. J. L. NEVIUS, D.D. . . . . . Presbyterian Missionary, Chefoo, China.

25. Rev. J. I. GOOD, D.D. . . . . German Reformed Church, Philadelphia, Pa.

26. Rev. J. F. ELDER, D.D. . . . . . . Baptist Church of the Epiphany, New York.

INDEX OF AUTHORS.

27. Rev. Donald Crawford . . . . . Church of the Disciples, New Glasgow, P. E. Island, Canada.
28. Rev. David Van Horne, D.D. . . German Reformed Church, Tiffin, O.
29. Rev. Andrew Longacre, D.D. . . Methodist-Episcopal Church, Baltimore, Md.
30. Rev. J. C. K. Milligan . . . . . . First Reformed Presbyterian Church, New York.
31. Rev. George Washburn, D.D. . President Robert College, Constantinople, Turkey.

August.

1. Rev. H. G. Underwood . . . . . . Presbyterian Missionary, Seoul, Corea.
2. Rev. S. H. Greene, D.D. . . . . . Calvary Baptist Church, Washington, D. C.
3. Rev. F. W. Conrad, D.D. . . . . Editor "Lutheran Observer," Philadelphia, Pa.
4. Rev. W. Ormiston, D.D. . . . . . Minister in the Reformed Church, New York.
5. Rev. W. Adams, D.D. . . . . First Presbyterian Church, Augusta, Ga.
6. Rev. F. H. Marling . . . . Emmanuel Congregational Church, Montreal, Canada.
7. Rev. Robert H. Nall, D.D. . . . First Presbyterian Church, Fort Worth, Texas.
8. Rev. James Chambers . . . . Calvary Presbyterian Church, New York.
9. Rev. T. Davis Ewing, D.D. . President Parsons College, Fairfield, Ia.
10. Rev. M. R. Vincent, D.D. . . . . Professor of Sacred Literature, Union Theological Seminary, New York.
11. Rev. G. F. Krotel, D.D. . . . . . Holy Trinity Lutheran Church, New York.
12. Rev. A. A. Reinke . . . . Moravian Church, New York.
13. Rev. Wm. Caven, D.D. . . . . . . Principal of Knox Presbyterian College, Toronto, Canada.
14. Rev. Anson P. Atterbury . . . . Park Presbyterian Church, New York.
15. Rev. J. M. Haldeman . . . . . First Baptist Church, New York.

16. Rev. Charles H. Hall, D.D. . . . Holy Trinity Protestant - Episcopal Church, Brooklyn, N. Y.
17. Rev. W. F. Junkin, D.D. . . . . . Presbyterian Church, Montclair, N. J.
18. Rev. Isaac Errett . . . . Church of Disciples, Cincinnati, Ohio, and Editor of the "Christian Standard."
19. Rev. F. L. Ferguson. . . . . Prytania Presbyterian Church, New Orleans, La.
20. Rev. W. N. Searles . . . . Washington Heights Methodist-Episcopal Church, New York.
21. Rev. J. W. Rosebro . . . . Tabb Street Presbyterian Church, Petersburgh, Va.
22. Rev. Wolcott Calkins, D.D. . Congregational Church, Newton, Mass.
23. Rev. I. S. McElroy . . . . Presbyterian Church, Mount Sterling, Ky.
24. Rev. Wm. Bayard Craig . . . . . Church of the Disciples, Denver, Col.
25. Rev. D. C. Hughes . . . . Trinity Baptist Church, New York.
26. Rev. H. W. Warren, D.D. . . . . Bishop in the Methodist-Episcopal Church.
27. Rev Chas. L. Thompson, D.D. . Madison Avenue Presbyterian Church, and Moderator of Presbyterian General Assembly, 1888, New York.
28. Rev. E. H. Barnett, D.D. . . . . First Presbyterian Church, Atlanta, Ga.
29. Rev. Halsey Moore . . . . Lexington Avenue Baptist Church, New York.
30. Rev. J. R. Burgett, D.D. . . . . . Government Street Presbyterian Church, Mobile, Ala.
31. Rev. R. K. Smoot, D.D. . . . . . . Presbyterian Church, Austin, Texas.

September.

1. Rev. Henry M. Field, D.D. . . . Presbyterian Minister, Editor "New York Evangelist."
2. Rev. W. W. Page . . . . New York Presbyterian Church, New York.
3. Rev. Robert W. Jones . . . . . . North Methodist-Episcopal Church, New York.
4. Rev Henry A. Powell . . . . . . Lee Avenue Congregational Church, Brooklyn, N. Y.

5. Rev. DAVID W. FRAZIER . . . . . . Presbyterian Missionary, Greenville, Sinoe, Africa.
6. Rev. T. CHALMERS EASTON, D.D. First Reformed Church, Newark, N. J.
7. Rev. J. R. KERR, D.D. . . . . . . Fourth Presbyterian Church, New York.
8. Rev. CARLOS MARTYN . . . . Bloomingdale Reformed Church, New York.
9. Rev. J. ELMENDORF, D.D. . . . . . Harlem Collegiate Reformed Church, New York.
10. Rev. L. T. CHAMBERLAIN, D.D. . . Classon Avenue Presbyterian Church, Brooklyn, N. Y.
11. Rev. W. N. SCOTT, D.D. . . . . . . Presbyterian Church, Galveston, Texas.
12. Rev. JAMES S. CHADWICK . . . . . Bedford Street Methodist-Episcopal Church, New York.
13. Rev. T. D. WITHERSPOON, D.D. . First Presbyterian Church, Louisville, Ky.
14. Rev. HENRY E. JACOBS, D.D. . . . President Lutheran Theological Seminary, Philadelphia, Pa.
15. Rev. L. A. CRANDALL . . . . Twenty-Third Street Baptist Church, New York.
16. Rev. H. T. MCEWEN . . . . Fourteenth Presbyterian Church, New York.
17. Rev. LEWIS FRANCIS . . . . Reformed Church, Greenpoint, Brooklyn, N. Y.
18. Rev. JOHN J. BROUNER . . . . North Baptist Church, New York.

19. Rev. RODERICK TERRY, D.D. . . . South Reformed Church, New York.
20. Rev. JOHN C. BLISS, D.D. . . . . . Washington Heights Presbyterian Church, New York.
21. Rev. J. S. RAMSAY . . . . Harlem Presbyterian Church, New York.
22. Rev. CHAS. W. FRITTS, D.D. . . . Reformed Church, Fishkill on the Hudson, N. Y.
23. Rev. C. P. MASDEN, D.D. . . . . . Madison Avenue Methodist-Episcopal Church, New York.
24. Rev. HORACE L. SINGLETON . . . . Member of Maryland Presbytery.

25. Rev. D. R. MILLER . . . . United Brethren Church, Dayton, Ohio.
26. Rev. J. A. M. CHAPMAN, D.D. . . Methodist-Episcopal Church, Philadelphia, Pa.

INDEX OF AUTHORS. 381

27. Rev. WM. H. ROBERTS, D.D. . . . Professor Practical Theology, Lane Theological Seminary, and Stated Clerk of General Assembly, Cincinnati, Ohio.
28. Rev. JOHN D. WELLS, D.D. . . . . South Third Street Presbyterian Church, Brooklyn, N. Y.
29. Rev. EDWARD T. HORN, D.D. . . Lutheran Church, Charleston, S. C.
30. Rev. A. H. CROSBIE . . . . Harlem United Presbyterian Church, New York.

October.

1. Rt. Rev. F. D. HUNTINGTON, D.D. Protestant-Episcopal Bishop of Central New York, Syracuse, N. Y.
2. Rev. C. R. HEMPHILL, D.D. . . . Second Presbyterian Church, Louisville, Ky.
3. Rev. O. H. TIFFANY, D.D. . . . . . St. James Methodist - Episcopal Church, New York.
4. Rev. C. SCHENCK . . . . Trinity Reformed Church, Plainfield, N. J.
5. Rev. L. W. MUNHALL, D.D. . . . Evangelist Methodist - Episcopal Church, Philadelphia, Pa.
6. Rev. W. B. JENNINGS . . . . First Presbyterian Church, Macon, Ga.
7. Rev. E. D. KEPHART, D. D. . . . . Bishop of the United Brethren Church, Toledo, Ia.
8. Rev. C. W. D. BRIDGMAN, D.D. . Madison Avenue Baptist Church, New York.
9. Rev. T. A. NELSON, D.D. . . . . . Memorial Presbyterian Church, Brooklyn, N. Y.
10. Rev. W. GLADDEN, D.D. . . . . . First Congregational Church, Columbus, Ohio.
11. Rev. J. H. READING . . . . Presbyterian Missionary at Gaboon, Africa.
12. Rev. BRADY E. BACKUS, D.D. . . . Protestant-Episcopal Church of the Holy Apostles, New York.
13. Rev. JESSE E. FORBES . . . . Adams Memorial Presbyterian Church, New York.
14. Rev. J. W. HOTT, D.D. . . . . . . Editor "Religious Telescope" (United Brethren), Dayton, O.
15. Rev. E. HUMPHRIES . . . . First Primitive Methodist Church, Brooklyn, N. Y.
16. Rev. JOHN GASTON, D.D. . . . . . First Reformed Church, Passaic, N. J.

17. Rev. J. H. HOADLEY . . . . Faith Presbyterian Church, New York.
18. Rev. GEO. S. CHAMBERS . . . . . . Pine Street Presbyterian Church, Harrisburg, Pa.
19. Rev. J. B. HAMILTON . . . . . . Simpson Methodist-Episcopal Church, Brooklyn, N. Y.
20. Rev. H. C. RIGGS, D.D. . . . . . . Congregational Church, Binghamton, N. Y.
21. Rev. A. H. CLAPP, D.D . . . . . . Secretary Congregational Home Mission Society, New York.
22. Rev. G. D. HULST . . . . South Bushwick Avenue Reformed Church, Brooklyn, N. Y.
23. Rev. G. ALEXANDER, D.D. . . . . University Place Presbyterian Church New York.
24. Rev. A. R. BENTON . . . . Church of Disciples, Indianapolis, Ind.
25. Rev. J. WEAVER, D.D. . . . . Bishop of the United Brethren Church, Dayton, O.
26. Rev. J. R. PAXTON, D.D. . . . . . West Presbyterian Church, New York.
27. Rev. W. MANCHEE . . . . Reformed Church, Hoboken, N. J.
28. Rev. P. F. LEAVENS . . . . Presbyterian Church, Passaic, N. J.
29. Rev. J. WITHERSPOON, D.D. . . . First Presbyterian Church, Nashville, Tenn.
30. Rev. H. N. COBB, D.D. . . . . . . Secretary Board of Foreign Missions, Reformed Church in America.
31. Rev. E. D. MORRIS, D.D. . . . . . Professor Systematic Theology, Lane Theological Seminary, Cincinnati, Ohio.

November.

1. Rev. J. M. THOBURN, D.D. . . . . Bishop Methodist-Episcopal Church, India.
2. Rev. JOHN B. DRURY, D.D. . . . . Editor "Christian Intelligencer," New York.
3. Rev. W. J. SHUEY . . . . Publisher of the "Religious Telescope," Minister United Brethren, Dayton, O.
4. Rev. W. H. THOMAS . . . . Israel African Methodist-Episcopal Church.

INDEX OF AUTHORS. 383

5. Rev. S. F. HOTCHKIN . . . . St. Luke's Protestant-Episcopal Church, Philadelphia, Pa.
6. Rev. J. L. CALDWELL . . . . First Presbyterian Church, Bowling Green, Ky.
7. Rev. W. H. PARMLY, D.D. . . . . Baptist Church, Jersey City, N. J.
8. Rev. E. A. BULKLEY, D.D. . . . . Presbyterian Church, Rutherford, N. J.
9. Rev. D. BERGER, D D. . Editor S. S. Literature, United Brethren Church, Dayton, O.
10. Rev. A. W. HALSEY . . . . Spring Street Presbyterian Church, New York.
11. Rev. P. T. POCKMAN . . . . First Reformed Church, New Brunswick, N. J.
12. Rev. R. W. KIDD . . . . Seventh Avenue United Presbyterian Church, New York.
13. Rev. J. P. LANDIS, D.D. . . . . . . Professor of Systematic Theology and Hebrew, Union Biblical Seminary, Dayton, O.
14. Rev. J. L. SCUDDER . . . . Congregational Tabernacle Church, Jersey City, N. J.
15. Rev. A. W. COWLES, D.D. . . . . . President Female College, Elmira, N. Y.
16. Rev. J. H. DULLES, Jr. . . . . . . Librarian Theological Seminary, Princeton, N. J.
17. Rev. G. H. SMYTH, D.D. . . . . . Harlem Collegiate Church, New York.
18. Rev. J. LESTER WELLS . . . . . . Bethany Presbyterian Church, Newark, N. J.
19. Rev. W. S. BOWMAN, D.D. . . . . Lutheran Church, Savannah, Ga.
20. Rev. M. H. BIXBY, D.D. . . . . . . Cranston Baptist Church, Providence, R. I.
21. Rev. JOHN CHESTER, D.D. . . . . . Metropolitan Presbyterian Church, Washington, D. C.
22. Rev. J. FORD SUTTON, D.D. . . . . Minister in the Presbyterian Church, New York.
23. Rev. M. H. POGSON . . . . Sixteenth Street Baptist Church, New York.
24 Rev. D. O. DAVIES, D.D. . . . . . First Presbyterian Church, Henderson, Ky.
25. Rev. J. M. TRIBLE . . . . Church of Disciples, Buffalo, N. Y.
26. Rev. WILLIAM T. FINDLEY, D.D. . Central Presbyterian Church, Newark, N. J.

27. Rev. JOHN HUMPSTONE, D.D. . . . Immanuel Baptist Church, Brooklyn, N. Y.
28. Rev. R. H. HOWARD . . . . Methodist-Episcopal Church, Townsend, Mass.
29. Rev. A. C. WEDEKIND, D.D. . . . St. John's Lutheran Church, New York.
30. Rev. G. S. PAYSON . . . . Mount Washington Presbyterian Church, New York.

December.

1. Rt. Rev. H. C. POTTER, D.D. . . . Bishop of New York, Protestant-Episcopal Church, New York.
2. Rev. D. WATERS, D.D. . . . . North Reformed Church, Newark, N. J.
3. Rev. W. L. PHILLIPS . . . . Summerfield Methodist-Episcopal Church, Brooklyn, N. Y.
4. Rev. D. WORTMAN, D D. . . . . . Reformed Church, Saugerties, N. Y.
5 Rev. J. R. FISHER . . . . Presbyterian Church, South Orange, N. J.
6. Rev. L. D. CALKINS . . . . Trinity Presbyterian Church, Brooklyn, N. Y.
7. Rev. I. J. LANSING . . . . Salem Street Congregational Church, Worcester, Mass.
8. Rev. W. W. ATTERBURY, D.D. . . Secretary of the Sabbath Committee, New York.
9. Rev. C. R. BARNES . . . . Methodist-Episcopal Church, Hoboken, N. J.
10. Rev. J. C. FRENCH, D.D. . . . . . Park Presbyterian Church, Newark, N. J.
11. Rev. J. E. C. SAWYER . . . . Methodist-Episcopal Church, Pittsfield, Mass.
12. Rev. E. C. MOORE . . . . Westminster Presbyterian Church, Yonkers, N. Y.
13. Rev. R. H. FULTON, D.D. . . . . Northminster Presbyterian Church, Philadelphia, Pa.
14. Rev. L. C. VASS, D.D. . . . . Presbyterian Church, New Bern, N. C.
15. Rev. A. ERDMAN, D.D. . . . . . . South Street Presbyterian Church, Morristown, N. J.
16. Rev. E. H. HARDING, D.D. . . . . Presbyterian Church, Graham, N. C.
17. Rev. JOHN REID, D.D. . . . . First Presbyterian Church, Yonkers, N. Y.

18. Rev. O. A. KINGSBURY . . . . Editor " Illustrated Christian Weekly," New York.
19. Rev. ROBERT LOWRY, D.D. . . . . Baptist Minister, Plainfield, N. J.
20. Rev. J. C. VAN DEVENTER . . . . . Reformed Church, Nayack, N. Y.
21. Rev. R. S. CAMPBELL, D.D. . . . . First Presbyterian Church, St. Joseph, Mo.
22. Rev. D. PARKER MORGAN . . . . . Protestant-Episcopal Church of the Heavenly Rest, New York.
23. Rev. H. C. ALEXANDER, D.D. . . . Professor of Biblical Literature and Interpretation of the Old Testament, Union Theological Seminary, Hampden, Sidney, Va.
24. Rev. T. RALSTON SMITH, D.D. . . . Westminster Presbyterian Church, Buffalo, N. Y.
25. Rev. C. H. SPURGEON . . . . Metropolitan Tabernacle, London, England.
26. Rev. ABBOTT E. KITTREDGE, D.D. Madison Avenue Reformed Church, New York.
27. Rev. HENRY M. DEXTER . . . . . Editor " The Congregationalist," Boston, Mass.
28. Rev. J. H. WHITEHEAD . . . . . . North Reformed Church, Passaic, N. J.
29. Rev. W. C. STITT . . . . Minister in the Presbyterian Church, and Secretary American Seamen's Friend Society.
30. Rev. G. W. F. BIRCH, D.D . . . . Bethany Presbyterian Church, New York.
31. Rt. Rev. W. W. NILES, D.D. . . . Protestant-Episcopal Bishop of New Hampshire, Concord, N. H.

ALPHABETICAL INDEX OF NAMES.

Adams, Myron . . . . . Mar. 7	Bonar, Andrew A. . . .	July 22
Adams, W. . . . . Aug. 5	Booth, Henry M.	July 5
Aikman, Wm. . . . . . . Jan. 7	Booth, Robt. R.	Feb. 16
Alexander, G. . . . . . Oct. 23	Bottome, F.	Feb. 12
Alexander, H C. . . . Dec. 23	Bowman, W. S.	Nov. 19
Alexander, S. D. . . . . July 12	Brackett, Gilbert R. . .	May 25
Allis, J. M. . . . . Apr. 7	Bradford, Amory H. . .	Jan. 4
Amerman, James L. . . . Mar. 12	Breed, W. P.	Mar. 30
Armstrong, Geo. D. . . . May 8	Brett, Cornelius	Mar. 28
Atterbury, Anson P. . Aug. 14	Bridgman, C. W. D. . . .	Oct. 8
Atterbury, W. W. . Dec. 8	Bright, J. S.	Jan. 23
	Brooks, Arthur	Feb. 3
	Brouner, John J.	Sept. 18
Backus, B. E. . . . . Oct. 12	Brown, Abel J.	May 29
Bainbridge, W. F. . . . Jan. 10	Brown, Hubert W. . . .	Jan. 24
Baird, H. M. . . . June 8	Bulkley, E. A.	Nov. 8
Baker, Smith . . . . . May 14	Bullock, J. J.	May 4
Baldwin, Geo. C. . . . Feb. 21	Burgett, J. R.	Aug. 30
Barnes, C. R. . . . . . Dec. 9	Burnham, Michael . . .	June 17
Barnett, E. H. . . . . Aug. 28	Burrage, Henry S. . . .	Jan. 8
Barrows, J. H. . . . . . May 6	Burrowes, Geo.	Mar. 29
Bartlett, W. F. V. . . . July 23		
Bausman, B. . . . . . . July 21		
Bell, Chas. D. . . . . Feb. 1	Caldwell, J. L.	Nov. 6
Benton, A. R. . . . . . Oct. 24	Calkins, L. D.	Dec. 6
Berger, D. . . . . . . Nov. 9	Calkins, Wolcott . . .	Aug. 22
Birch, G. W. F. . . . . Dec. 30	Campbell, R. S.	Dec. 21
Bishop, Geo. S. . . . . Apr. 16	Capp, T. H.	July 2
Bixby, M. H. . . . . . Nov. 20	Caven, Wm.	Aug. 13
Blaikie, W. G. . . . . Mar. 17	Chadwick, J. S.	Sept. 12
Bliss, Daniel . . . . . Feb. 25	Chamberlain, L. T. . . .	Sept. 10
Bliss, John C. . . . . Sept. 20	Chambers, G. S.	Oct. 18
Blodget, Henry B. . . . July 14	Chambers, James . . .	Aug. 8
Boardman, Geo. Dana . . Apr. 13	Chambers, T. W. . . .	Jan. 2
Boardman, Geo. N. . . . June 13	Chambers, W. N. . . .	May 3
Boardman, Sam. W. . . . Jan. 30	Chapman, J. A. M. . .	Sept. 26
Bomberger, J. H. A. . . June 10	Chester, John	Nov. 21

Alphabetical Index of Names.

Clapp, A. H.	Oct. 21	Field, H. M.	Sept. 1
Clark, Bishop	Mar. 1	Findley, W. T.	Nov. 26
Clark, W. H.	Apr. 11	Fisher, J. R.	Dec. 5
Clark, W. W.	Feb. 17	Forbes, Jesse E.	Oct. 13
Clever, Conrad	May 16	Francis, Lewis	Sept. 17
Cobb, H. N.	Oct. 30	Frazer, D. R.	Mar. 6
Coe, Edward B.	May 21	Frazier, David W.	Sept. 5
Cole, David	Apr. 8	French, J. C.	Dec. 10
Conkling, N. W.	Mar. 11	Fritts, Chas. W.	Sept. 22
Conrad, F. W.	Aug. 3	Fry, Jacob	May 18
Cookman, John E	Mar. 22	Fulton, R. H.	Dec. 13
Cowles, A. W.	Nov. 15		
Crafts, Wilbur F.	Jan. 28		
Craig, W. B.	Aug. 24	Gaston, J.	Oct. 16
Crandall, L. A.	Sept. 15	Gladden, W.	Oct. 10
Crawford, Donald	July 27	Glass, Harvey	June 7
Crosbie, A. H.	Sept. 30	Good, J. I.	July 25
Crosby, Howard	Jan. 5	Gordon, A. J.	May 5
Cuyler, Theo. L.	Mar. 4	Grant, A.	Apr. 12
		Greene, S. H.	Aug. 2
		Gregg, D.	Mar. 14
Dana, M. McG.	Jan. 15	Grenell, Z.	Jan. 21
Davies, D. O.	Nov. 24	Guerrant, E. O.	May 27
Davies, Thomas	May 7		
Deems, C. F.	Mar. 10		
Demarest, D. D.	Feb. 11	Haldeman, J. M.	Aug. 15
Denison, J. H.	Apr. 2	Hall, C. C.	June 28
Dexter, H. M.	Dec. 27	Hall, C. H.	Aug. 16
Douglas, G.	Feb. 6	Hall, John	July 1
Dulles, J. H.	Nov. 16	Halsey, A. W.	Nov. 10
Drury, J. B.	Nov. 2	Hamilton, J. B.	Oct. 19
Dwinell, I. E.	Mar. 18	Hamilton, S. M.	May 23
		Handley, L. S.	June 26
		Happer, A. P.	Apr. 21
Easton, T. C.	Sept. 6	Hardin, O. J.	Apr. 20
Eaton, T. T.	Feb. 5	Harding, E. H.	Dec. 16
Ecob, J. H.	June 6	Harsha, W. J.	June 12
Elder, J. F.	July 26	Hart, B.	Feb. 9
Elmendorf, J.	Sept. 9	Harvey, W.	Apr. 5
Erdman, Albert	Dec. 15	Hasselquist, T. N.	July 9
Errett, I.	Aug. 18	Hastings, T. S.	May 1
Ewing, T. D.	Aug. 9	Hays, Geo. P.	Feb. 14
		Hemphill, C. R.	Oct. 2
		Henry, B. C.	June 16
Fenwick, K. M.	Apr. 22	Hoadley, J. H.	Oct. 17
Ferguson, S. D.	Apr. 27	Hodge, J. A.	Apr. 17
Ferguson, F. L.	Aug. 19	Hoffman, C. F.	Jan. 25

ALPHABETICAL INDEX OF NAMES. 389

Hoge, M. D.	July 19		Ladd, H. M.	Mar. 2
Hopkins, S. M.	June 5		Landis, J. P.	Nov. 13
Horn, E. T.	Sept. 29		Lansing, I. J.	Dec. 7
Hotchkin, S. F.	Nov. 5		Lansing, J. G.	May 20
Hott, J. W.	Oct. 14		Leavens, P. F.	Oct. 28
Howard, R. H.	Nov. 28		Leavitt, G. R.	Mar. 21
Howland, J.	Feb. 23		Lee, E. T.	Mar. 15
Hoyt, T. A.	Feb. 10		Locke, W. E.	May 31
Hoyt, W.	Mar. 9		Longacre, A.	July 29
Hughes, D. C.	Aug. 25		Lowry, R.	Dec. 19
Hulburd, M.	May 24		Ludlow, J. M.	June 19
Hulst, Geo. D.	Oct. 22		Lupton, J. W.	June 20
Humphries, E.	Oct. 15			
Humpstone, J.	Nov. 27		Mabon, W. V. V.	July 15
Huntington, Bishop	Oct. 1		MacArthur, R. S.	July 13
Huntington, W. R.	Mar. 13		MacCracken, H. M.	Mar. 26
Hutton, M. H.	Jan. 19		Mackay, A. B.	Jan. 22
			Macloskie, G.	Jan. 11
			Manchee, W.	Oct. 27
Ingersoll, E. P.	Mar. 3		Mandeville, G. H.	Feb. 4
Ingham, Bishop	June 1		Marling, F. H.	Aug. 6
			Marquis, D. C.	May 17
			Martyn, C.	Sept. 8
Jacobs, H. E.	Sept. 14		Masden, C. P.	Sept. 23
Jeffrey, R. T.	Jan. 12		McElroy, I. S.	Aug. 23
Jennings, W. B.	Oct. 6		McEwen, H. T.	Sept. 16
Jessup, H. H.	Apr. 29		McKenzie, A.	Feb. 15
Jones, R. W.	Sept. 3		McVickar, W. N.	June 25
Junkin, W. F.	Aug. 17		Meredith, R. R.	Apr. 9
			Merrick, F.	June 18
			Meyer, F. B.	Apr. 18
			Miller, A.	Apr. 10
Kelley, W. V.	Apr. 14		Miller, D. R.	Sept. 25
Kellogg, S. H.	Feb. 7		Milligan, J. C. K.	July 30
Kephart, Bishop	Oct. 7		M'Leod, Thos. B.	Feb. 22
Kerr, J. R.	Sept. 7		Moffett, R.	July 4
Kerr, R. P.	June 30		Moment, A. H.	Jan. 26
Kidd, R. W.	Nov. 12		Moore, E. C.	Dec. 12
Kieffer, J. S.	July 20		Moore, Halsey	Aug. 29
King, H. M.	Jan. 6		Morgan, D. P.	Dec. 22
King, J. M.	May 11		Morris, E. D.	Oct. 31
Kingsbury, O. A.	Dec. 18		Mott, Geo. S.	Jan. 20
Kittredge, A. E.	Dec. 26		Munhall, L. W.	Oct. 5
Klopp, D. E.	July 16			
Knox, J. H. M.	July 17			
Koenig, R.	Mar. 20		Nall, R. H.	Aug. 7
Krotel, G. F.	Aug. 11		Neil, J. W.	June 14

ALPHABETICAL INDEX OF NAMES.

NELSON, T. A.	Oct. 9	RIDDLE, M. B.		July 8
NEVIUS, J. L.	July 24	RIGGS, E.		Apr. 6
NEWTON, F. J.	May 19	RIGGS, H. C.		Oct. 20
NEWTON, J.	Mar. 5	RIGGS, J. F.		May 15
NEWTON, W. W.	May 30	ROBERTS, W. H.		Sept. 27
NICCOLLS, S.	June 24	ROSEBRO, J. W.		Aug. 21
NICHOLSON, BISHOP	July 11	ROSSITER, S. B.		Apr. 23
NILES, BISHOP	Dec. 31	ROWLAND, A. J.		Feb. 19
NOYES, G. C.	June 21			
		SABINE, W. T.		Jan 18
OFFORD, R. M.	Feb. 29	SAMPLE, R. F.		Mar. 8
ORMISTON, W.	Aug. 4	SANDERS, H. M.		Feb. 28
OTTS, J. M. P.	June 15	SAPHIR, ADOLPH		Feb. 24
		SAWYER, J. E. C.		Dec. 11
		SCHENCK, C.		Oct. 4
PAGE, W. W.	Sept. 2	SCOTT, W. N.		Sept. 11
PARKHURST, C. H.	Mar. 23	SCUDDER, J. L.		Nov. 14
PARMLY, W. H.	Nov. 7	SEARLES, W. N.		Aug 20
PARSONS, H. M.	Mar. 27	SHEDD, J. H.		Feb. 2
PAXTON, J. R	Oct. 26	SHINDLER, R.		Apr. 24
PAXTON, W. M.	May 22	SHUEY, W. J.		Nov. 3
PAYSON, G. S.	Nov. 30	SINGLETON, H. L.		Sept. 24
PENICK, BISHOP	Jan. 31	SMITH, J. T.		June 9
PESCHAU, F. W. E.	July 7	SMITH, T. R.		Dec. 24
PHILLIPS, W. L.	Dec. 3	SMOOT, R. K.		Aug. 31
PIERCE, B. K.	June 27	SMYTH, G. H.		Nov. 17
PIERSON, A. T.	Mar. 19	SOMMERVILLE, R. M.		July 3
PITZER, A. W.	June 11	SPAETH, A.		May 12
PLUMB, A. H.	June 2	SPURGEON, C. H.		Dec. 25
POCKMAN, P. T.	Nov. 11	STAPLE, M.		Jan. 29
POGSON, M. H.	Nov. 23	STEARNS, L. F.		Apr. 19
POTTER, BISHOP	Dec. 1	STIMSON, H. A.		Feb. 8
POTTER, E. N.	Feb. 20	STITT, W. C.		Dec. 29
POWELL, H. A.	Sept. 4	STODDARD, C. A.		May 9
POWER, F. D.	June 22	STODDARD, E. L.		Apr. 3
PRIME, WENDELL	Jan. 9	STRATTON, J. B.		June 4
		STRONG, J.		June 29
		STRYKER, P.		Feb 18
		SUNDERLAND, B.		April 1
RAMSAY, J. S.	Sept. 21	SUTTON, J. F.		Nov. 22
RANKIN, J. E.	Apr. 28	SWARTZ, J.		Apr. 25
READING, J. H.	Oct. 11			
REED, E. A.	May 2			
REID, J.	Dec. 17	TALMAGE, G		Mar. 31
REINKE, A. A.	Aug. 12	TALMAGE, J. V. N.		May 10
REMENSNYDER, J. B.	Mar. 16	TALMAGE, T. D.		Jan. 3

ALPHABETICAL INDEX OF NAMES.

TAYLOR, WM. J. R.	May 26	VIRGIN, S. H.	Feb. 26
TAYLOR, W. M.	Jan. 1	VOSE, J. G.	Apr. 4
TERHUNE, E. P.	June 3		
TERRY, R.	Sept. 19		
TEWKSBURY, GEO. A.	May 28	WARFIELD, B. B.	Jan. 13
THOBURN, BISHOP	Nov. 1	WARREN, BISHOP	Aug. 26
THOMAS, W. H.	Nov. 4	WARREN, E. W.	Jan. 14
THOMPSON, C. L.	Aug. 27	WASHBURN, G.	July 31
THWING, C. F.	Jan. 17	WATERS, D.	Dec. 2
TIFFANY, C. C.	Apr. 26	WATTS, R.	Mar. 25
TIFFANY, O. H.	Oct. 3	WEAVER, BISHOP	Oct. 25
TODD, J. E.	Jan. 27	WEDEKIND, A. C.	Nov. 29
TRIBLE, J. M.	Nov. 25	WELLS, J. D.	Sept. 28
TRUMBULL, D.	July 6	WELLS, J. L.	Nov. 18
TWITCHELL, J. E.	Feb. 13	WHITEHEAD, J. H.	Dec. 28
TYLER, B. B.	July 18	WILSON, J. R.	July 10
TYLER, J.	Feb. 27	WITHERSPOON, J.	Oct. 29
		WITHERSPOON, T. D.	Sept. 13
		WOODBRIDGE, S. M.	June 23
UNDERWOOD, H. G.	Aug. 1	WORRALL, J. M.	Apr. 15
		WORTMAN, D.	Dec. 4
VAN CLEEF, PAUL D.	May 13		
VAN DEVENTER, J. C.	Dec. 20		
VAN DYKE, HENRY	Jan. 16	YERKES, S.	Mar. 24
VAN HORNE, D.	July 28		
VASS, L. C.	Dec. 14		
VINCENT, M. R.	Aug. 10	ZABRISKIE, F. N.	Apr. 30

www.ingramcontent.com/pod-product-compliance
Lightning Source LLC
Chambersburg PA
CBHW051248300426
44114CB00011B/939